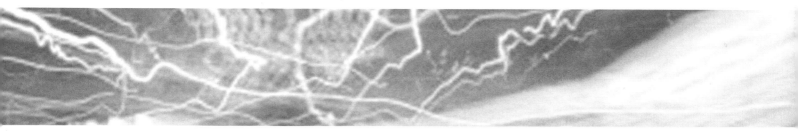

THIS IS NOT A RAVE

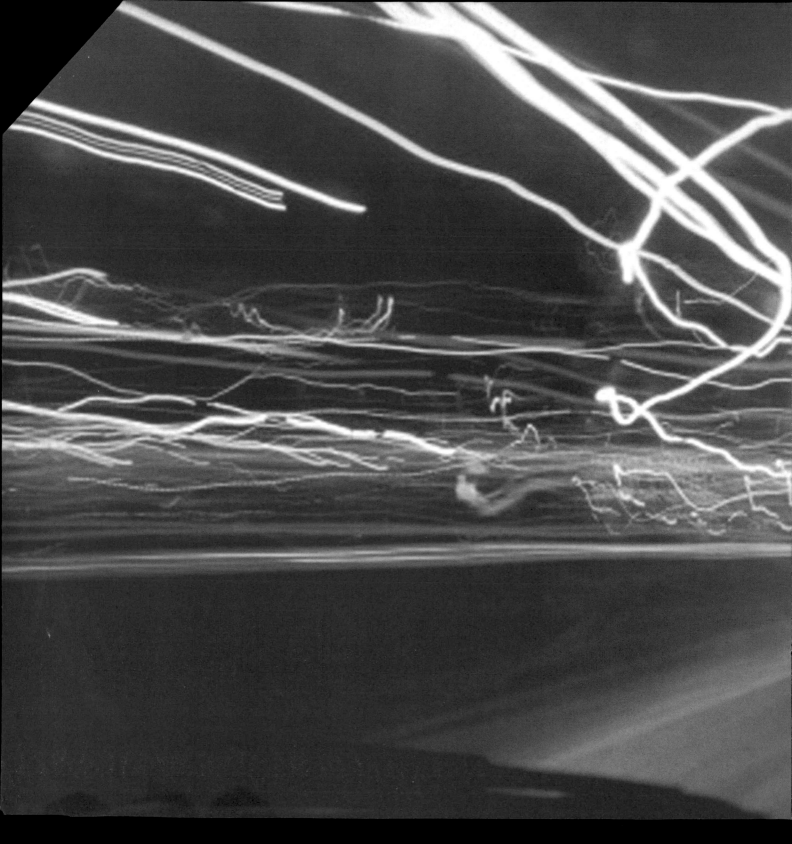

THIS IS NOT A RAVE

IN THE SHADOW OF A SUBCULTURE

TARA McCALL

THUNDER'S MOUTH PRESS
NEW YORK

THIS IS NOT A RAVE: IN THE SHADOW OF A SUBCULTURE

© 2001 by Tara McCall

Published by
Thunder's Mouth Press
An Imprint of Avalon Publishing Group Incorporated
161 William St., 16th Floor
New York, NY 10038

Edited by Graham Fiddler
Copy edited by Richard Almonte and Adrienne Weiss

The publisher and author gratefully acknowledge the support of the
Canada Council, the Ontario Arts Council and Department of Canadian
Heritage through the Book Publishing Industry Development Program.

Library of Congress Control Number: 2001098806

ISBN 1-56025-395-9

9   8   7   6   5   4   3   2   1

Designed by Pauline Neuwirth, Neuwirth & Associates, Inc.

Printed in Canada
Distributed by Publishers Group West

To everyone who helped create moments memorable enough to inspire these pages.

THANKS TO EVERYONE WHO COLLECTIVELY MADE THIS BOOK POSSIBLE. Kevin McCall, Paul Cairns, Mum & Dad, Mu, Pattie, Libby, Nana, Will Straw, Graham Fidler, All at Insomniac, Majero Bouman, Margaret Collins, Tara Roy-DiClemente, Robin Dwarka, Monique Bergeron, Max Izod, Juliana Hodgson, Mark Bryan, Juan Atkins, David Mancuso, Larry Heard, Gerald Simpson aka Guy Called Gerald, Beverly May, Ian Guthrie, Jason Ford, SNUG, Syrous for letting us in to shoot, T.H. Jackson Huang, Will Paterson, Tobias Van Veen, Tyler Stadius, Komrade Eric, Martin Lauzé, Jacques Chamberlain, Karl Borst, John Crosley, Denny, Jean-Michel, Jean-Marc, Skube, Dolphin-Boy, Nelson Fernandes, Wendy Petersen, Kuowei Lee, Tom Varesh, Alan Kapler, The Ravemobile, Woody, Tessa, and all those that have made an impact on my raving days.

A SPECIAL THANK YOU TO ALL THE "UNKNOWN" RESPONDENTS WHO HAVE SHARED THEIR VOICE IN MY BOOK BY ANSWERING MY EMAIL SURVEY OVER THE LAST COUPLE OF YEARS. *star*, 2e, Alex Pitsirilos, Alji, BLUE, Brian Stanish, Bunny, CandyLove, Captain Nutmeg, Casper, Charlie, chewd0g, Christina C. Snider, Special K, Devonshire Boy, DJ Akommodate, DJ Psonyk, DJ QT, Gartner, Fluffy, Fu Man Chu, Gnat, HatGrrl, Ilam Nebrann, Izflwr, DJ_S2C, Jamiee, Jernet, Jodi "fraggel" McGee, Justin Howell, K. Charpentier, Katie, kid*NaSa, Kitten, Kortni, KRAN, Lauren Guilkey, Little Zero, Leet, Leslee Carothers, lil'chic, Lite Brite, maJic Myk, Max, Messycat, Miguel, MoN, Nahtanha Borland, Nicole Brenza, Nikole, ORION, Peanut71, Psychedelic phD, PriNcEsS LiNdZy, Princess Nikitta, Princess Pez Kandy, Pwl, RT, Scottish raver, Seth, Sharon Shor, Shloopy, Stan, Star-eee, Synapse, Tamara Ross, Zima and all the anonymous respondents.

These respondents are attributed throughout the book by the following:
NAME OR NICKNAME; CITY, STATE, PROVINCE, AND/OR COUNTRY THEY ARE FROM; AGE; GENDER; AND THE NUMBER OF YEARS THEY HAVE BEEN RAVING OR PARTYING.

ACKNOWLEDGEMENTS

Something magical happens to me during those twilight hours on Sunday morning. It is on the Sabbath that I always find my god. I am as nomadic as the others wandering from warehouse to warehouse to have my soul awakened. The music thunders through my flesh, the notes swim within my veins. DJs spin their scriptures with eloquence, zest and assurance. The bass rattles my lungs and beats in unison with my heart. If I close my eyes I can watch my flesh melt away and my soul rise between the spaces of sound.

I have agonized to no end trying to find a concrete definition of the word "rave." How do you define something that can only be experienced? By defining something you place parameters around it and limit what it can and cannot be. If I say I attend raves you will automatically make assumptions about what kind of person I am, what music I like and what drugs I take. The media has provided you with these assumptions. Even people who take part in rave subculture undermine the labeling of rave.

It seems these days if you're over 18 and have been going to events for more than a year, you cringe at the thought of being called a raver. You don't want to be part of what you now consider mainstream, because you were once a renegade, part of the underground. Through its existence rave has slowly become defined as a massive event filled with teens who are more than likely under the influence of ecstasy. They wear big beads and candy around their neck, inhale Vicks Vapo Rub smeared inside white dust masks, and twirl glowsticks in frantic circles and squiggles while they dance frenetically. I wore big beads, I wore phat pants, I used to love Vicks massaged into my back while I took a break from dancing. So was I a raver then but not now because I've abandoned those cultural signifiers? Often when something is assigned a definition it's abandoned by those who were a part of it before it was defined. Accepted and understood by the mainstream is an obvious contradiction to being underground. Regardless of definitions, what is essential is the connection through dance. DJs help us find expression and liberation between the beats. Maybe we'll call it something else and then we'll be renegades once more.

CONTENTS

NOVEMBER 22, 1997: a rave called **OZ**.

I picked up my tickets at a trendy clothing store in Santa Monica where I am given a map to the location of the party (the promoter's final attempt at maintaining an underground, old school charm). The location is a decrepit downtown hotel. Among the kids on the sidewalk a man lies belly up. A woman walks by in fluffy pink slippers carrying her baby, a ghostlike apparition of poverty and decay. Hundreds of colorful teens wait outside as the music pumps through the walls, rattles the windows and escapes into the street. They are bobbing and swaying anxiously on the sidewalk, needing so much to get inside to dance.

00

INTRODUCTION

INTRODUCTION

Drugged-up kidz making asses out of themselves while good music is wasted on them.
NIKOLE, Alpharetta, GA, age 18, F, 4 yrs.

Well, the word sure has changed from its simple, original sense, but I now use it to describe a specific type of event that is not a regular occurence at a club, and something a little bigger and flashier than a party. Essentially, a large party one-off, that attracts a medium to huge number of people, that focuses on one or more genres of electronic music. **MAX, Toronto, ON, age 30, M, 10 yrs.**

Our culture defines it as anyone who attends specific underground parties but anyone who is involved with the underground scene understands that there have always been different types of underground parties. Which of course would make the word "rave" or "Raver," like so many stereotypical terms, too broad of a statement to hold any validity. **FU MAN CHU, Eatontown, NJ, age 21, M, 7 yrs.**

My first stop at the party is the bathroom. The only one is upstairs. The stairs are packed with ravers. Crazy to say the least. They squish by one another on the staircase full of bodies, sweat, color and energy. Some are traveling up the stairs, some are going down. Those going up are simultaneously pushing the others down, and the only way to move is to catch the momentum of everyone else. Everyone does a whole lot of squeezing, and the feat of getting to the bathroom seems unattainable. As awful as it may seem, it's lovely. You just don't get this close without having sex. Total strangers, boys and girls and undescribables, pressed together in the pursuit of music, inebriation, liberation and dance. Everyone appears in Technicolor. Every cartoon character in existence seems to be mashed together in one frame. As we pass by one another we radiate our colors, only to suck back the energy we project with a smile.

What does the word "rave" mean to you?

A. It is a media-hyped word which is only used by people who don't rave. **Fu Man Chu, Eatontown, NJ.**

Rave = a bunch of drugged-out kids listening to trance music. **MIGUEL, Detroit, MI, age 19, M, 5 yrs.**

After the party ends at about 6 a.m., we are ushered outside like cattle. Some sing, most bob to the music now imprinted in our brains. Two teens are delicately pushed into a police car. Most of us watch in horror realizing that they could be us . . . the illicit substances still surging through our blood. I watch as the color seems to drain out of their childlike ensembles. Before getting into our car and surrendering to the impending morning, I dance on the top floor of an outdoor parking lot. There are a few colorful leftovers clinging to the remains of the night as music pumps out of the cars. I watch the sun come up through the nasty downtown core. In the distance there are mountains trying their damnedest to remain beautiful within the picture of smog and concrete.

Here in the epitome of America, I witness the epitome of rave. Handfuls of teens not sure how to cope with the decaying world around them. Simultaneously a "fuck you," and a rejoicing in life itself. It may be called a celebration of music, a celebration of drugs, or even a celebration of celebration, but for me it's a celebration of dance. As I continue that dance in the refreshing morning air, I realize that the feeling of rave can transcend borders; it doesn't always matter if the music isn't ideal, if the space is dingy, and that there are dodgy characters lurking in the corner. What matters is that I am at a rave 3,000 miles from Toronto and yet somehow I feel as though I am . . . home.

Rave is about connection. It's about feeling at home, welcomed, alive, happy and joyful. A rave is somewhere you will not only hear music but also feel it. It will penetrate you and consume you until your chest cavity rattles. The sounds will be foreign, alien, beautiful and mechanical; offering rhythms that will make you move in ways you never imagined possible. Rave is a place where you can offer a massage to someone you've never met before and they won't assume you're hitting on them.

Cultural and musical milestone for the 21st century. A revolution @ 33 1/3 RPM. The message? Acceptance and mutual love for electronic music worldwide. The medium? 20,000 watts of sound and lightning. **DJ PSONYK, Montréal, QC, age 30, 8 yrs.**

To me, the word "rave" conjures up images of a surreal playground, a parallel universe that we all create [and] share. The frantic music, the pulsing lights, that delicious smell of fresh sweat, Vapo Rub and ganja. A rave isn't like a concert. There is no audience at a rave—we all entertain each other. **SYNAPSE, Toronto, ON, age 27, M, 8 yrs.**

It just means I have something to do on the weekend . . . **MoN, Sydney, Australia, age 17, F, 2 yrs.**

Semantically, some kids today cringe at the sound of rave . . . around here it's kind of a no-no to call it a "rave." The word "party" is usually used to describe it. I guess the word "rave" sort of took on a negative connotation after society began to associate it with glowsticks and excessive drug use. To me, "rave," whether others would approve of the use of the word, is what my social niche has been for a while. **LAILA, New Jersey, age 18, F, 2 yrs.**

Sadly, not what it used to [be] . . . it now just means bad, cheesy parties where no effort to do anything other than profit is made . . . **CAPTAIN NUTMEG, Vancouver, BC, age 26, M, 8 yrs.**

INTRODUCTION

Kick-ass techno, friends, love, peace, being young and having fun, being free, being happy, coming together to form an ultimate experience. **STAR-EEE, Hamilton, OH, age 18, F, 3 yrs.**

Rave means a dark atmosphere with techno-type music and glowsticks. **LIL'CHIC, Grant, AL, age 18, F, 0 yrs.**

I disagree with the word "rave." It used to mean fun and excitement but now it means drugs and cops. The true meaning is lost. **CHRISTINA C. SNIDER, Royal Oak, MI, age 21, F, 3 yrs.**

Rave really has no meaning anymore. Nowadays it's little teens comin' to them to do drugs . . . but it means to come together and accept one another for who they are. **JODI "FRAGGEL" MCGEE, Pittsburgh, PA, age 19, F, 4 yrs.**

Freedom of expression. A gathering of many subcultures into one. **RT, Tampa, FL, age 25, M, 11 yrs.**

It's a place where you'll enjoy giving a massage as much as receiving one, because you've never been able to share in this way with a complete stranger. Raving is about making a friend because you thought their hair was neat. It's about dancing so hard for so long, that you feel like you're going to pass out if you don't get a sip of water. It's about asking that guy over there for a sip of his water and him saying, "Of course. You OK?"

PLUR is one of the unofficial rave credos. The acronym stands for peace, love, unity and respect. Its lineage is not easily pinned down but rave mythology suggests that Frankie Bones initially talked about PLUR at one of his Stormraves in the early 1990s in New York. As rave dogma was embraced by participants worldwide, PLUR undoubtedly stems from the welcoming, loving, unifying atmosphere that is spawned by the drug Ecstasy. That's not to say that those who choose to be drug free don't follow PLUR. An ideal rave is a haven where all participants feel peace, love, unity and respect.

Raving is about getting in touch with yourself. Meditating through movement so that you crawl deep inside the crevices of your own head, experiencing pure internal joy as if you were a child again. It's about knowing all the thoughts behind someone's smile because you've connected so strongly with them just by dancing to the same beat. Raving is about enjoying how good it feels to be alive at this very instant, when the build in the music is so intense that the energy in the room is about to explode into simultaneous tribal, primal, urban rejoicing. Raving is about being disoriented so you can be re-oriented. It's about abandoning who you thought you were, what you look like and how you normally interact. It's about doing drugs to help you let go, connect and empathize with those around you. It's also about learning you don't have to do drugs to get there.

The word "rave" instantly conjures a multitude of images, attitudes and reactions. It is a scene that is ripe with dichotomies: beautiful, utopian moments that exist in tandem with accusations of underworld criminal activity. For some veterans, the word is devoid of meaning, describing a scene that has become cliché. They no longer embrace the scene or simply deny the classification of rave because for them it has become mainstream. For newcomers and those less jaded, the word invokes an inviting community where peace, love, unity and respect – PLUR – flows as freely as it did in the beginning.

FEDS CRACK DOWN ON 'RAVES'

Anyone who uses the word 'rave' to market an event could be inviting a federal investigation. . .

ABCnews.com, Jan. 13, 2000

Raves have been accused of enticing society's youth into a mass scale crack house with the drug ecstasy as the Pied Piper of the decade. Others have praised

What does the word "rave" mean to you?

Family.
CASPER, Bayonne, NJ, age 21, M, 7 yrs.

Dancing, lights, talent, meeting new people, having so much fun you feel like you're going to burst, dancing for almost seven hours nonstop! **LESLEE CAROTHERS, Bloomington, MN, age 16, F, 0 yrs.**

A rave is a party where you can be yourself, be acccpted, loved, and make new friends but mostly the word rave means HOME to me.
SPECIAL K, Ft. Wayne, IN, age 19, M, 4 yrs.

To be together as one. To be enlightened by great music. No fights, people just being real with each other.
KATIE, Orlando, FL, age 20, F, 4 yrs.

Well, rave, what it means to me is just a big party. **JUAN ATKINS**

For me a rave is the release of all the stress in my life!
STAR, Covina, CA, age 18, F, 3 yrs.

INTRODUCTION

this dance playground as a creative space for youth identity and exploration. Some promoters reject the label "rave" completely in order to legitimize their business and book venues without hassle and possible police busts. As much as young participants embrace the culture, they'll often deny involvement to their parents. Rave is at once a beautiful expression of the freedom to dance and yet a parental nightmare for those who have bought into the media's moral panic which focuses solely on rave's criminal and illicit reputation. A word that has existed for decades is now infused with a number of contrasting connotations.

For its regular participants, rave has almost sacred connotations. Yet since its beginnings over a decade ago, journalists, politicians, parents and participants have fumbled around cumbersome descriptions and depictions of the essence of rave. For outsiders rave symbolizes difference, defiance, escapism and meaningless hedonism. For insiders rave can mean transgression, transcendence, freedom, unity and meaningful fun. Rave has always had numerous definitions. In 1960, "raver" was used as a condemning description of jazz fans. The same word appeared in a 1960s documentary to describe hysterical teen female fans. The

phrase "All Night Rave" was used in 1966 for a psychotropic event which featured acid rock bands Soft Machine and Pink Floyd. In the Bible the term "to rave" is to prophesy. In 1958 Buddy Holly sang about "That crazy feeling" in a song called "Rave-on." The word "raving" has roots in Jamaica that allude to letting loose on the weekend. Dictionaries have traditionally defined a raver as an "uninhibited pleasure loving person," while a "rave-up" was simply a "lively party." Mainstream knowledge and participation in a definitive rave culture is evidenced in the latest *Canadian Oxford Dictionary* (1998) definition of rave: "a large, often illicit all-night party or event, often held in a warehouse or open field, with dancing to loud fast electronic music."

R is respect for everyone around you, no matter who they are **A** is achievement in knowing who you are **U** is vibes, feel all vibes, good and bad and pursue the good always **E** is for everyone, it doesn't matter who you are or what you look like. **KORTNI, Atlanta, GA, age 18, F, 3 yrs.**

The definition of rave should be as lucid and amorphous as the event itself. It can exist for a few hours, a whole night, or an entire weekend. A rave can be an indoor party with 50 people or an outdoor happening with 15,000 people. Participants can be 15 or even 45, gay or straight, and any ethnic background. There may be two DJs or more than 20; spinning banging techno music, uplifting trance or happy hardcore. Some ravers may take ecstasy, LSD, marijuana; some take nothing at all. Other than DJs, electronic dance music, willing participants and a venue, what can be called a rave defies parameters. Rave has come to signify a culture that is in continual flux.

At a rave, the lights, the lasers, the stomping feet, the DJ and the ceaseless beats synchronize in a unifying pulse. Rave's façade may seem mysteriously communal, but the experience is wholly personal. The feelings one encounters at a party are as varied as its participants. Somewhere between the frantic feet and arms raised in ecstatic bliss, something meaningful is going on. This book aims to articulate this meaning. People are connecting, communicating, networking, falling in love and making new friends. What is forgotten or ignored in most rave discourse is that all of this meaning begins and ends with dance.

Rave is by no means the first subculture to be both embraced and rejected by society. In the late 1960s hippies saw themselves as enlightened and spiritualized while onlookers saw them as misfits and druggies. Punks in the late 1970s were viewed by the public as street urchins addicted to hair dye and heroin. Internally they were a community that consciously abandoned the norm and relished this subversion. All subcultures seem to follow this formulaic pattern. Initially, as the media and society catch wind of "deviant" activity, moral panic is generated. Absent within this panic is the active "meaning" found by the subcultural participants. What they seek and how they seek it is unintelligible to the outside culture. Why people participate in a subculture is secondary to how they look and what deviant acts they partake in. Just as early 1960s mods are remembered for their tailored suits, thin ties and ska music instead of for their all-night dance fests, so ravers are known as druggies and not as dancers.

The formulaic pattern continues as the subculture is eventually quietly infused into mainstream cultural industries. The "look" is swallowed by fashion, the sound is absorbed into everything from pop music to car commercials. Hippie culture was sanitized in the 1980s as peace signs and daisies, while punk culture seeped onto fashion runways on models adorned with safety pins in the mid-1980s. Once the cultural artifacts within the subculture become commodified, the subculture as it once existed fades and mutates into a number of different forms and sub-scenes. What makes rave stand apart from this formula of moral panic to quiet acceptance is its global dimensions and cyclical renewal. Rave has been disseminated to virtually every corner of the globe; as it grows in one area it decays in another and morphs into another sub-scene, dress code, venue, and soundscape. With each cycle, rave's old-timers proclaim its death as the new recruits rejoice in their discovery. This cycle has been repeated since rave's birth in England in the late 1980s.

While England was getting ready to rave, my interest in industrial and new wave music was starting to peak. I was 13 when I begged my older brother and his best friend to take me with them to see Skinny Puppy on tour. For my first concert I got all decked out. I crimped my hair and safety-pinned the sides of my black jeans and put my black eyeliner on, as did my brother. At the concert I remember smelling wafts of pot. As alien as this crowd seemed I was excited to be invited into something that I knew was anything but mainstream. During the song "Assimilate" the crowd thrashed around in unison. It was a sea of movement, energy and sheer intensity. There's nothing quite like the first time you realize that other people love the music you love with as much passion and verve. You have instantly connected with a total stranger just by bouncing simultaneously beside them.

This is what lies at the foundation of rave: everyone in tune with the same rhythm. Once you feel this connection you bare part of your soul by dancing your dance. Once you get inside the music it's like a heartbeat in a womb. It validates your existence with a constant reminder that you are quite literally connected to all that encompasses you.

ALTHOUGH RAVE HAS a specific lineage and distinct birthplace, it was conceived out of a culmination of musics and scenes. Rave began as a very amorphous collection of people in Britain. Its predecessors were the English Northern Soul scene which started in the late 1960s and New York's gay disco scene of the 1970s.

01

ROOTS OF RAVE

Northern Soul. Before Americans were dancing to disco and the earliest forms of house music there was a burgeoning underground in Northern England that embraced Black American music from the previous decade. Its participants were working class youths from the dull, bleak industrial outer limits of England's northern cities: Wigan, Manchester and Blackpool. Living it up on the weekend made living during the week bearable.

You could not have squeezed one more person in that club . . . It was so hot and packed, the sweat was rising off people's bodies as condensation and dripping back onto them from the ceiling. **IAN LEVINE talking about the Torch, a Northern Soul club, as quoted in *Last Night a DJ Saved My Life*, 89**

Hedonistic hopefuls from as far away as Scotland would go on pilgrimages for a taste of these underground all-nighters. Northern Soul offered a contrast to the rock and glam rock typical in Southern clubs. The scene provided a more community-oriented, friendly atmosphere than the usual alcohol-induced aggression of London clubs.

The music these hopefuls sought was American soul and Motown from Detroit and Chicago. This music was already outdated or even obscure in its homeland, but was embraced by participants and DJs of this new British subculture. Like rave music, success didn't depend on chart acclaim. For the most part, the music was unrecognized by the mainstream market.

Northern Soul events were usually alcohol-free all-nighters where a variety of amphetamines would fuel hours of acrobatic dancing. The backflips, spins and clapping of Northern Soul dancers were forerunners of early break dancing, with their fusion of jazz and swing. The dress code was geared more toward comfort and ease of movement rather than fashion. Polo shirts and bowling shirts, extremely baggy pants and Adidas sports bags filled with necessities such as talc to sprinkle on the dance floor and a change of clothes after sweating for hours. The look of Northern Soul and the intensity of the dancing was without a doubt a blueprint for the days of rave.

The main Northern Soul clubs were the Twisted Wheel in Manchester and the Wigan Casino close to Scotland. The Twisted Wheel had been host to all-night soul events for a number of years and was the perfect breeding ground for this new specialized scene. It was one of a number of Manchester clubs catering to youths that had come under close scrutiny by the police in the mid-1960s. A moral panic was prompted by the city's chief constable J.A. McKay, who believed a lot of the clubs were unclean, dark and filled with young mods and beatniks high on speed and hash. The Manchester Corporation Act of 1965 granted Manchester police greater powers to shut down clubs. Foreshadowing the crackdown on rave, the Twisted Wheel's reputation for drugs meant it could only remain open with a prominent police presence. It was eventually shut down in 1971. The Wigan Casino attracted the biggest crowds and by today's standards would be considered the most mainstream. In 1977 *Billboard* magazine called New York's Paradise Garage the world's best discotheque, and in 1978 the same magazine gave the Wigan Casino the same distinction. Blackpool's Mecca was the more "purist" of the big Northern Soul clubs.

Northern Soul marked the first British scene to revere the DJ. DJs and the rare albums they would play would be advertised on posters to entice a crowd. The Northern Soul DJ was more collector than innovator or mixer. Unlike the American disco DJs at the time who were stretching technology by adding new layers of computerized sounds, mixing tracks together and manipulating rhythms, Northern Soul DJs were obsessed with the purity of tradition and embraced the "old." Since no new Northern Soul music was actually being produced, the longevity of the scene was solely dependant upon seeking out more obscure and never-before-heard albums. A desirable DJ was the one with the rarest albums. Music was played track to track as opposed to being mixed. There

BEAT MATCHING is the synchronization of beats from two or more different tracks. In the late 1960s when beat matching originated with the likes of Francis Grasso, there was no pitch control on turntables. There were also no slip mats which would allow a DJ to hold a record while the table spun beneath it. A DJ simply had to catch these two beats at exactly the right time. Grasso would sometimes use two copies of the same record in order to extend the track. In the mid-1970s, remixer Tom Moulton was about to press one of his mixes but had run out of 7-inch blanks. Instead he used a 12-inch which produced a remarkable sound. Moulton started pressing 12-inch versions of tracks and the trend slowly caught on. When grooves on a record are farther apart, the volume and quality increases allowing a DJ greater control. 12-inch singles were also desirable in the dance-oriented disco scene because they allowed tracks to play out longer.

What started to happen at one point, I would say around '77, some places which I won't mention, their policy was, they'd make sure drugs were available. They controlled it and they made sure drugs were available when you got there. Even though they controlled the situation, they're not allowing people to make the best choices . . . People should be intelligent enough to prepare themselves, bring what they want to bring with them or not bring with them. Once you get to a situation, this happening that happening, you might be inclined to do something that you normally wouldn't. They made it more available. Doing that hurt the scene a lot. I believe it did. **DAVID MANCUSO**

would be cheers and claps between songs much like at a concert. Conversely, participants would stop dancing, boo and shout if they were unhappy with a DJ's selection. Dancing also determined the order in which DJs would play songs, building the music up to a plateau for a few records then slowing it down for a breather.

Prescription amphetamines were the fuel for the dance floor. They would sometimes be stolen from pharmacies or bought from dealers at an event. The scene wasn't without its casualties because of this. The music would have to be fast enough to maintain the momentum of the gymnastic moves of speed-freaks who were known to literally run up the walls. Because speed-induced dance styles dictated a particular tempo, certain scenes became limited. Northern Soul also became limited by its demands on musical obscurity and rarity. There was a limited supply of unheard songs because the music was old and no longer being produced. Another contributing factor to the demise of Northern Soul was that as the scene grew and embraced larger clubs like the Wigan Casino, the DJ was separated from the crowd, causing the precious symbiosis between music giver and receiver to become lost. The scene fractured in a way that foreshadows current divides in rave culture, with a fight between the original purists and the new progressives.

Disco is Born. Contrary to popular, sanitized memories of the polyester-wrapped music of Abba, the Bee Gees, the Village People and the film *Saturday Night Fever*, the scene and music which accompanied the disco era actually began as a rebellion. In New York City in the early 1970s there was a burgeoning gay pride movement which had been sparked by the Stonewall riot of 1969 after the brutal police invasion of a gay café and club. Disco became the anthem to this pride movement and promised a haven where Blacks and gays could be free from public scrutiny and stereotypes. Disco was the music of social change and freedom from heterosexist mainstream society. Many New York clubs had been under scrutiny for violating alcohol and drug laws. This scrutiny gave rise to alcohol-free all-night juice bars which began attracting ostracized gays, Hispanics and Blacks. These all-night spots offered a community atmosphere where gay patrons could be "out" comfortably. The acid rock of the 1960s had never been intended to find a home on the dance floor, and this left a void to be filled. Along with an influx of Hispanics and Blacks in clubs, this void gave rise to dance music tinged with Latin and R & B.

Disco ushered in an era of singles being recorded solely for dancing; it also pioneered the idea of mixing one record into another for a seamless flow of music and therefore a more continuous dance experience. Because of this desired continuity, DJs were learning how to beat match in order to make a smooth transition between tracks. Programming and remixing techniques were born and synthesized effects were being used. The DJ was becoming a creator rather than just a collector. Another disco-propelled milestone in the advancement of music technology was the rise of the now ubiquitous 12-inch. The idea of mixing one track into another for a continuous flow of music was changing the way people danced. Without the breaks between music to seek out a dance partner, dancing alone and in groups was becoming more prominent. This early disco scene offered a pharmacopoeia of drugs: downers such as quaaludes, amphetamines and psychedelics such as acid. Urban myth has it that high profile DJs such as Frankie Knuckles and Larry Levan had their first disco-related jobs at the Gallery Club, and spiked the punch with LSD.

One important figure in the disco scene was David Mancuso, a host and DJ who held private parties for two decades in his loft, which became known simply as The Loft. The money raised at these invitation-only affairs was intended to go towards the rent of the loft. These parties offered a refuge to a counter-culture clientele; in essence they were well-planned house parties with an incredible sound system and DJ. Parties at The Loft exuded love, togetherness and belonging. There was a mix of music with

David Mancuso

When I got the loft I decided at one point to do parties there because I had this really large space. I would make tapes and invite friends over and that sort of went on and off between 1965 and '70. So I decided to take the space and I was always into sound and by then I had a more elaborate sound system. So I decided to move some furniture around and make more of a dance area and started to try and make rent parties to survive. My friends had no problems with that, they supported it. It started off at $2. They would come to the party and everyone would just support it and of course we were quite happy with that. Because I never meant to go into the business, i.e. the club business. That was not where I wanted to go. So it grew from that and I always maintained it that way. It was always private, it was always where I lived.
DAVID MANCUSO

> One of the things that I liked about the parties was the economic background. You didn't know if a person was wealthy or poor or whatever. **David Mancuso**

People connected on very common grounds . . . That you had more money or less money did not mean that you could have more drinks, because you could bring your own alcohol, or that you'd get more food, less food, or that you had to dress, because there was no dress code . . . People would connect to each other for each other, and not necessarily for how they dressed or this or that because they had more money . . . To go someplace and not have to carry that luggage with you, then some progress is made. People who were very well known would come to the parties. When they weren't there, they were very high profile, what they did so far as their work goes, show business or whatever. And when they came there it wasn't like, ohhh so and so's here. It was very calm; everybody gave each other space. It was very interesting.

DAVID MANCUSO

threads of Latin beats and soulful vocals, and parties would often last the entire weekend. Although Mancuso learned to mix, he wished to remain true to the purity of a recording by playing each track seperately and in its entirety, allowing the recordings to speak for themselves. It was his choice and placement of records within a set that told a story.

Disco is Dead. The renowned Studio 54 had begun to expand disco's patronage to a more mainstream and high class crowd, exuding the opulence that disco is now remembered for. It was disco for the stars, with a clientele including Andy Warhol, John Travolta, Elizabeth Taylor and Grace Jones. The disco scene that was iconized in the late 1970s by the movie *Saturday Night Fever* was actually a homogenized version of the original gay disco scene. It was no longer about transgression and emancipation from labels and stereotypes, but instead it was about being cool enough to bypass a club's line-up, flaunting excesses, platform shoes, glitter, polyester suits, hetero couples dancing, flash dance floors, sex and cocaine. By the late 1970s there was a noticeable and familiar fracture within the disco scene, between the purists who would go on to initiate new scenes and mass disco culture, which would flood the market until it drowned.

Disco Reincarnated at the Garage. In contrast to Studio 54, the Paradise Garage attempted to embrace an underground spirit with its member- and guest-only policy. Opened in 1977, this alcohol-free club was housed in an overturned parking garage, a raw space with an incredible sound system. It was a discotheque built upon the same rules of gay acceptance and inclusivity that had rooted the original scene. It was here that Larry Levan, a disciple of David Mancuso's, made his mark as resident DJ. Levan would go on to inspire up-and-coming DJs such as Danny Tenaglia, David Morales, Junior Vasquez and Joe Clausell. Levan was known to switch off all the lights, even exit signs, just to build intensity. He was a master controlling his environment. Levan offered music without boundaries by creating sets with solid gold disco, elements of pop, rock, electronic weirdness, soul, funk and even rap. The Paradise Garage survived disco's death and continued well into the 1980s when the music began mutating from disco into a blend of soulful house music bearing part of the name of its creator-club: "garage." Today's garage music represents only a small portion of Levan's repertoire. The genre today is characterized by soulful disco rhythms with gospel-tinged vocals and jazz influences.

House. Existing in tandem with the Paradise Garage was an underground club in Chicago aptly named the Warehouse because of its industrial locale. Opened in March of 1977, this three-storey factory building offered a weekend escape for a predominantly Black, gay crowd. The party would begin on a Saturday night and typically continue through to Sunday afternoon. Although the space was only intended to hold around 600, a reputed 2,000 would often squeeze inside. The Warehouse exuded a community atmosphere of familiar strangers. Free water, juice and snacks were offered in lieu of alcohol.

It was here that DJ Frankie Knuckles's career skyrocketed after his move from New York. Knuckles took the spirit of the disco he knew from New York and imported it to Chicago. His mix was eclectic, ranging from Philadelphia Soul to gospel vocals, jazz and Euro-disco, all mixed with synthesized sound effects. Knuckles altered music through his mixing and editing. By the 1980s Knuckles was incorporating post-disco sounds from Italy and was experimenting by editing and remixing old songs by extending intros and adding new sounds, bass lines and rhythms. Not unlike

LARRY HEARD, house music innovator, otherwise known as Mr. Fingers, was best known for the groundbreaking house single "Can You Feel It?"

My main influences had to be the music that I came up on. The tunes that were on the radio during the late '60s through '80s. Anything from Steely Dan to War to Stevie Wonder to Marvin Gaye to Curtis Mayfield to MFSB to The Mamas and the Papas to Rush and stuff like that. There seemed to be more variety on the radio then than there is now. You could hear Albert King and Hall and Oates and Kraftwerk on the same station back then. On the different programs you could tell that a different DJ was playing. It may as well be a jukebox now. **LARRY HEARD**

Q. What role do you think house music has played in creating a global dance culture such as rave?

A. The blueprints that were used in the formation of all the other sub-genres that are now or once were popular were all extracted from the basics contained in the music that came out of New York, Detroit and Chicago. For rave music, rock elements seem to have been added. **LARRY HEARD**

House Music's main appeal WAS its sincerity and rawness. **LARRY HEARD**

A Guy Called **GERALD** is one of electronic music's most prolific innovators, successfully making transitions from house, to techno to acid house. Most recently, he has found acclaim as a drum and bass producer.

Q. How influential/ successful was your single "Voodoo Ray"?

A: "Voodoo Ray" was '80s. It's so weary that people would go on about it like it was that good. It was just different for that time. I had no intention to make anything other than stuff to dance to. The media blew it out of proportion. To this day I don't see what the big deal is with that track. It just makes me think no one really listens to music, they just listen to what other people say.
GUY CALLED GERALD

. . . the house movement is determined to have no stars. It is 'in the face' of a recording industry that needs egos and idolatry in order to survive.
DOUGLAS RUSHKOFF, *Life in the Trenches of Hyperspace*, 121

Larry Levan, he was master at controlling the environment and the crowd. Knuckles was known to turn off all the lights and play the sound of an oncoming train as though it were screaming through the crowd.

Initially house wasn't aligned with a particular genre of music but rather with an attitude and a feeling. House signified a rebellious edge and an underground vibe. House then became known as a musical style that paid homage to its home, the Warehouse. House was the sound being played by Knuckles—his own particular manipulation of what was once disco. Faster and more driving than the garage sound from New York, house inspired a fast jerky dance style known as "jacking." Many house tracks alluded to this type of dance such as JM Silk's "Jack Your Body" and Rhythm Control's "My House" which talks of "the House that Jack built." To accommodate the freedom of movement inspired by the music, and to overcome the intense heat generated by bodies at the Warehouse, a relaxed clothing style became evident, including baggy and comfortable sports gear, often worn with no shirts because of the heat. The drugs that accompanied this Chicago house scene were typically acid and MDA (a variant of MDMA). By 1982 Knuckles left to open the Power Plant and the Warehouse was renamed The Music Box and had a new DJ, Ron Hardy.

What began as an underground and marginalized club culture grew to include a broader cross-section of clientele. Eventually straight white kids started going to the Warehouse because of its after-hours allure. House music began revolutionizing the way music was being made. House aficionados who were inspired by the clubs they attended now could become musicians. With a few simple pieces of music equipment like a Roland TB 303 bass line machine, Roland 909 or 808 drum machine and a four track recorder, amateurs began making music in their homes.

Acid House. DJ Pierre and his group Phuture created new hyper synthetic, high frequency, bubbly, gurgly sounds by maxing the sound from a 303 bass line machine. These new sounds were tested by Ron Hardy's

Q. **What exactly is jacking?**

A. It's just a body motion, that they did, when you know, when you danced to house music . . . like jerking your neck, you know, like a jerk motion . . . if you were to get hit from behind in an auto accident . . . that would be similar to jacking. **Juan Atkins**

followers at The Music Box, where the early morning drug crowd reportedly went nuts. Since acid was the drug of choice for these frantic dancers, the record that resulted was named *Acid Tracks*. The music on this album was the catalyst for the first sub-genre of house. By 1987 New York City outlawed after-hour clubs and The Music Box closed in 1988. Like Levan of the Paradise Garage, Hardy became another casualty of the disco/house scene, his demise reportedly aided by excessive drug use. The clubs that had given birth to house were slowly disappearing, and the music began to be exported to Britain.

We Call It Acieed by D-Mob reached #3 in Britain and was the impetus behind the BBC banning all songs with the word "acid."

Techno. In Detroit in the early 1980s, three Black DJ/producers were experimenting with revolutionary science fiction-esque beats. Inspired by trips to the Music Box in New York and obsessed with technology, Kevin

A great DJ is like a storyteller. The music played sets you in a mood [and] carries you through the hours of dancing. A great DJ is also like a great lover, seducing you with his or her music, teasing with the mix, bringing the next song in just enough then taking it back a bit and when you can stand it no more—SPLASH! [and] that song is in and the next one's on the way. **SYNAPSE, Toronto, ON, age 27, M, 8 yrs.**

Q. **How do you think electronic dance music or rave music started?**

A: Probably when someone some day figured out that the computer can be used for more than just writing letters and calculating stuff. **IZFLWR, Denmark, age 16, F, 3 yrs.**

ROOTS OF RAVE

juan atkins has moved me on many dance floors. The recent rise of the DJ to stardom made me a little nervous about talking to him. This was the man they called the godfather of techno— one of those pioneers who has inadvertently influenced all the music we dance to today at raves. But talking to him on his cell phone in Los Angeles, listening to him order a chocolate fudge sundae at a McDonalds drive thru, I realized that he's just a really nice, modest guy . . . who happens to really love music.

Saunderson, Juan Atkins and Derrick May, who met at junior high, are said to be the godfathers of techno. Techno was an underground dance music that borrowed the energy of disco and the electronic sounds of New Wave European bands. According to Stuart Cosgrove, who wrote one of the first articles about techno in the May 1998 edition of *The Face*, these three DJ/producers created a sound that was a ". . . hybrid of post-punk, funkadelia and electro-disco." Even though the genre was first known by music writers as Detroit house and reputedly even referred to as acid disco, the sound was closer to European synth-pop by bands like Kraftwerk and Gary Numan. This highly repetitive, often lyricless and strangely hypnotic new music was largely disregarded in its birthplace, but found support in Chicago at The Music Box and in England.

> . . . I've always called my music techno, from day one, even with Cybotron we called that techno. **Juan Atkins**

Q. How do you feel about being called the godfather of techno?

A. Well, I mean you know, it's cool . . . You know, I've been called worse . . . I just make my music and I can't mentally get caught up into [it] . . . By the same token I'm sure it has affected me . . . I'm sure subconsciously somewhere in my mind you know I've said to myself, gosh I've gotta live up to this title.
JUAN ATKINS

Although Juan Atkins had considered his music techno from his early production days in 1981, music marketers were still calling the genre house music. The compilation album *Techno! The New Dance Sound of Detroit* was originally going to be called *House! The New Dance Sound of Detroit* until Atkins made it clear that the music they were making was techno not house. He created a track for the album called "Techno" which ultimately swayed the change of name. Unlike garage and house music, techno wasn't aligned with a particular club. The sound began to have its own partly marketing-based philosophy, as music journalists equated it with the cold, bleak ambience of Detroit. More producers than DJs in these early years, all three techno initiators had their own projects. Juan Atkins headed the group Cybotron on his Deep Space label, and had three hits in Detroit in the early 1980s, "Alleys of Your Mind," "Clear" and "Cosmic Cars." Atkins was later known as Model 500 on his second label Metroplex, and eventually produced under other aliases such as Infinity. Derrick May performed as Rhythim is Rhythim and had two major singles, "Strings of Life" and "Nude Photo" as well as his record label Transmat. Kevin Saunderson had the most commercial success with his group Inner City: his tracks "Big Fun" and "Good Life" became huge U.K. hits. These three producer/DJs proved very influential in the growth of techno and electronic music. They directly inspired a second wave of Detroit techno artists: Richie Hawtin, Carl Craig, Stacey Pullen and Kenny Larkin.

Techno as Catch-all Term.

Since the term techno was coined by its godfathers in Detroit, it has been used as an umbrella term for a number of electronic genres. The mainstay of techno, like most dance genres, is the single. Techno's foremost intention is danceability, and it marks the first genre of popular music that is built around a voiceless, faceless artist. Although many have suggested similarities between rave and hippie culture, rave can also be compared to disco. Music criticism from both eras makes accusations that are virtually interchangeable. Just as disco was accused of being "monotonous, boring, mechanical," "faceless," "formulated, restrictive" and having "predictable rhythms," rave music has been described as "repetitive and cold," "faceless, computer-generated dance music," and "soulless machine music." [1]

Technology has altered the crucial role of the musician. As the live act was disintegrating, DJ culture was born. DJs use other artists' music (sometimes with their own) to create a signature piece through their mixing. The process causes the music to continually evolve. Records and samplers have become the instruments of the rave experience, with DJs often using two or three turntables to create their music. As music has progressed into the computer age and the importance of the five-piece

It didn't have anything to do with any magazine interview. It was like we've always called it techno . . . When a record company does a campaign on an artist, and they come and say, Heh, this is what we're doing, this is the new sound, people take heed to that. And basically Virgin records with their sublabel Ten Records I believe is more responsible for the techno movement than any other label. This guy Mick Clark who was the A & R guy from Ten records when they did this compilation from Detroit, they were calling this thing . . . "House!: The New Dance Sound of Detroit." They were calling it Detroit house and I was hey, we're not doing house music, this is techno. So I even did a track under that name for the album. So when Mick Clark checked out my track, my track was one of the last tracks, he decided to change it to "Techno!: The New Dance Sound of Detroit." And at that point all of the marketing and everything said techno music. And that's what happened.
Juan Atkins

My favorite album of all time is Computer World by Kraftwerk, and also I would have to say Parliament's Funkentelechy vs. The Placebo Syndrome. **Juan Atkins**

My biggest influence I would say, is of course P-Funk and Kraftwerk . . . My father probably had a big influence, he used to listen to a lot of jazz. So, I got some jazz stuff in there, hence the name of one track, "Jazz Is the Teacher," I did. A lotta Miles Davis . . . George Duke, things of that nature.

ROOTS OF RAVE

Juan Atkins

Well see, you gotta remember when I first started making music I was making music for urban America. My first records came out and were played on urban radio . . . it got received really really well. I mean we got three huge records on Black radio in Detroit. The first one was called "Alleys of Your Mind," that was the one I was recording as Cybotron. And the second one was "Cosmic Car" and the third one was "Clear." And, you know, I mean even "Clear" went to the top of the Black R&B chart. Well, not to the top but you know . . . the top 40.

Juan Atkins

band has faded, it has experienced a vast transformation from voice orientation to a lyrical void. For the most part, rave music is lyricless. It manipulates repetitive rhythms to involve the dancer, not a catchy tune or lyrics. Some DJs would argue that the music at an event is the symbiotic relationship between this "vibe" and the DJ. The DJ has often been coined a shaman, controlling the crowd. At the same time the crowd determines what the DJ will play and how it is played through the energy it creates.

Terrence Parker making calls on the job again.

[22]

Detroit has always been a progressive music city. So what you had was almost like a fifty-fifty mix of Black kids and white kids. Even in the early days of the music institute, I would say even then it was more probably seventy, eighty per cent Black. But they listened to progressive house or techno dance music. And that's the one thing about Detroit that you probably won't find in any other city in America. Outside of maybe New Jersey, maybe Chicago. Where you'll find a totally Black audience dancing to and listening to what we call quote unquote house or dance music, electronic dance music. And that's a very unique thing, that you don't find in many other cities, you know. **Juan Atkins**

THERE HAS BEEN a continued symbiosis between England and America when it comes to music. Each country has provided a home for the other's music. Motown and soul from Detroit and Chicago were the impetus behind the English Northern Soul movement. Brithish synth-pop by bands such as New Order and Cabaret Voltaire was not only played in New York clubs but was part of the inspiration along with European bands such as Kraftwerk, for American producers. This new American music, reinvented as techno and house, then found its second and arguably more influential home in England.

My first rave was 2000 WEMF. We danced till the sun came up. The next day we just walked around talking to everybody. Then I got separated from my friends, so I started dancing around the Destiny hangar looking for them. I ended up dancing with an old man [who] had to be at least 70, and his grandson maybe he was 10 [and] then a group of girls started dancing with us. I guess they saw how much fun we were having. Anyway, about 20 minutes later I was having sex in a porta-pottie with Samantha—one of the girls. She gave me her phone number and address in T.O. but in all the fun and excitement I lost it and I never saw her again. My friends don't believe me to this day, but if some girl gives you a similar story give her my e-mail address, PPLLEEAASSEE!!!!!! That's about it except [on] the bus ride home everybody looked like zombies.

KRAN, Newfoundland, age 22, M, 2 yrs.

For me what was so beautiful about raving initially was that there was only myself, my brother, and his best friend. It was so wonderful to connect on another level with two people that I was already so close to. It was not only an affirmation of how much we cared about each other, it was a profound realization that we could connect on multiple levels that we hadn't previously been made aware of.

BUNNY, age 27, F, 6 yrs.

02
BLISSFUL BEGINNINGS

Q. **Why do you think techno and a lot of electronic genres have to go though the U.K. and Europe before they can really get a more mainstream acceptance in North America?**

A. Well, I think, it's you know, history repeats itself! Right? If you look at, you know even like the Motown era, you take groups like the Beatles and the Rolling Stones, to me they were just emulating Motown! I think even the Beatles... did a couple of Motown covers didn't they? So I think you just find that history is repeating itself.
JUAN ATKINS

The first ecstasy-influenced album was Soft Cell's *Memorabilia* in 1981. The song "Non Stop Ecstatic Dancing" pays homage to this.

ME AND MY peeps jumped into a Blazer with our visers on and candy neckleces (this was like 3 years ago when it was still mostly underground, compared to now), glow-sticks in our pockets and cruised to downtown Detroit to a warehouse. I don't think I ever sat down the whole night. I met all the DJs (plus it was the first time I ever learned how to spin). I laughed and danced all night. When we left the sun was coming up. So we all piled back into our Blazer and went to Dennys to eat break-fast. CHRISTINA C. SNIDER, Royal Oak, MI, age 21, F, 3 yrs.

Q. **Describe the best time you ever had at a party.**

A. When everyone thought I was so beautiful and wanted me to bless them with my wand and I got kisses all night. **PRINCESS PEZ KANDY, Batesville, Arkansas, age 17, F, 1 yr.**

Well, maybe we're not ravers. We just love the scene. My husband (40) and I (35) went to our first rave last summer (Mega Buzz or Buzz Fest, something like that) in the foothills of Calaveras County in Northern Cal. Even though I was a little nervous because of our ages, we had an excellent time. Everybody was so friendly and so real; there was nothing but good energy all around. We totally loved the music and danced all night. Even though we had some E, we didn't even dose, because the vibes were so high we felt like we didn't need it. So we want to do it again. But this time we want to go to an indoor rave. **K. CHARPENTIER, SILICON VALLEY, CA. AGE 36, F.**

In 1986 London DJs Norman Jay and Judge Jules traveled to New York and the Paradise Garage and were inspired to collect house and garage. Back home in London there was a trend toward slower, more downtown funk coined "rare groove." The two DJs would spin 1970s American soul and host all-night warehouse parties in disused and empty buildings to crowds of up to 5,000. Jay would discretely advertise these events on his pirate radio show as raves and keep the venue as secret as possible. The sound and lights would be hooked up to generators and reportedly even street lamps, in true renegade style. This rare groove scene was more than quietly suggestive of the full-blown rave scene that would soon follow.

This new English dance music was often coupled with the drug ecstasy that had been brought over from the U.S. by music and club types such as Boy George. Ecstasy is an amphetamine-based drug that creates feelings of empathy and happiness and increases sensations of touch and sensuality. Although it would be unfair to assume that everyone participating in raves indulges in ecstasy, it would be unrealistic not to acknowledge that the combination of ecstasy and house music was the inspiring factor in rave's development. As early as 1981 the British group Soft Cell had someone rapping the praises of ecstasy on the remix of one of their earliest tracks. They had discovered the drug when recording their album in New York. In the mid-1980s ecstasy was enjoyed by an elite Soho crowd in London, as well as at Manchester's huge club the Hacienda, where there was a strong presence of house music. The most prominent sub-genre to grow out of the Hacienda's house music ecstasy scene were the so-called "Madchester" bands like Stone Roses and Inspiral Carpets. The Happy Mondays were said to throw E pills out to the crowd. In 1991 the Happy Mondays even had a song called "Rave On." But it wasn't at the Hacienda or even in Manchester that the secret of the new combination of house music and ecstasy had first crept into the mainstream.

It was a group of London vacationers including Paul Oakenfold, a hip-hop DJ, and Danny Rampling that discovered the powers of ecstasy during a trip to Ibiza in the summer of 1987. Ibiza, an island off the coast of Spain, had been a prime vacation hot-spot for years and was originally

Whoever it was that brought house music, ecstasy and amphetamines together is a total genius and I want to shake that man's hand. **ANONYMOUS.**

When times get tougher, people tend to escape down the rabbit hole, through the K-hole, past the doorman, down the corridor and into Wonderland . . . the acid house and rave scenes were about a generation denied a place in society as a whole creating a space in which they could express themselves. **SHERYL GARRATT,** *Adventures in Wonderland,* **321**

March or April of 2000, [a rave] by AWOL at a warehouse they own called the Candy Factore (Las Vegas, NV). What really made this party great for me was the feeling and vibe I got from it. I was driving down the street trying to find a parking spot—my car loaded with all my friends—and we could see kids walkin' to the end of the street. We could hear the pounding beats a lil' bit away—kids I didnt know sayin' hi and what's up to me. We could feel the vibe of the party miles away on the way to the party. I've never seen so much love at a party—you could feel the energy of all the past parties that were held there. The city of Las Vegas has since taken away all the permits of the Candy Factore to have any parties—it's missed. To this day, you walk into the Candy Factore, you can still feel the love and vibe there. AWOL is hoping to turn the Candy Factore into a café/art gallery place. *Crossed Fingers* ORION, Las Vegas, NV, M, 20, 2 yrs.

It was my first rave and I was 13. I had told my parents that I was sleeping over [at] a friend's house. It was such a rush that no one knew where I was or what I was doing except for me and my close friends. Once I got in I knew it was going to be the best night of my life. My favourite DJs all played and I was with my best buds. **ANONYMOUS, Sydney, Australia, age 14, F, 2 yrs.**

We'd come through E, and what we were into was smoking joints and chilling . . . For me, at the raves it was all sheep. Everyone would look the same, dress the same, expect to hear the same big tunes. **DJ PAUL OAKENFOLD as quoted in Adventures in Wonderland, 243**

Q. What was your impression of the huge raves in England in the late 80s and early 90s?

A. They stirred masses of youth who were unaware of the problems they caused the goverment. So to be on the safe side, the powers that be passed laws stating that any group of 20 or more gathering in a public place was breaking the law and should face stiff penalties . . . so that kind of pissed on the bonfire. **Guy Called GERALD**

popularized by hippies in the late 1960s. In Ibiza these Londoners encountered a somewhat bizarre yet inspiring mix of people: English vacationers, celebrities and gays who had all discovered this drug that lowered inhibitions and created an astoundingly warm, friendly atmosphere. In beachfront open air clubs such as Amnesia, DJs combined an eclectic mix of house music with more popular dance and club anthems. Astounded by his vacation discoveries, Danny Rampling attempted to recreate his Ibizan holiday bliss by opening a small after-hours club in London called Shoom in October of 1987. Shoom's goal was to capture the feeling, spirit, energy and eclecticism of Ibiza by adopting a similar

The Summer of Love in 1967 epitomized the hippie's culmination of self-awareness and wakening through public displays of "uniformity," and was seen by many as the height of psychedelic drug flow within this culture's lifespan. It was the summer that America discovered the hippie.

blend of music, now known as Balearic after the group of Spanish islands of which Ibiza is one. Rampling passed out flyers for Shoom adorned with yellow smiley faces, a cheeky indication of the happy pills that would more than likely be involved. With only enough room for a few hundred people, those at Shoom had either been to Ibiza or were friends with those who had. News of Shoom events, like most underground venues, was reserved for those in the know. After the regular clubs closed, those in the know indulged in ecstasy pills, danced and hugged the night away. Shoom was the impetus behind a number of London acid house clubs that followed, including Paul Oakenfold's Spectrum. At the time, acid house became an umbrella term for most of the house and techno that was embraced by these clubs.

In the far western fringes of London, there was another burgeoning underground scene. Free all-night parties under the name Hedonism were taking place in an empty warehouse. The promoters of Hedonism were not inspired by Ibiza, but by New York's Paradise Garage. Unlike the happy, huggy nature of Shoom-inspired clubs, Hedonism was raw, dark and had a more rebellious air. Hedonism's fifth event was also its last because of police pressure on the promoters to shut the club down. Together, these two English scenes were the embryonic stage of rave. They offered a refreshing alternative to the stuck-up and sometimes exclusive London clubs that closed at 3 a.m.

Rave Flourishes. One of the original Ibiza crew, Nicky Holloway, started a club called The Trip in 1988. It was decidedly more mainstream than Shoom and started bringing ecstasy aboveground. Some acid house promoters started experimenting with spontaneous outdoor events in the summer of that year which came to be known as the "Summer of Love." These smaller outdoor events acted as catalysts for the illegal events of mass proportions that would follow. There was a new breed of promoter by 1989 in England who jumped on the acid house bandwagon, motivated by the prospect of a huge tax-free income from these spectacular events. Outdoor events with no stated venue started with Tony Colston-Hayter's company Sunrise, whose first event was raided by police. The shutdown of his first party prompted Hayter to withhold announcement

Q. What normally happens if you find drugs on someone?

A. Unfortunately once we find the drugs, we can't let the customer return the stash to his or her car in exchange for entrance. It is too easy to hide drugs on your person, and it is only the really stupid people who get caught anyway. Large quantities of drugs are never confiscated as they may belong to a dealer or runner who in turn may retaliate. Drug czars are dangerous enemies.

Anything other than pot will result in immediate expulsion. For pot we like to give people a warning first, but upon a second offence the customer will be ejected. The problem for security is if they take a relaxed attitude about drugs, word spreads quickly that we have a drug friendly venue, and then drug use becomes unmanageable. Next, the police hear about the drug use and suddenly we don't have jobs.
ILAM NEBRANN, Club/Rave security guard for 6 years.

BLISSFUL BEGINNINGS

Q. Describe the worst time you ever had at a party.

A. Greenville, SC at the Civic Center, when the asshole promoters or club owners thought they'd be cute and turn off the water to the sinks in the bathrooms. AND decided to charge $3 for water. How legal is that??? It was midwinter and people were SICK. It was hot as hell inside, people couldn't wash their hands, germs were everywhere . . . and of COURSE I came home with the WORST sinus infection and DEHYDRATION I have ever had. I must have spent $20 on bottled water that night. [I] ended up in the emergency room the next day (due to dehydration from dancing and sweating and not drinking enough water . . . No drugs were consumed!!!) **JAMIEE, ASHEVILLE, NC, age 21, F, 2 yrs.**

of his upcoming rave locations until a couple of hours before the event in order to avoid police closures. Other promotion companies followed suit under the names Energy, Biology and World Dance. These massive outdoor gatherings came to be known as raves and became increasingly spectacular, showcasing lasers, strobe lights, massive inflatable bouncy castles and special effects.

In order to avoid police closures, raves were secretly advertised on pirate radio stations and flyers were disseminated to those in the know. Cell phones and advanced messaging systems helped create a circuit of last minute directions to either meeting points or the actual locale that would remain undisclosed until the last minute. Parties grew to massive proportions with attendance increasing into the thousands while ticket prices inflated from around £5 in 1988 to £20 a year later. In 1989, a Biology event attracted 12,000 participants. Britain's rave scene had flowered into something that was barely recognizable from the initial Ibiza crew's acid house. It wasn't long before the secret, underground world of rave started being taken over by the masses. Acid house moved into larger, privately owned and sometimes disused warehouse locations where ravers and promoters could overcome the restricting hours of licensed clubs.

As rave grew so did the ecstasy distribution network that now involved serious criminals. Eventually, "firms" were demanding a cut of the action and threatening some promoters. Corruption and moneymaking schemes were also evident in legal club spaces. With the knowledge that water was the primary and necessary rave drink, some club owners began turning off water taps in an effort to increase their bar earnings. As the media and police caught on to these huge illegal events there were crackdowns, new laws and even special police units like "the pay party unit" set up strictly to abolish raves. The Bright Act put forward by Tory MP Graham Bright in 1990, increased penalties up to £20,000 for promoters throwing unlicensed events and up to six months in jail for unlicensed events and started forcing raves to be licensed. With the risk of having an event closed by police and of being charged themselves, promoters started bringing rave to mainstream clubs. It was too huge to let it die because of government crackdowns. The end of 1990 saw a second wave of rave promoters holding large scale commercial raves in legal venues. By the summer of 1992 British raves were drawing crowds exceeding well over 20,000 people.

Rave Spreads. What separates rave from other music-based subcultures is that it hasn't remained isolated in the area in which it is initiated. By the time rave was passé in some parts of London, similar scenes were emerging not only in other cities but across oceans. In the late 1980s in Germany there were many events that were in some ways akin to the raves that were taking place in the U.K. The event that became the most renowned internationally was the Loveparade. The first Loveparade took place on the streets of Berlin in 1988, four months before the Berlin Wall came down. An array of the city's techno DJs and various promoters demonstrated peace, love, unity and respect with techno music, one truck and 150 participants. It was called *Friede, Freude, Eierkuchen* which loosely translates as happiness and well-being. The Loveparade became an annual event, rapidly gaining in size each year. By its fourth year an estimated 15,000 people attended with 15 trucks of music. In 2000, the parade attracted a whopping 1.3 million people with 53 floats. Loveparade was expanded with sister parades in the U.K., South Africa and Austria.

Los Angeles. It took a few years for the music that had originated in Detroit and Chicago to be sold back to the States. The key American cities in the introduction of rave to the rest of the country were New York, Los Angeles and San Francisco. After these three scenes emerged it didn't take long for rave promoters to pop up in most American cities. It was an ex-Brit, Steve Levy, who had been to London and witnessed the acid house scene there, who used this experience as the template for starting events in Los Angeles. Steve and his brother Jon held parties for thousands under

If you are traveling to the U.K. [and] you want a good rave, come to Scotland, England is crap for raves! **SCOTTISH RAVER, Glasgow, Scotland, age 15, 3 yrs.**

Only 6 million Israelis in the country and the biggest rave took place with 15,000 clubbers on trance music in '97. And these days we have the Israeli Loveparade [with] 250,000 [people attending]. **SHARON SHOR, Israel, 28, M, 15 yrs.**

Q. **How did England's early rave crowd compare to what you've witnessed in the U.S. and Canada?**

A. The first rave I did in the U.S. was in 1991. You could not get in with trainers on. They soon got the hang of it though. **GUY CALLED GERALD**

What does plur mean to you?

False hope. **MIGUEL, Detroit, MI, age 19, 5 yrs.**

A hyped-up overused term. PLUR is supposed to stand for "peace, love, unity, respect" but the only people who use such terms usually have no idea what such grandiose concepts really mean. You cannot love or respect everyone, especially in an environment [where] any random riff-raff can be amongst you, [and] such concepts [as] peace and respect fall to the wayside. PLUR was a nice idea so long as parties were restricted to people who only found out about [them] because someone else who already had been going decided that that person would fit in and brought them. When raves and ravers were all part of a secret or underground club it was easier to assume that everyone there was . . . someone you could try to respect, perhaps even love.
FU MAN CHU, Eatontown, NJ, age 21, M, 7 yrs.

I see it as a goal to achieve. PLUR is often misinterpreted as people being genuinely good, affectionate and respectful of each other. If it is witnessed in parties, it means it exists within people of various backgrounds, old and new. There is a potential in human beings for being good to each other that is most often seen in raves and within ravers. In effect, PLUR is the 21st century equivalent of the '70s' "Peace and Love." It is a mantra, a train of thought to follow, nothing more.
DJ PSONYK, Montréal, QC, age 30, M, 8 yrs.

the names Truth, Orbit and Moonshine, beginning in 1989. In 1992, Steve Levy started a record label, Moonshine Music, that would eventually be home to artists like Keoki and Carl Cox.

New York. While the Levy Brothers were introducing the essence of British rave to the West Coast, Frankie Bones was pioneering a rave scene on the East Coast. Already a prominent New York DJ in the late 1980s, Bones became inspired by an event in England's early days of rave called Energy where he DJed to a crowd of 25,000. He came home to New York and was intent on re-creating the overwhelming experience. He began with small gatherings of a few hundred people held outdoors or in warehouses that would often be broken into. Bones then collaborated with his brother and girlfriend to create his highly influential Stormraves. Flyers would direct people to a meeting point where they would be given a map to the most unlikely of places: a brickyard, the woods in Queens, anywhere but the obvious. Bones's events were purely hardcore and featured DJs such as Richie Hawtin, Sven Vath and Underground Resistance. In 1992 Stormraves were happening every month and were starting to pull in thousands of partygoers. Rave legend suggests that at a Stormrave in 1992 that drew over 5,000 people, Frankie Bones spoke about peace, love, unity and respect, initiating what would become the unofficial rave credo of PLUR.

San Francisco. A couple of years after Los Angeles's first introduction to underground parties, Dianna Jacobs and Preston Lytton held a series of alley parties in San Francisco with cartoon-inspired names like Babar's Banana Boat. Mark Heley, an ex-Briton, then came along to complete the trio and started the infamous ToonTown parties. The first event happened in April, 1991 in a warehouse. Small weekly parties eventually turned into larger scale monthly events. By New Year's Eve of that year their party drew 7,000 people. ToonTown was a melding of club kids, the gay and straight disco scene and computer techies that sported huge Los Angeles house DJs such as Doc Martin and Jenö. In contrast to the hardcore scene in New York, the San Francisco rave scene reflected a spiritual, new age, hippie yet cyber-infused attitude. A ToonTown character called Earth Girl served Smart Drinks at some events which would become a North American trend.

Toronto. The initial stage of rave in Toronto began in the early 1990s with a tiny club crowd much like what had happened in Britain. Exodus was a night in a small semi-underground club initiated by some of Toronto's original techno DJs such as Mark Oliver and Malik X, and two British techno fans John Angus and Anthony Donelly who had heard about raves in the U.K. While this after-hours rave night lasted five months, Toronto's first official one-off rave, appropriately named Rave On, happened in August 1991 at the same club. The promoters tried to maintain the illusion of British rave by citing all the DJs from their hometowns in Britain and by advertising the promoter as the U.K.'s Exodus Productions. Soon, a company called Chemistry became Exodus's competition. Chemistry held events in varying venues and was responsible for Canada's first outdoor rave.

Locations were kept secret in true British rave style. As in the early days of British acid house, knowledge of events was strictly word of mouth and typically limited to those in the know. Raver "John" explains that he found out about his first rave simply because he was in an alternative record store buying techno singles when the salesperson handed him a flyer from under the counter and recommended that he attend. This particular rave event was held in a parking garage and according to John, "there was no style back then, it was just jeans and T-shirts, people were just going because it was this new thing... There were about 500 people, which was big back then."

Nitrous started in 1992, and blatantly advertised itself as an "all-night rave" on its flyers. Nitrous was criticized by many for its mainstream appeal, showcasing large international acts like 2unlimited. Still, Nitrous

I have never came accross that word. **SCOTTISH RAVER, Glasgow, Scotland, age 15, M, 3 yrs.**

PLUR is bullshit—shove some gabber up ya ass. **2E, Sydney, Australia, age 18, M, 2 yrs.**

PLUR is a joke. It is just one more thing for e-tards to talk about while they get massages from strangers. There is no such thing as PLUR. It would be nice, but, let's face it . . . this is the real world. **NIKOLE, Alpharetta, GA, age 18, F, 4 yrs.**

PLUR is a good idea, good things to keep in mind. PLUR for me is as simple as meeting everyone with an open heart. I think this is found in pockets in the larger rave scene but I'm not sure as much. It tends to get diluted in larger venues. **LEET, Toronto, ON, age 25, M, 8 yrs.**

PLUR is people looking out for each other, taking care of someone who looks like they're tripping bad, or maybe simply in need of a hug and some good energy. And extending this love to everyone at the party, not just those in your circle of friends. **SYNAPSE, Toronto, ON, age 27, M, 8 yrs.**

I found out about the gay warehouse parties—the Sears warehouse parties and the white parties. I think those parties were happening from about 1991 to about 1994. They were very illegal. You would have to go into an alley and find this van and buy a watch, get the receipt, then go to this house, show them the watch and you'd get in and . . . everything was free. So it was quite shady, quite illegal, but I think it added some energy to it that really worked. Those parties were really creative . . . really cool. They were happening in these dirty warehouses and there was just these fun things going on that you couldn't get anywhere else. Fun visuals, fun atmosphere, the music was pretty progressive house for the time, very tribal. They would change the decor for them each time and it was really wild. And also what they had at those parties that they don't have now is they had dark rooms, which was just a room that was pitch black for people to go into and either meet people or they would take the person that they'd just met on the dance floor back there to take the party to a new level I guess. **JASON FORD, promoter.**

was undoubtedly responsible for expanding Toronto's scene. Not unlike the scene in Britain, the initiators in Toronto resented outside money-hungry infiltrators on "their" scene. Chemistry's Alex Clive explained in a 1993 interview with *Trance 5000* magazine why he left the scene when it was still relatively new in Toronto. "Basically," Clive says, "I wanted to quit while we were ahead . . . The events are getting larger and larger and everyone is trying to outdo each other on production and who can spend the most money." [2]

It was early in the night. The space wasn't very crowded. I was tripping hard and dancing in my socks on this carpeted area. I thought it would be fun to lie down on the nice fluffy carpet and watch the lightshow. This guy came by to see if I was OK and I said yes. He sat me up and gave me the most invigorating backrub, then helped me up all the way and danced beside me for a while. Throughout the night, people were all so friendly and generous. I made a lot of long-time friends that night.
Synapse, Toronto, ON, age 27, M, 8 yrs.

Montréal. News of England's acid house scene and raves seeped into Montréal in the early 1990s. Tiny events were often held in the basements of bars and clubs well away from the prying eyes of the police. Montréal's gay community was also instrumental in initiating Montréal's rave scene with small house parties in the late 1980s. Montréal's first rave-type event, Rave New World, was held on February 4,1993 at the Metropolis Night Club with huge acts such as Moby and The Prodigy headlining. Just over a month later a rave called Solstice was held at what was then the Museum of Contemporary Art. This event paved the way for large rave circuit parties with its large color flyer and infoline. Montréal's third big rave was also the first to be raided by the police. On May 1, 1993 an event called H20 at the Palais du Commerce ended with unprecedented police

Photo: Celine Saki **Courtesy:** Guvernment

Q. Was there one person/promotion company or club that started rave-oriented nights/events?

A. The gay community is solely responsible for the rave scene in Montréal. THEY are the ones who popularized (much less invented) house music and started holding small house parties in remote venues. Personally I will always recall my first rave experience at a gay club called the Royale which held such illegal basement after-hours. The total capacity was of about 50 people at most and consisted of staying deep inside the bar as owners explained the ropes to the very few chosen to go underground while locking the doors. Otherwise, you had access through a door on the side of the building and were led inside VERY carefully. That night, we stayed nailed to the wall in a very small room with stars in our eyes, as if our parents let go of our hand in a five-storey Toys R Us, and witnessed for the first time stuff we never thought existed: 50 or so people really into the music, our first whiff of Vicks Vapo Rub (the word "ecstasy" as a drug hadn't entered our vocabulary at the time) and one very beautiful girl dressed with orange and pink plastic overalls . . . and no top underneath. THAT NIGHT, I knew where I belong. And that is precisely how it went from MY perspective.
DJ PSONYK, Montréal, QC, age 30, M, 8 yrs.

The best party I personally have ever attended was "O.D.C." on New Year's Eve of [2000]. The largest room—though not very large—was mostly techno and breaks and the crowd was really fun and friendly. Lots of black light and funky decor. There was a small hardcore room for those who like it hard and downstairs—and this was fun—they had another room that was more trance and less heavy music but you had to take your shoes off to enter the room. No smoking allowed. There were tam-tam players playing along with the DJs and one end of the room (though I think it had topped by the time I finally discovered this room) had massage tables and people giving massages. It was an amazing night! The music was good, the drugs were great, the people were wonderful. I made friends that night—that I'm still in touch with and that doesn't happen very often! It was also my first night ever spinning poi and I got a lot of attention and on-lookers for that. I wish every party could be as good as that one. But nothing has compared to it since. **MESSYCAT, Montréal, QC, age 24, F, 2 yrs.**

brutality. Police officers wore riot gear. Rave promoter Neksus started taking rave to another level with huge flyers and street posters for the events they held throughout 1994. Not only did Neksus start bringing in larger crowds, its success spawned competition from a plethora of up-and-coming promoters: Enigma, Beat2Beat, Liqueeen, Channel, 514, Millenium, Shock and Experience. Crowds for these events were mostly made up of white youths from the suburbs, while venues were typically massive warehouses well out of the city's core. As rave began gaining popularity, biker gangs saw there was a huge new market to tap into and started encroaching on the scene through drug and event control.

The predominantly francophone techno night held at Foufounes Electriques called Dimanches Technos was one of the initial rave-oriented club nights in Montréal. After-hours clubs were also spawned by raves: Playground opened in late 1994, and when it closed Storm and Sona took its place by early 1996. By the late 1990s new laws and stiffer venue regulations meant mega raves were forced to be held in the most commercial of venues such as the Olympic stadium. The gay party circuit had also become huge in Montréal with massive events such as the Black and Blue and Wild and Wet parties that went on to gain national and even international attention.

AS RAVERS' ECSTASY use increased and other drugs were being added to the rave menu, music and musical tastes were quickly being altered. It was arguably the increase in amphetamine use and its direct effects on ravers' movement that caused a divergence in rave music.

The way the music makes my heart race with life. I walk into a place that is sporting my music and my body starts to move without any hesitance. It's all about the music. Without music where would we be? Music inspires the best out of people.

Christina, Royal Oak, MI, age 21, F, 3 yrs.

03

**BREAKING DOWN
THE BEATS**

Q. **What is your favorite kind of electronic music and why?**

A. Happy hardcore because no matter how sad I am it ALWAYS cheers me up. **LAUREN, INDIANA, age 18, F, 1 yr.**

Hardcore. House music was too soft for this new hardcore crowd. A different kind of music started to be played, reflecting the extremity of these followers who relished more frenetic rhythms. Some DJs started accommodating some ravers' need for speed by increasing the pitch control. Frantic beats were accompanied by chipmunk-like voices. Tracks like "Go Speed Go" by Alpha Team and "Sesame's Treat" by Smart E's epitomized hardcore's strange mix of sheer speed and childhood nostalgia. In Britain, and later in North America, specific rituals developed around the hardcore scene. These included whistles to be blown along with the music, baggy jeans for increased ease of movement, glowsticks to be held in the hands for visual effect while dancing, soothers to gnaw on when on speed and Vicks Vapo Rub to massage fellow ravers. White gloves looked trippy under the lights and made hands more obvious when doing snaky things.

> Ravers had once taken drugs because they enhanced the feeling of the music; now the music seemed made to enhance the feeling of the drugs.
> **SHERYL GARRATT, Adventures in Wonderland, 265**

Q. **What is your least favorite kind of electronic music and why?**

A. Happy hardcore. It is very annoying. If I want to listen to chipmunks sing I would have kept my Chipmunks Christmas album. **PRINCESS NIKITTA, Cabot, AR, age 19, F, 2 yrs.**

The insides of dustmasks would be smeared with Vicks, the mentholated vapors clearing air passages and enhancing the E buzz. Usage became so great that Procter and Gamble had to warn the public of the dangers of misuse. In North America specifically, hardcore ravers helped initiate the now ubiquitous rave trends of backpacks, Teletubbies, Winnie the Pooh, and all the other cute and cuddly aspects of rave culture. By the early 1990s in Britain, hardcore started moving into the mainstream. There were TV ads for hardcore compilations, and hardcore bands appeared on *Top of the Pops*, England's most commercial music TV show.

Gabba. The most extreme development in hardcore was Gabba. Dutch and Belgian in origin, Gabba found most of its devotees in the Netherlands and Scotland. With beats per minute rising well over 200, Gabba expressed a militant aggression that totally diverged from the happy hardcore scene. Some have accused Gabba of having skinhead and neo-fascist followers. With a hard and extremely fast four-beat, Gabba is not for the faint of heart or the Teletubby rave crew—it's for those who have aggression to lose on the dancefloor by going mental. The scene has helped to develop artists with names that reflect Gabba's darkness. Atari Teenage Riot, whose first single was called "Hunting for Nazis," Speed Freak and DJ Bleed are examples of this techno hybrid.

Trance and Techno. The 1990s saw techno coming out from under the confines of the Detroit sound. European producers were creating their own techno, combining the Detroit sound with the European synth and industrial sounds that had led to Detroit techno in the first place. Belgium's R & S Records produced New York's Joey Beltram, C.J. Bolland, and Speedy J., while Berlin's Tresor Records produced Detroit stars such as Underground Resistance, Jeff Mills, and Eddie "Flashin" Fowlkes.

Also hailing from Germany was trance, a mutation of acid house and techno. One of trance's early stars was Sven Vath. A DJ in Frankfurt's underground, Vath was renowned for his marathon sets, some of which lasted longer than 12 hours. Vath founded Harthouse Records in 1992, just as trance was gaining a greater audience. Characterized by fast repetitive beats usually in 4/4 time, most trance tracks typically build to an ethereal, washy, beatless plateau, which seems to intensify and enhance the ecstasy euphoria. It is usually at this point in a trance track that everyone is forced to stop dancing because of the deliberate suspension of beats and notice how hard they are "rushing." By the late 1990s trance began to infiltrate the U.K. scene. It had diverged to become less hard than its German predecessor and was coined "progressive." In North America

Q. Can you describe why and how dancing is important to you?

A. U can release ya aggresion—gabber stomp it out. **2E, Sydney, Australia, age 18, M, 2 yrs.**

DJ Noah, who does a show on CiTR, used to do a night at Graceland on Thursdays in the early '90s that really moved the club from a gay club to one focused on rave/dance music. He used to play a lot of rave hardcore and early trance and techno (back when it was all one big blob of a genre). Markem took over from him with his infamous night, "Sol," playing more of the then-established trance sound. Noah played rave hardcore music (think old techno à la Joey Beltram, old Prodigy, Orbital, that U.K. sound—James Brown Is Dead, etc.) and Markem moved it over into trance as that genre took off on the West Coast. **TOBIAS V, Vancouver, BC, age 23, M, 7 yrs.**

There's definitely a link between trance music and acid . . . Acid lends itself more comfortably to the mood on the dance floor at trance events. The music is very visual, with lots of changing frequencies. Acid exaggerates the sounds, which are made for people in that headstate as their ears are so much more sensitive to what is happening. **SIMON BERRY, of the trance label Platypus, as quoted in "Acid Reign," 47**

I would almost say that . . . gay music is more about people and . . . rave is more about escaping, more out of the body. So the gay music is like you are trying to find something within yourself or within the people around you and the rave is . . . more like you are trying to find something a little more distant. I think they are just borrowing things from each other. **JASON FORD, promoter.**

Appendix 3.a
Suggested Electronic Music Genealogy.

● **Note.** This chart is only intended as a guide.

Jazz Dub Ambient Hip
R&B Synth Indus
Soul Dub Disco Elec
blues Rock Steady Gara
Ska
Funk

Q. How do you feel about the naming of a multitude of house/techno subgenres?
A. I think it's a ploy the industry uses via the press to fragment something too hot to handle.
Could you imagine how much power dance would have if it was just one movement, independent and moving
at speed through a very stagnant industry? That's why you get everything from
deep house to tech rock . . . go figure . . . it's all in my house. **A Guy Called Gerald**

Starting Approx. 1970   **1975**   **1980**

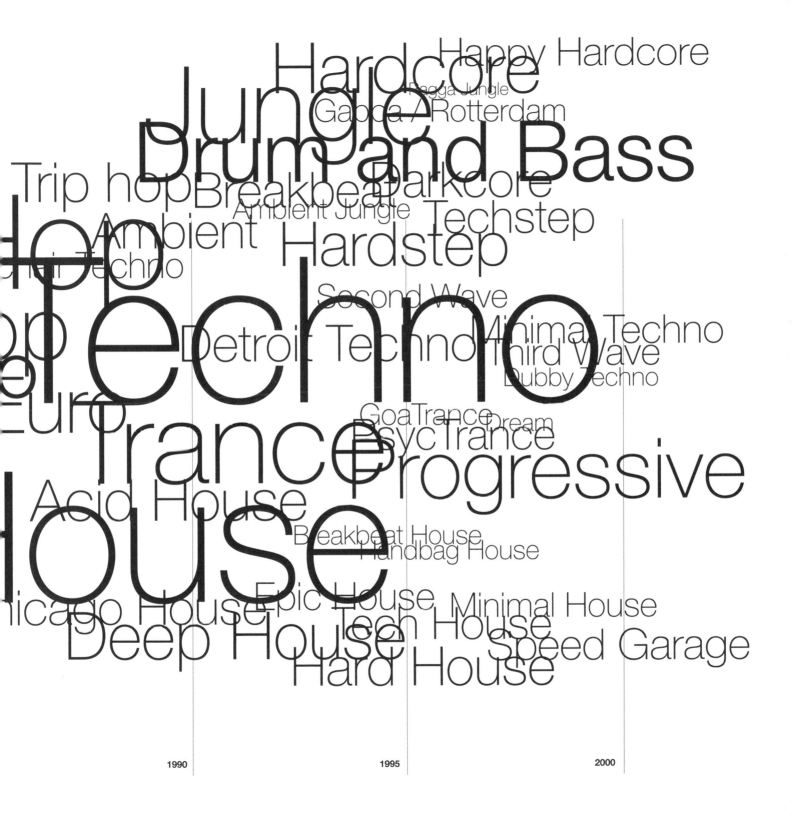

I like the floaty, lost in space nature of trance but also the raw rave sounds and sexiness of hardhouse (yes, sexiness in that "I'm going to bounce up and down for four hours" way). I love to close my eyes and let the music take me away and the melodies in trance and the swooshy sounds of house just work perfectly for that. Music can make you want to hug the world! **FLUFFY, London, England, age 22, F, 2 yrs.**

I like it all but if I had to pick one it would be trance because of the level it takes you to and then drops you on your ass. I feel trance to the core of my heart. **CHARLIE, Mobile, AL, age 22, M, 3 yrs.**

Q. What is your least favorite kind of electronic music and why?

A: Acid Trance, because it's the same beat for every song—boom boom boom boom . . . etc. **KRAN, Newfoundland, age 22, M, 2 yrs.**

Q. What is your favorite kind of electronic music and why?

A. Trance is my guide, house is my soulfood. **chewd0g, Gastonia, NC, age 18, M, 1 yr.**

trance became prominent in California and Florida with the likes of DJ Christopher Lawrence in Los Angeles, and Kimball Collins in Florida who helped initiate rave in Orlando. In Britain, DJs like Sasha and Paul Oakenfold and Danny Rampling were bringing trance to a much more mainstream audience.

Another offshoot of trance is Goa. The Ibiza of India, Goa has been a club, drug and hippie hangout since the 1960s. The LSD in Goa left over from hippie days helped create a more psychedelic edge to the original hard European trance sound. Goa trance combines Indian mysticism and instrumentation such as electronically produced sitar sounds with major labels such as Blue Room, Dragonfly and Platypus. Return to the Source events brought Goa to the masses in England and produced three compilations. Goa parties in North America are often held outside in an attempt to replicate its beachside origins. Goa trance is responsible for bringing the fluorescents that were part and parcel of the acid house experience back into rave. Goa is a scene that relishes black lights, fractal imagery and a strong community spirit.

Jungle. The many plateaus in trance music are generally the most opportune moment to judge how good one feels on E. This usually entails holding hands and/or hugging those beside you. Listening or dancing to trance not under the influence of ecstasy or another psychedelic drug makes the music sound predictable. Without the E-rush the epic moments of beatless bliss seem formulaic while the need to hug, hold hands and massage one another can seem superficial. For those on pot, speed or psychedelics, it isn't about flowers and hugs anymore. The rituals that are part of the ecstasy experience seem a little too false. Hard techno and jungle seem to fit this more serious mood.

How do you feel about being called an innovator?

It's all just showbiz talk, words they use to sell stuff in the grand scheme of things. I'm just here to make product, anything you see or hear of me has been devised to move units. Look into the history of jazz. There were lots of "innovators." **Guy Called Gerald**

Currently I'm into dark atmospheric drum 'n' bass. I've been getting more and more into fast break beats and the logic in sequencing percussion, but what really makes me listen is the amount of control these guys have over bass below 100hz. They create, shape and play with sounds that have a definite physical effect on you, the room, the speakers, everything. The little flips and warpiness in the bass is the result of hours and hours of playing with synth settings, samplers and sequencing.
LEET, Toronto, ON, age 25, M, 8 yrs.

Hardcore further diverged from house and techno into breakbeat hardcore with producers in England such as Shut up and Dance. Eventually, producers such as Omni Trio and 4 Hero started paving the way for breakbeat to morph into jungle. By 1992 jungle was beginning to break. It could be argued that it was the first rave oriented sub-genre that was developed completely in the U.K. Regardless of its hip-hop roots, jungle was literally breaking beats and dividing the scene into another faction.

All-consuming because of its sheer velocity and penetrating beat, jungle pulls you in then spits you out over and over again. Aggressive, accented, driven: some people find it intimidating, the snares too fast and erratic. It's like jazz. You have to find the balance, allow yourself to drop in and out of it.

With its half-time bass lines, frenetic rhythms and multiple break

Q. What is your favorite kind of electronic music and why?

A. By far jungle. There's no other style out there that can blend so many styles, cultures, and feelings together so eloquently and harshly.
Kid*NaSa, Milwaukee, WI, 17, M, 2 yrs.

Q. How did you progress from being part of one of England's first house bands to being a drum-n-bass innovator?

A. I was the first because I wanted to share something new with everyone, that's what art's all about. **GUY CALLED GERALD**

Sutpens Jungle . . . this was when I was in love with drum 'n' bass. The music was off the hook, the vibe was so strong and I just remember listening to Dieselboy's set and watching these tribal dancers spitting fire and they had a little drum circle going on. It was so intense and I was just so overwhelmed by the moment that I actually got tears in my eyes . . . that was the only time that ever happened and I'll never forget it. **LAILA, New Jersey, age 18, F, 2 yrs.**

OK, here is something I have noticed a lot in the rave culture. Many many many people were former punk rockers, listening to punk and a lot still do, myself included. Why is it that people go from liking punk rock to liking electronic music? Maybe it has to do with them both being (sort of) underground scenes. Also I think maybe it has to do with [the fact that] they are music that someone can create themselves, without the use of a studio and record companies. Someone can create a punk song in their garage, and it can be 10 times as good as anything you hear on the radio. Also, someone can produce a techno track in their bedroom, using just a personal computer, and it can be loved by millions. Both are great scenes, and I don't think I will ever lose the love for punk or electronica! **BRIAN, Portage, IN, age 20, M, 1 yr.**

structures, jungle is music's version of controlled chaos. It is dark, thick and foreboding. Jungle dancers move with lightning speed; their impressive footwork carries them across the floor in short spurts. Even on large amounts of speed, this style of dance is exhausting. Jungle saw the rise of MCs, chanting to the crowd in rapping outbursts. Jungle also fractured into a number of more subtle sub-genres: drum and bass, a dance hall reggae-oriented counterpart called jump-up and a softer, gentler drum and bass called intelligent drum and bass (also known as ambient jungle). The jungle scene in England developed artists such as Fabio and Grooverider, A Guy Called Gerald and Goldie, and labels such as Metalheadz and Moving Shadow. Like hardcore and other sub-genres, jungle was initially reliant on pirate radio play in England. In the U.S. and Canada, jungle spread purely through college radio, raves and record shops.

Some have claimed that the onset of jungle between 1992 and 1994 saw most of the remnants of "raveyness" disappear from the scene. All that remained now was the velocity of the music. Jungle was less demonstrative bodily and emotionally and had fewer glowsticks and even fewer smiles. Breaking from the parameters laid out by house music and ecstasy, jungle came to be labeled as dark and evil. Some jungle scenes in England became the antithesis of rave's initial ideals because of their suggested associations with violence and bad drugs such as crack cocaine. The onset of jungle created yet another division within the scene.

What is your favourite rave toy?

What the hell do I need toys for when there's girls?! **SETH, Las Vegas, NV, age 18, M, 3 yrs.**

My fantastic, expanding and contracting plastic DayGlo mesh ball! You see them hanging from the ceiling in fancy "educational" toy stores. **SYNAPSE, Toronto, ON, age 27, M, 8 yrs.**

Well, I'm not into all that stuff but I must say watching kids play with the little expando ball thingy is too funny. The best was when I saw this guy get his head stuck in one so me and my friends refer to those balls as raver prison. **LAILA, New Jersey, age 18, F, 2 yrs.**

Toys are for pansies. **2e, Sydney, Australia, age 18, M, 2 yrs.**

My fave rave toy isn't actually mine, it's my friend's toy [and] she brings it to raves all the time. It is a cute little soft duck [that] she gives . . . to me to hold. He is now my mascot for when I DJ—I sit him up near the right turntable . . . he is a very supportive duck. Tee hee. **DJ QT, Sydney, Australia, age 24, F, 8 yrs.**

My spiky rubber lighter that glows like some kind of sea anemone under UV light and doubles as a rather nice massager. Cool conversation starter when people ask you for a light. **FLUFFY, London, England, age 22, F, 2 yrs.**

Well besides the rave must-haves (water, gum, lip-stuff, etc.) my favorite toy for a while was my laser pointer. What can I say—hours of fun! Must get another one of those things. **MAX, Toronto, ON, age 30, M, 10 yrs.**

It used to be my pacifier, it was great to have when you were on E. I also liked to have candy to give to people. **KITTEN, New York, NY, age 21, F, 7 yrs.**

AT THE END of public school and the beginning of high school I stood out because I didn't fade in. I wanted to be the opposite of what was mainstream and didn't want to engage in the "I" I was supposed to play. At 13 I wore black eyeliner pulled out to small points at the corners of my eyes. I wore short, crimped boyish hair and tartan kilts with multiple pins. I put two more piercings in my ear for a total of four. I would pay homage to the obscure music groups I admired by wearing their T-shirts. I relished the idea that only a select few liked the music I liked. I realize now this early behavior was not different than attending a rave wearing pigtails and overalls, no make up and fuzzy animals attached to my backpack at 22.

04

EMERGING FROM THE UNDERGROUND

Both times I was negating who I thought I was supposed to be. At 13 I was trying not to be a kid, at 22 I was trying not to be an adult. When I started to go to raves, I didn't want to accept I had finished university because I didn't feel ready to embark on this new path called adulthood. Raving was obscure, hidden and therefore desirable. I couldn't tell most of my friends I was part of this secret underworld. Two of my closest friends lectured me for hours about why I shouldn't go to raves. I was a rebel at a time in my life when I was supposed to be starting a job, moving out and getting a life.

What does vibe mean?

A feeling. The vibe is when the music, the surroundings and the people all become one, an amazing sensation or feeling. **MIGUEL, Detroit, MI, age 19, M, 5 yrs.**

Vibe is the energy or excitement you get from being in an environment which you find stimulating. A vibe is created when more than one person, possibly thousands of persons, get mentally stimulated by an environment which . . . can cause one to feel quite good. The problem is that at some point the environments, no matter how stimulating they once were, will no longer stimulate you and . . . you will not get that feeling of euphoria that can sometimes be associated with partying. **FU MAN CHU, Eatontown, NJ, age 21, M, 7 yrs.**

Club vs. Rave. It is difficult to describe the epic proportions and spectacle of a rave to someone who has never been in attendance. The rave event is like a piece of complex machinery with intricate parts all working in unison. Unlike traditional music events like concerts and festivals, at a rave the audience is the spectacle. The "vibe" at parties, growing out of the mix of people, music and energy, can be so strong that some say it's tangible. It is this overwhelming sense of collectivity that creates a community atmosphere at most raves. This uniformity of energy is what stands in stark contrast to the sometimes alienating club environment. Run-of-the-mill dance clubs offer a variety of moods often facilitated by alcohol. Dress codes limit those who can or want to attend, while the general aura is one of overt sexuality as opposed to friendship and camaraderie. Those who cannot find an outlet in these clubs or who can't identify with the music being played will venture into the underground where the music is usually more obscure and the atmosphere more community-oriented. In the late 1980s in England this underground was acid house. In the early 1990s in Canada and the U.S. it was rave.

Many people are of the view that being underground means that you're part of an authentic culture. Most music that is labeled underground is faceless: you have to be in the know to be aware of it. This elitist need for what is original and authentic hasn't been overcome by the supposedly welcoming and inclusive culture that is rave. But for any movement to survive

It's not something that's necessarily tangible, sure you can look at people's faces and see if they're smiling and you can watch whether people are dancing and energetic but really it's more of an intense rush you get that makes you think "Yeah, this is why I keep coming out." **LAILA, New Jersey, age 18, F, 2 yrs.**

Vibe derives from vibration, energy changing forms. Electrons vibrating to higher energy levels and releasing light, heat [and] sound as they come back down. Vibe is energy, flowing from DJ to the beat to the heart of a crowd, and back again. Incredible. **Gartner, Toronto, ON, age 30, M, 3 yrs.**

it has to welcome new members. As long as these new participants' intentions are pure and adhere to the original meanings found within the scene, the scene's essence will be maintained. Those that are of the underground feel that once something is popular it can no longer be good, authentic or pure. To be loved by many means that it has been sold to the masses.

Balearics vs. Ravers. In England, the acid housers and ravers positioned themselves against the status quo and the mainstream club crowd. They saw a need to maintain their scenes' underground status. To be part of an underground culture meant that you stood apart from the norm. It indicated that you belonged to a sacred and secret community that was safe from commercialization. If you were part of the underground

VIBE is something that people have—kinda like their soul—but more along the lines of their energy—and in a way, [it has to] do with PLUR. People come to a party in a mindset to be free and have fun and enjoy and celebrate life and everything around them. When those people come together, they bring with them a VIBE or energy that you can feel when you go to a party. **ORION, Las Vegas, NV, age 20, M, 2yrs.**

It's the feeling that makes 500 people cry when a certain tune is played. It's the feeling that you can trust everyone around you, that everyone is sharing in somehow touches them deep in their soul and that you all understand each other. Terribly hard to explain, but I know how to help make it happen!
FLUFFY, London, England, age 22, F, 2 yrs.

It is the energy at the party—the feeling that you belong and you'd rather be nowhere else if it is a good vibe.
PEANUT71, Toronto, ON, age 29, F, 4 yrs.

Psychic feeling of community about an event. **DEVONSHIRE BOY, Toronto, ON, M, age 37, 22 yrs.**

The vibe, man, is the emotional atmosphere of a party. **LEET, Toronto, ON, age 25, M, 8 yrs.**

you were part of a chosen group. Set apart from the mainstream, these early ravers bonded with one another by exhibiting small signs such as specific articles of clothing that could be "read" by those in the know, signalling that they belonged. Day-glo, fluorescent outfits and bright, comfy vacation wear often suggested you were an insider. Eventually, a number of acid house clubs opened up in London leaving the original crew feeling resentment toward the newcomers who were turning their seemingly secret world into a business.

Just as punks had plastic punks or safety-pin people, rastas had burr-head rastas and hippies had weekend hippies, the Ibiza crowd had acid Teds. A year after the original British acid housers or Balearics had posited themselves against the mainstream club scene, they were forced to reposition themselves against a new mainstream: the acid Teds. Ted was a by-word for the average male. It could be argued that the media hype caused by the initial police crackdown on raves created an even bigger audience: a new breed of unhip and inauthentic ravers exhibiting outdated, stereotyped rave antics. Thus began the fight between the elitist/underground and populist/mainstream camps in rave culture.

The scene fractured into sub-scenes and sub-genres, each diverging from rave's original path. The hypocrisy of rave was beginning to show. The scene that initially purported to be about unity, love and equality, now exhibited a number of restricting not unifying attitudes relating to class, drug choice, musical preference and clothing style. Clubs like Shoom now imposed strict door policies that ran contrary to their own initial ideology of unity and acceptance. Ironically, despite the new restrictiveness imposed by the originators, the new young recruits to the hardcore rave scene were enjoying the same innocent euphoria that the Ibiza crew had experienced a couple of years earlier. The original crew didn't abandon their scene, they abandoned what they were calling it. By 1993 rave had peaked in England with crowds of 25,000 at Fantazia and Vision events. The honeymoon had ended for some, but was only commencing for others.

Even though the amount of people doing ecstasy and going to raves steadily increased, the original acid house crew now withdrew from the big outdoor raves viewing them as too commercial, impersonal and their followers too young. Rave was in a tug-of-war between the mainstream and the underground, the hip and the regular, those part of something new versus the sheep-like followers. One year after rave began in England, two distinct rave factions had developed, leaving the definition of rave highly contested.

North America. In the U.S. the transition from initiators to followers was also taking place. In New York, Frankie Bones's Stormraves were becoming successful. As the raver base grew there was enough room in the scene for entrepreneurial spirit and more than one promoter. Michael Caruso started having warehouse events that catered to a somewhat different crowd than the Stormraves crowd. Caruso's crowd was reportedly a little rougher and into more aggressive music. In 1992 Caruso held hardcore nights at both the Limelight and the Palladium in New York. These events were accused of being more commercial than Stormraves, and the headbanging and slamdancing suggested the environment wasn't as loving as at an old-style rave. In the summer of that year another club came to the fore that attempted to bring the underground back to rave. Ex-Londoner DJ DB, who had opened Breakbeat Science, the first exclusively jungle record store on the East Coast, opened his renowned club NASA in 1992. NASA brought a hardcore edge to New York's primarily techno and house rave scene. Within a few months NASA's crowd was initiating the fashion that would become synonymous with North American rave. Tinged with elements of New York hip-hop, the look included baggy pants hanging well off the waist and the childlike accessories of backpacks and pigtails.

Also in the early 1990s San Francisco's ToonTown events were attracting audiences into the thousands. Their success inspired many commercial spectacle-oriented raves, some of which even had virtual real-

The biggest change has been the influx of new faces and the outflux of old ones. With that change of course come many others but that is the major cause for most of the changes. The problem with this influx is that those who are newer to the scene never get to see how positively beautiful it can be and as such they don't respect it, and because they don't respect it those coming after them only see people who don't respect it and repeat the process. They don't understand that our scene was based on music and dance. Instead they only get to believe it was based on drugs and violence. I can't blame them but I can in the least do my best to show the error of their ways which is why I founded a dance team. **FU MAN CHU, Eatontown, NJ, age 21, M, 7 yrs.**

I don't think underground means a specific percentage of the people. I think underground means a culture that is ostracized from the mainstream and is not allowed, is not accepted. And that's what this culture was in the beginning. **BEVERLEY MAY, promoter.**

When the myth became reality, when the plebes turned up en masse for the party in 1991-92, rave became a dirty word; Ecstasy was passé, undignified. **SIMON REYNOLDS, *Generation Ecstasy*, 181**

Too many people getting drunk and not understanding house music, and throwing stuff at the DJs . . . far to many "beer boys" invading the scene and spoiling it. **Alji, Oxford, England, age 42, M, 24 yrs.**

[53]

Q. Describe the crowd at these initial events/nights?

A. Nothing like what it is today. Clothes were somewhat similar (phat denim pants, printed tees, visors, colorful plastic jewelry) but the mentality was totally different. Secrecy was the word back then. Ravers felt exclusive, they felt like they were part of some secret, forbidden underground society. We felt like renegades and rebels. People would be in shock and disbelief as we would walk past by them with our large, oversized pants. Today, with the novelty and exclusivity gone, it's just about wearing the right clothes, finding the right drugs and staying up all night. Don't get me wrong, people can still party like never before! Hell, I'm still out there every month. **DJ PSONYK, Montréal, QC, age 30, F, 8 yrs.**

ity stations. Full Moon parties took an almost extremist grassroots approach to their events that contrasted sharply with the mass ToonTown raves. These spiritually-oriented events were free, away from the city core and always outdoors. While the San Francisco scene was embracing nature, techno-shamanism and spirituality, the Los Angeles scene was following the progression that had happened with England's rave explosion. After Moonshine had proved the success of rave-oriented events, events became more grandiose in their production and their locales. Les Borsai took rave in Los Angeles to the next level. In the quest for the most extravagant production, he held one event with a fully foamed dance floor and another with a full carnival. Daven-the-Mad-Hatter-Michaels was another promoter who continued the process of one-upmanship for the most spectacular events. In June 1991 Daven threw the first outdoor rave in Los Angeles which would help initiate the city's reputation for desert raves. The rave scene in Los Angeles became so huge that by 1992 the city had a radio station dedicated to techno called Mars FM.

> As [an] ex-raver gets older, a bit of cynicism sets in. I have tried to maintain a good attitude about it and to reject the depressed kind of whining that you hear so often about how good the scene used to be. It's kind of true, but I really feel that attitude is mostly just a refection of the individual's state of mind and current situation vis-a-vis the scene. **Ian Guthrie, promoter.**

Toronto. You didn't need drugs to experience it, or fancy clothes, or even your friends around to experience it. You simply needed to be free enough to allow yourself to not only hear the music, but to feel it, consume it and allow it to consume you. Without drugs, or with ecstasy no longer having the effect it once did, it becomes more difficult to feel. You have to work at it. Finding that one spot in the crowd where people aren't going to encroach in your space, where there are enough people dancing like mad around you, where you feel no one is watching you, where you can feel that you are a part of everything around you. At that very instant you are as free as you've ever been. A feeling that I can no longer find at the massive events because I no longer feel welcome. All of a sudden it seemed that there were too many people, too much of a spectacle and too much to look at. That sacred space was no longer mine, it was everyone's.

Like the Balearics in England who resented the acid Teds, self proclaimed "originals" in Toronto condemned new, younger recruits and the commercially-oriented raves they attended. Ian Guthrie of *Transcendance* magazine in Toronto suggested in 1996 that rave had simply become another youth culture. Old ravers accused the new, younger generation of being too concerned with fashion and drugs. Some participants were starting to deny that the events they attended were raves. For some, the word rave now signified a mainstream commercial event with which they didn't want to be associated.

The quiet divide between Toronto rave promoters was evident even when there were only two production companies. Exodus produced the original underground events and Nitrous produced the more commercial events. The third event by Nitrous offered an all-night midway in a field north of Toronto with eight local DJs, a ferris wheel, bumper cars and an octopus ride. Each Nitrous rave tried to outdo the last with increased spec-

A cheerleader from my school went to her first rave and someone told her to do five rolls and she did and I just felt so bad for her . . . she didn't OD or anything but she was just acting so ignorant and that just ruined the party for me to think about the rave culture getting so mainstream that cheerleaders were going to it and compromising it all because they are ignorant and will eat anything. **PRINCESS NIKITTA, Cabot, AR, age 19, F, 2 yrs.**

Q. What is your favorite type of venue for a party and why?

A. I love parties that are outdoors because you really feel your connection to the earth and that is part of the whole rave ideal. **KITTEN, New York, NY, age 21, F, 7 yrs.**

I would have to say a cave. I went to a party one time that was in a cave [and] the music was echoing everywhere! **KORTNI BUTLER, Atlanta, GA, age 18, F, 3 yrs.**

Places that you're not supposed to party in, like empty department stores, bingo halls or abandoned churches. The juxtaposition between the mad flashing party, and the space's original . . . use adds to the surreal, parallel universe effect. **SYNAPSE, Toronto, ON, age 27, M, 8 yrs.**

Vancouver Island, in the middle of a forest, nowhere near anywhere else . . . loud, loud, loud . . . **CAPTAIN NUTMEG, Vancouver, BC, age 26, M, 8 yrs.**

Jim Trickett's Full Moon parties—every month on the full moon, no matter when that was—so sometimes like a Tuesday, if that's when it fell! Always outdoors. Outdoors in B.C. means at least a 1.5-2 hour drive, up past Squamish or Whistler and then up a logging road. Always an adventure, [and] if it was good weather it was amazing. Usually on a riverbank, a beautiful panorama of forest and water . . . amazing sunrises. **TOBIAS V, Vancouver, BC, age 23, M, 7 yrs.**

I think we (along with a few others), were just in the right place at the right time with the right attitude. People were looking for something that they felt was a little deeper than the others. Transcendance came about at the crest of what I call the first wave of cynicism, where partiers were just starting to realize that some aspects of the scene were not all they were cracked up to be. **IAN GUTHRIE, promoter.**

tacle appeal. Their "Full-E-Charged" rave was held in a 90,000 square foot warehouse with an indoor fireworks display and laser show that managed to blow out the power for the whole area. In contrast, smaller promoters like Exodus, who sometimes gave a portion of their proceeds to charity, had smaller venues, fewer DJs and less entertainment features.

As early as 1992 there were promoters who championed themselves as being underground. These promoters complained about the sensational excesses of Nitrous events. New companies like Sykosis prided themselves on being an underground solution to the mega raves. The flyer for the first Sykosis event in September of 1992 promised "Classic rave anthems without the mainstream commercial shit. Taking rave where it should be . . . back to the underground." Ben Ferguson of Sykosis announced during a college radio interview: "We want to bring things back to where they began. While other companies are worrying about bouncy castles or meeting points, we've been focusing on the music." [3] Much like the originals in England, some people in Toronto accused the scene of being dead and reminisced about the good old days in an effort to demonstrate their early allegiance to the scene and therefore their own superiority as an original.

A good party has to be more that just a DJ and a couple lights. I think it has to be an experience of the senses. Something that gives you a lot to look at, a lot to feel. I don't like the sort of rave thing where everyone faces the front and everyone looks at the DJ and the lights are all up front and the sound's all coming from up front. **JASON FORD, promoter.**

By 1994, Toronto's scene was large enough to allow smaller promoters to get a piece of the action. There were divisions now not only between promoters but between participants who were usually aligned with a particular division within the scene. Those who frequented smaller events often argued that the nurturing aspects of rave couldn't take place at massive venues. Some smaller events attempted to bring a more spiritual side to raving, others wanted to duplicate the mass rave environment but scaled down. Companies such as Transcendance were extremely successful, while others would have one-off parties.

Competition Mounts. In the mid-1990s, rave's growing prominence could be measured by the sheer volume of flyer art being distributed. The promoter had been transformed from a discreet messenger into a pushy salesman, battling for punters' attention. Exiting an event, ravers found themselves in a virtual tunnel of promoters bidding for their patronage by yelling out their upcoming headliners: "Kimball Collins!" "Derrick May!" "Josh Wink!" A sea of flyers would adorn the pavement outside clubs and raves. The following year I had my own event to flyer for. Many mornings I joined the tunnel of solicitation. "Please take my flyer, it cost 40 cents!" my eyes tried to scream. One raver grabbed a flyer, perused its glossy pictures, then threw it at my feet. With that defeat, I decided that I didn't have the ironclad constitution necessary for the new, commercialized business of rave promotion.

The sheer increase in rave events helped turn the noun "flyer" into a verb. As the more commercial raves grew to become more spectacular, so too did their flyers, showcasing the latest in graphic art technology. Flyers from the large parties often included outdated rave credos in the spirit of peace and love with typical slogans such as Liberation, Utopia, Kind and

Transcendance had a mandate to be more intense . . . than your typical event. We tried to have intellectual/ artistic themes that would be selected as a group [and] encompass all aspects of an event from flyer design to decor and music. As the years went on, our musical acts' quality also sharpened. We brought in artists that many others wouldn't have thought of, and would put them on at "peak hour." There was also a very powerful feeling of community around Transcendance, so powerful at times that it was almost frightening!
IAN GUTHRIE, promoter.

To a seasoned raver, the flyer will tell you whether it's your kind of gig or not. Simplistic imagery, straightforward fonts, less color and a smaller size will typically suggest a more techno-oriented event. Loud and boisterous in both imagery and size will often indicate a hardcore massive, while psychedelic imagery, Mandelbrots, fractals or East Indian motifs may be intended to entice trance-heads.

It tends to be the case that a promotional company books one good DJ and then builds a party around that with the same old tired-out list of cheesy shitty DJs, time and time again . . . and charges at least $35 to get in, "more at the door" plus "special VIP passes available." Anyway, as for spaces, Vancouver did a pretty good job of shutting everything down, leaving a few, horrible box-shaped venues with bad sound and fascist security . . . most of the crowd tends to be either girls-who've-never-done-E-until-omigod-now! who cannot dance and want you to impail yourself on their radioactive glowsticks; cracked-out crystalheads; people trying to sell you the aforementioned crystal and gangs standing around posing at each other. Scary and un-PLUR as possible.
CAPTAIN NUTMEG, Vancouver BC, age 26, M, 8 yrs.

The worst experience was definitely a Halloween party at the Docks. It was one of those huge raves (approximately 14,000 in attendance) thrown by Lifeforce. The only reason that I agreed to go to such a big party was because EPMD was going to be performing in the drum and bass tent. Having never had a chance to see them back in the day, I was very excited. We called the information line to make sure that we would be on time to catch them. EPMD was scheduled to come on at 12, so we got to the venue by 10. We ended up standing in line for over two and a half hours. During that wait, we had asshole security guards yelling at us and pushing us

Summer of Love. These flyers would advertise star DJs and public appearances from the U.S. and Europe. As attendance for these events climbed well into the thousands so did the DJs' fees. Only fully established promotion companies guaranteed to draw mass crowds paying $25 to $50 a head would risk the massive DJ fees and set-up costs. Companies would try to outdo one another by increasing the number of DJs at their events.

> **Q. Describe the worst time you ever had at a party.**
>
> **A.** NYC parties (Turkeyball in particular), when the promoters over-pack the venue and you can barely move or breathe in the place; when they cut off the water from the sinks so that you have to buy water at $5 a bottle; when everyone there doesn't give a shit about the music or dancing and is just bombed on dirty drugs like angel's dust; and when no one at the party could even spell the words vibe or PLUR. Thats when a party sucks.
>
> **ALEX PITSIRILOS, New York, NY, age 22, M, 2 yrs.**

In the early stages of rave in Toronto, promoters would often thank each other on their flyers for support and simply for being part of the same scene. This goodwill soon began to evaporate. Rave had become a battle of egos where bigger meant better: the biggest venue, the biggest acts, the most acts, the biggest crowd. Kind's New Year's 1997 rave was the first intended to be held in Toronto's SkyDome. Competing companies reputedly sabotaged this event by convincing SkyDome management that a rave held on their premises would put their reputation at risk because of illegal activity that would undoubtedly take place. After relocating, Kind then had to react to accusations from other promoters that their DJs weren't officially booked. They posted their DJ contracts on the Internet. Kind promised 14 headliners, four live public appearances, a staggering 57 local DJs, a bouncy castle, clowns, stilt-walkers, massage booths and virtual reality set-ups. Toronto's three biggest promoters banded together in an attempt to outdo Kind's efforts that night. The outcome was two massive spaces that were barely full. The tug of war that took place that New Year's was not only sad, but it left rave's purported ideals of unity and respect in question. Competition this fierce was the eventual impetus behind the amalgamation of Toronto's four largest rave companies in 1998. The new company, called Lifeforce, was capable of producing parties so huge that it was futile for anyone else to compete with it on the same night. The exception was if you were part of the smaller, niche party circuit that attracted a completely different crowd.

The niche scenes that became prominent by the mid-1990s encompassed a number of different subgroups. Some of these small parties were spiritually, new age or hippie-influenced, some were purely experimental, while others catered to a more elite and older rave crowd. Transcendance was one of the more successful smaller companies that stood in opposition to the burgeoning mass rave scene. Their small party flyers often had little information on them and were much less extravagant than those advertising large raves. Often they would have only one or two obscure headliners; some didn't even list DJs. These flyers were generally less enticing to newcomers or very young ravers seeking mass rave spectacles.

so that we would form a tighter line, (a line that was over 20 people wide and a kilometre long) though this was impossible as there was a mob of people waiting. Then to top things off there was a drunk tourist . . . who proceeded to make racist and homophobic comments to many of the people in line, and who rounded off his performance by singing obnoxious songs at the top of his lungs and pulling out his John Thomas and peeing on the rails right in front of us. Finally, when we got in, we managed to catch the last two songs that EPMD had left. I'd love to say that the rest of the night got better but it did not. What a waste of $35! **PEANUT71, Toronto, ON, age 29, F, 4 yrs.**

"Rave New World" most certainly spear-headed the entire movement in Montréal but in terms of taking it to the next level? The Nexus parties ('94) established raves in fairly large warehouses. Then came along 514 Productions who single-handedly managed to bring raves into the mainstream light, attracting thousands and thousands of people to their "Swirl" and "Cream" events through extensive public-ity. Because of them, raves are now a casual [thing] to do on a Saturday night. On the positive side, it has forced smaller parties deep into the underground where smaller, more devoted groups can be found. **DJ PSONYK, Montréal, QC, 30, M, 8 yrs.**

Rave left a bad taste in many mouths as it started encompassing what it initially denied, the excesses of clublife. As a reactionary measure, Beverly May started Ritual in 1996 and tried to escape the trappings of rave by executing a more purist event that maintained musical integrity in an artistic production. Ritual events generally appealed to musical purists and older participants. These "non-rave" raves shunned the glow-stick brigade by having a no glowstick policy printed on their flyers. Tiny in comparison to typical rave flyers, the Ritual flyers were usually black or dark blue with little design or flourish. The fact of being held in licensed venues helped to ensure that any under-age "E-mongers" would not attend because alcohol was indisputably un-rave. For Beverly May, rave is a particular aesthetic, a particular community, a particular music and a particular delivery of that music. Like in Britain, the division of elitists versus populists, the underground versus the masses, had fractured the Toronto scene, leaving the definition of rave in question.

Mass Raves. As the size and number of parties increased, compa-nies started becoming more specialized musically. Participants started enjoying one particular sub-genre of house and techno and would often seek out promotion companies that would cater to their tastes. In Toronto at a Destiny party you would expect mostly trance, while at Better Days or Dose parties it would be progressive house. Syrous was jungle and Hul-labaloo was typically hardcore. The number of rooms at raves also changed dramatically over a few years, growing from one room events to one room plus a traditional chill-out room with slower more ambient-oriented music where participants could come-down off their drugs and rest. Later there was a move toward two dance rooms plus a chill-out room, the main room being the promoter's usual brand of music and the other smaller room offering a variant. Syrous for example, would generally have jungle in the main room, and house in the small room. Companies like Phryl would typically have techno in the main room and jungle in the

Your description of mass raves today?

A. I can sum them up in a few words: "Rave-in-a-box." **Ian Guthrie, promoter.**

smaller room. With many participants on amphetamine overloads, the need for chill-out rooms decreased until eventually they were only evident at small parties. By the mid-1990s entrance lineups could often be two or more hours long, while bathroom and water lineups could be up to a half-hour long. Ominous bouncers would frisk entering ravers while security guards would shine their flashlights at anyone sitting around or looking "suspicious." By 1999, large events often attracted more than 15,000 people and had up to four rooms. Crowds exceeded capacity and were often left with barely enough room to dance while condensation would drip like rain from the ceilings.

Occasionally at parties the issue of going to the bathroom can be a challenge, to say the least. Sometimes the raves I went to were held in warehouses, where there were only two toilets for hundreds of people; and as you can imagine, you could be waiting in a line up for about an hour. On other occasions, some promoters were smart enough to rent porta-potties, but those are quite nasty, and sometimes you also had to line up for those. The worst, the absolute worst warehouse party toilet experience I've ever had took place in a Toronto suburb in 1996. The promoters went to the trouble and the cost of setting up a very impressive rotating DJ stage that was located in the middle of the dance floor. But what they seemed to forget was the importance of washroom facilities! After waiting in a very long line up, I was extremely disappointed to find that there were no toilets, and that in their place were plastic garbage pails! Most of the guys that were there took advantage of these pails, but needless to say, I held onto my pee all night! And believe me, that is a very difficult thing to do when you're really high on E! **SHLOOPY, Toronto, ON, age 28, F, 6 yrs.**

the jaded raver survey

You snicker when you hear someone say "PLUR"
You finally realize that phat pants are heavy and impractical
You blame candy kids for everything retarded in the scene
You find out how much better European electronic music really is
You realize how cool Drum 'n' Bass is
You realize how lame progressive trance is
You find out that American DJs are completely overrated
You have close friends that don't give a fuck about raving
You think that maybe you don't give a fuck either
The smell of Vicks makes you physically ill
You can't help but laugh when someone tries to give you a "glowstick show"
You learn to break
You drink beer at parties
You quit collecting flyers
You wouldn't mind if that kid with the whistle accidentally swallowed it and died
You are actually called by your real name
You realize the general public shouldn't be blamed for hating raves
You talk s?!t as much as possible
You DESPISE happy hardcore
You DESPISE candy
You no longer feel the need to advertise your "rave-ness" to the world
You party sober and now understand how stupid you looked when you didn't
You know who PRODUCED your favorite tracks, not just which DJ bought it and put it on a mix CD
You think that dancing like you're running in place has all the skill and style of a penguin waddling with a stick up its butt
You have day dreams that involve Teletubbies and a large rusty chainsaw
Your parents gave up on you ever becoming normal a long time ago
You hate rave hoes
You begin to notice how often big DJs blow mixes
You think sweaty guys running around the party shirtless should get their asses kicked out
You act like a punk-ass bitch to security, police and any other authority
You say "ill" a lot
You know that raving is all about the music, but RAVERS are not
You've "accidentally" kicked people sitting in the middle of the dance floor
You find the jungle room more appealing now
You can actually DANCE to jungle
You realize that ravers aren't nearly as genuine as hippies were
You see guys from your high school football team at a party (refer to aformentioned "sweaty guys without shirts")
You know raving is mainstream as fuck
The bigger the flyer, the less you want to go
You can re-tell the story of how raving came to America quite accurately
Your sleeping and eating habits are completely f?!ked up
You are amazed that you are somehow still alive
You can't remember the last time you went to a party and didn't think it sucked
You can't remember much in general

from www. ravers.org/surveys/general/jaded.shtml

a rave called nonentity.

SOMETIME IN 1996.

3-4 p.m. On any given Saturday there's usually a choice of a few different events. Today it's a choice between a smaller party, possibly better vibe or a larger event with some of my favorite DJs. I opt for the DJs as usual. Small parties are nice but the music just has to rock for me to have a wicked time. I rush to a downtown record store to buy our tickets before they sell out.

5 p.m. I worked this morning, so I try to nap in order to make it through the night.

7:30 p.m. My brother and I go out to dinner with my parents. They're very suspicious that we're not having wine with them tonight. How do you explain to your parents that alcohol is somewhat taboo in the rave scene? E and alcohol don't seem to mix. Alcohol makes you stupid, tired and forgetful; E makes you aware, highly sensitized and alert. We tell my parents we're going to a concert that will be going very late, a slight stretch of the truth. It's too difficult to try and explain what a rave is without having them worry!

9 p.m. A huge difference between attending a club for a couple of hours and attending a rave is the amount of gear and preparation involved in going to a rave. With clubs usually closing at 3 a.m. the maximum time I'd be there is about three hours. At a rave I could be there up to 10 hours, sometimes even more. Setting up home base was kinda like setting up a campground for the night. I'd need to come fully prepared with all the rave-camp essentials:

Toilet paper / I'm not sure if there will be 'real' toilets or porta-potties which may have paper but are usually so dark that you can't find it, or don't want to in fear of someone having pissed on it. If the event does have real toilets chances are by 2 a.m. there will be no paper left anyway. **Camera** / everyone deserves their picture taken at a party! **Hard candies** / I'm not a candy raver but candies are always fun to share with people. **Gum** / when jaws are grinding, gum is a good thing. **Pen, paper** / meeting people and exchanging numbers and email addresses is inevitable. **Oranges** / I'll never forget the first time someone gave me an orange in the morning at a rave. It was absolutely heavenly! **Muscle Rub** / I'm pretty sick of the smell of vapo rub, it actually makes me nauseous. I still like the occasional massage and this does the trick for dance ache! **Ear plugs** / I opt for a little less sound quality in hopes of still having hearing when I'm old.

9:30 p.m. The outfit. I decide on my blueberry scratch 'n' sniff Japanimation baby tee and my phat jeans. I put my hair into Princess Lea buns, a small star sticker on either temple, glitter on my arms, eyelids and neck. The finishing touch is my big beads that I've hand-painted to match my shirt. And of course my dancing shoes: my patent red Airwalks with the silver pom-poms I glued to the ends of the laces. They make me feel like I'm dancing on a cloud! Some people will recognize me for the way I do my hair, others will know the shirt. Rave ensembles are childlike in the sense that the details became meaningful, like the boisterous color of your shoes.

10 p.m. Drug prep 101: We phone around and see who has what goods. Angels, doves or crowns, we opt for the faithful angels from the dealer we've come to know and love. I never rely on finding stuff at the party—too expensive, too risky. They could be duds or they could be laced with god knows what. I pull off two tabs of acid from the sheet we bought a while back. I also pack a baggie of Tylenol for those morning headaches I get so often.

11 p.m. I phone the info line to find out where tonight's festivities are taking place. A warehouse in the West End that hasn't been used before . . . always a good sign. We drive around aimlessly looking for the event. The chase is part of the fun—like a scavenger hunt. We've already got the tunes pumping in the car and I feel nauseous with expectation—the good butterflies.

12 p.m. We see other cars filled with ravers. We're there at last. The line-up is monstrous . . . it will be at least an hour till we get inside. We wait shivering as the windows shake with sound teasing us all with the fun that lies ahead. It will be a night tinged with many anticipations, plateaus and releases.

anticipation while in the line, to get past the bouncers
anticipation before you pop the pill
anticipation before you peak
anticipation to hear your favorite DJ

12:45 a.m. We're getting close so I hide my drugs. One little baggie goes in my underwear, another baggy goes inside my shoe under the arch of my foot. This is the moment when the butterflies start eating away at your stomach as the eagerness turns to the anxiety of passing the bouncers. You know they won't find anything, but that doesn't ease your fear. I just pray they won't ask me to take off my shoes or feel my crotch!

1 a.m. I'm in! Anxiety melts away and morphs into sheer relief and pure elation. As I surrender my ticket and walk into the space, I'm hit by a wall of sound. This is the point of the night I'm on the outside, still an observer and not yet a participant. We wander around in awe of the crowd, the space and the intensity of the moment. The music is like a soundtrack at this point, it hasn't completely absorbed me. It's only surrounding me. It's like being on the edge of a whirlpool; I know my being sucked in is completely inevitable and strangely desirable. The energy from the room starts bubbling inside me.

1 : 15 a.m. Attending an event has become ritualized—especially ones in warehouses such as this which lack the ease and security of a coat check, running water and toilets. These are the raves where condensation of recycled body heat and sweat drop as rain from the rafters. After casing the main room we find home base, that security zone where if any of us get lost we will come back to and find each other; the place where our stuff will be safe and the vibe seems good. We fill our plastic garbage bags we brought with our jackets and extra gear. The garbage bags will help keep our clothes dry from the floor that will inevitably become sopping wet, and will also serve as a wonderful pillow. By 5 a.m. I know nothing will be more heavenly than having our own plastic bag mattress filled with puffy jackets . . . a godsend for those moments my feet will feel as though they weigh at least 200 lbs each. The floor will more than likely get so dingy that only those completely comatose will be brave enough, or fucked up enough to sit down.

We start planning our "trip," coordinating when we'll "drop" in order to peak together and at the right point in the night. A playlist will tell us who's spinning when and in which room. We buy our water; I buy my glowsticks. I start feeling at ease and completely familiar with the event. I recognize faces, outfits and dance moves. I am awash with a willingness to let go and take what comes. I'm no longer concerned about losing my friends; there is a complete realization that I'll be taken care of. If I run out of water, someone will give me some; if I need gum someone will offer. I'm free enough to lose myself in the chaos of the moment. The whirlpool of sound pulls me in like a piece of debris . . . I'm sucked in and there is comfort within the chaos.

2 a.m. I've been holding off going to the can, in avoidance of the lineup and the stench of the porta-potties. Boys and girls mingle in the bathroom line, chat and connect. There is no separation of gender in a raver bathroom. Finally inside, it's so dark I can't see where I'm "going," so dank I can barely breathe. The plastic walls shake a split second after the beats. It's like being in an odd plastic womb, or more appropriately the bowels of the whole party.

This piss seems to take forever. How long have I been in here?
I'm starting to feel it, I've got to get out of here, there couldn't be a worse place to peak!

2:30 a.m. My fingers tingle. I feel slightly chilled by the sweat on my body. The tingle rises up my arms and then it's through me. There is a familiar warmth that comes from within and envelops me whole. Angels start dancing inside my body. I'm so overwhelmed I can't even move. I just want to relish how my body feels. I reach for the hand that's nearest to me (it happens to be my brother's) and squeeze it tight. We look at each other, shake our heads, smile, exhale and close our eyes . . . it's here! It's such a beautiful thing to share this moment of synergy with someone I'm already so close to.

The rush of energy inside me is like a freight train pulsing through my veins. The beats are now made of liquid and permeate the bodies they encounter. The room has become MUSIC. Thoughts dissipate and all that remains is bodies in motion.

A smile from a stranger indicates that they know the rules. I could ask them for water and they'd share. These are the people I'll likely bump into later and acknowledge a connection has been made by a smile and a nod, possibly a hug. I learn about people by how they move, not what they say. The more open and free they are, the more enjoyable they are to watch and the easier they are to connect with.

3:00 a.m. A huge silver ball is bounced around above everyone's head. A girl with massive curlers in her hair blows bubbles everywhere. She sprinkles talcum powder on the floor to make the floor less sticky and easier to dance on. In the smaller techno room everything is completely black. Then I notice glowing yellow hair with little horns made out of tinfoil accentuated by the one tiny black light. I tell him his hair looks amazing and we delight in the fact that we're wearing the same silver nail polish. We exchange email addresses; a strong connection is made. I don't realize this now but this bond is indefinite.

Sound becomes distorted by thoughts, visuals and lights. Strangers start looking completely familiar, everyone looks brighteyed and beautiful. There have never been so many elated people in one room. My mind becomes a rapid succession of thoughts in time with the music and then they just melt away . . . another build of energy.

There are sheer masses of movement. Herds of people migrate from room to room, to the bathrooms, to get water. The swirls of movement are enticing to watch. I turn toward the stage and notice a sea of hands in the air. I'm obviously not the only one excited! Everyone seems to simultaneously predict the upcoming build in the music. Together we anticipate the music's climax and suddenly . . . explosion! Whistles blow, people cheer, glowsticks slice through the smokefilled air. The music takes on new meaning. The rhythms are fluid. The crowd is a pulsating mass, a physical rejoice of the music that is in us. We're all completely in tune with the DJ's flows and ebbs. Enraptured by the beat. I experience a whole new range of emotion that I don't allow myself to in a normal environment. It's just too high. A flailing, dancing arm bumps into me, pulling me out of my trance. It's jarring but wonderful.

The crowd has changed without my realizing. It's more intense. The lightweights and the club crowd that are used to leaving events at 2 to 3 a.m. have left. Rippers (peelers) arrive after a hard night's work. Everyone's drugs, whether natural endorphins or synthetic highs, have all kicked in.

There is a refreshing openness to the crowd. We are organized around different signifiers of meaning from everyday life and club life. Status is no longer a signifier of value. Movement becomes a signifier. What is important is my rhythm and my body language, rather than my spoken language: my intensity, rather than my words.

Because we can't hear or see each other very well, we rely on another way of communicating. We give ourselves a chance to be de-socialized. There are new norms here. We are strangers squished together as close as in an elevator or subway car but we allow ourselves the freedom to connect and share and not be strangers. The value of simple things such as candy, water and smiles takes on a whole new importance.

4 a.m. For the 1 1/2 to 2 hours after you've dropped you're too fucked up to care what time it is. Time is fluid and has no meaning—your experience is now and completely of the moment. I no longer have the same points of reference; there is psychological and physical distortion.

Different people catch different rhythms and beats in the same music. Some connect to the highs, some to the low beats. All these different movements are manifesting the music and its multitude of ranges. Everyone's in time as long as they catch one of the music's elements. Our variety of dance interpretations to the sound creates a symphony of movement; it's fantastic to watch.

4:30 a.m. I see this girl playing with a tiny, stuffed pink bunny rabbit. I realize I've met her before, at my work of all places. Seeing her in this environment immediately indicates we can be friends. Connections are what I love about raves.

I look up and see that there are people dancing with their heads inside the speakers, a few others are even dancing on top of the huge speaker stack.

5 a.m. In the chill out room I see a guy sitting by himself. He looks like he needs a massage so I give him one. Afterwards we hug, chat and exchange numbers. I've made another friend.

I realize the pain in my legs. I only had four hours of sleep the night before, and taught dance all day. As I reach into my pocket to pull out my drug of choice, an extra-strength Tylenol, I am all dodgy and shifty. I realize how pitiful it is that I have to hide my painkillers as if they are illicit.

6 a.m. A glimmer of light starts to come through the warehouse windows that have been covered in paper. I love this time at a party: the second wave. A new DJ changes the energy completely: their music is lighter and less intense—more floaty and slower. People are forced to move and dance differently to this new rhythm. The DJ has recognized that the crowd is becoming tired and can't move with the same intensity. A good DJ will always be gentler with the crowd in the morning.

7 a.m. The crowd has dissipated. Those that have stuck around are recognized as the hardcore: full of life and energy, or drugs! They have the desire to keep things going and ignore the fact that morning is here. There is ample room to dance now. People seem to be gaining back their usual sense of reality. The entire space is less chaotic because everything seems familiar, including the faces. I know the room, I feel like I know everyone in it, I'm relaxed, comfortable, at ease. The tension of the night has broken and is permeated by a sense of resolution. I feel that I've shared something with everyone that remains. Most of us have allowed ourselves to interact in ways that are foreign in our 9 to 5 lives. We're all basking together in the afterglow of the evening's ecstatic moments. Some of us have been here over seven hours already. We all try and give one last burst of energy in homage to the DJ, the music and the night. We know this will be the last plateau of bliss.

8:30 a.m. There is an overwhelming sense of satisfaction making it to the end of a rave. It's as though you've completed a marathon. There is a strong, unspoken connection with the people that are left. We've communicated all night through our movements, our smiles and our sharing of water, hugs, massages and candies.

9 a.m. Abruptly, the lights come up. We all clap and cheer for the DJ. Everyone seems a little dazed, a little confused, not quite prepared for the task of getting home. I realize everyone that looked so shiny and beautiful now looks a little tweaked and haggard. Many people are obviously a little too fucked up to make eye contact in this harsh brightness. Some still look a little speedy, sketchy and jittery; others seem slightly awkward and deflated. The euphoria has left and the harsh reality of the party's end is now setting in. It's all over for at least a week.

A really cute boy that I've been watching dance all night asks if I'm going to the after party. I decide I'm in love. I tell him I don't usually go to afterparties because I like my sleep and want the night to end on this wonderful, positive note. I give him my card though and hope and pray that he calls. Who says raves aren't meeting places? I've always thought that afterparties, which can start as early as 10 a.m. and go until 11 p.m. or later Sunday night, are for a different breed. They cater to the very hardcore, the speed freaks, the sleep deprived.

The bouncers start yelling at us to get out. I scramble to find my stuff that I know I left by some pole if I could only figure out which one. I feel like I've gone traveling, tired but satisfied. Everyone's ushered abruptly out the door as we say good-bye to one another. It feels as though we've spent the weekend together… I guess we kind of have. There is a feeling of contentment knowing that I'm likely to see most of these people again. The air outside is cold and brisk but the sun is shining. These mornings are beautiful.

9:10 a.m. The running of the flyer gauntlet. The act of flyering has progressed considerably. Initially a few promoters would hand you a flyer inside the party while you went from room to room or when you were leaving the event. It felt like an invite because it was usually the promoter distributing them. I used to love getting flyers when there were only a few distributed on any given night. I'd start planning my next event. Then promoters stopped letting competitors in with flyers so they were forced to solicit outside. Now the process has progressed to as many as 20 people ramming flyers into your hands. It was no longer the actual promoter, it was a flyer monkey paid $8/hour to distribute four or five different events. They battle for the hard sell like used car salesmen, yelling out the DJ names of their events so you'll take their flyer. I don't feel as though any of these flyers are invites, they are simply solicitations. The sidewalk has become a colorful sea of flyer refuse.

9:30 a.m. We drive home. Quiet, serene, content. Exhausted.

10:00 a.m. My neighbors are out gardening . . . I know they think I'm a vagrant. My dad's awake when I walk up to my room; I hope I don't look as sketchy as I feel. Trying to sleep with the sun already beaming through my curtains is always a challenge. Sunday has begun for the neighborhood, my Saturday is just ending. When I close my eyes I still feel the throng of the party. My ears are ringing, the beats still seem to be playing from the recesses of my brain. I dance myself to sleep.

Sunday I sleep right through until 5 p.m. My mom wakes me up to make dinner. I don't think I can stomach much food, but I try for the sake of appearances.

Monday I spend the day reminiscing; relishing memorable moments with those I went with. My world is back to "normal" and feels unbearably boring. Recovering from the sheer high of the event is always a challenge. I feel emptiness. I wish I could share my secret world with everyone I know and love. Having been so high, so joyful, so in love with the moment . . . Will I ever get there again? I'll try next weekend.

Bunny, age 27, F, 6yrs

AS EARLY AS age three I was enraptured by the stage. Being a very shy child, the stage allowed me to disappear into myself and reappear as someone else. On stage, I was in complete control of who I was and who others saw me as. I was beginning to learn the meaning of the stage, the place of simulation. I was six when I performed my first dance solo. I had already been dancing for three years, but this moment was magical. I can still remember my costume. It was red with white polka-dots and my tap shoes were black patent leather. I also recall my initial fear turning to excitement, then elation, as the audience melted away and I realized I was in my own spotlight. My feet seemed to move more quickly than ever before and suddenly I was free.

05
MEANINGFUL MOVEMENTS

Dancing lets me feel my true energy and lets me release my pain. When I hear the music outside my stomach turns; I get so excited like I just want to start dancing right outside all the way through the doors to heaven. I really hope heaven has DJ's! =) **KATIE, Orlando, FL, age 20, F, 4 yrs.**

Dancing at raves allowed me to express aspects and facets of my life and myself that I didn't have an outlet to express in everyday life. It allowed me to experience myself not as a reflection of other people's judgements but as an expression of my freedom. **PSYCHEDELIC PHD, Toronto, ON, age 25, M, 6 yrs.**

I was 21 when I danced at my first rave. I remember my outfit: I wore denim overalls, Nike running shoes and my hair in pigtails. I experienced the fear and excitement of taking part in something that was deemed underground and possibly immoral. I was transported by a small ferry to the Island Airport hangar where the event was taking place. The butterflies in my stomach calmed as the crowd melted away and I drew in the lights and absorbed the bass. Suddenly my feet moved without me telling them to and I was reunited with the freedom I felt as a child dancing on stage.

Dance serves no purpose that can be qualified or quantified. It is simply a feeling expressed in motion. Dance is poetry of and by the body. A dance simultaneously starts and ends with movement. Impulses simply float off your fingertips into the air. A body gives dance a life and then watches it disappear. It is the most virtual of the arts. The only evidence that a dance ever lived is the sweat on your back and the race of your heart.

Dancing is about expression, it's about feeling, it's about the individual. There are no words.
Tamara Ross, Kelowna, BC, age 16, F, 3 yrs.

The feelings one experiences when dancing are difficult to articulate. When dance is subjected to analysis, the outcome is generally a rationalization of the social arenas surrounding dance or the philosophical underpinnings of the cultural art form. Typically the dancing body becomes lost in a sea of theoretical jargon and rationales. Cultural theorists, dance scholars, and dancers-turned-scholars have repeatedly tried to find meaning in motion. Perhaps motion doesn't create meaning through any outcome, but is meaningful in itself.

Of a myriad of convoluted theories of dance, it seems the integral question, "Why do we dance?" is often ignored. Perhaps the question is too basic for theorists, akin to asking why we walk. Because we can. A three-year-old has a need to move in a free-form, unregimented manner. The child hears music and needs to move to it. We call this movement dance whether it's a recognized dance movement or not. Through successive definitions of what dance is in artistic terms, Western culture slowly helps shut the doors to free movement and assigns instead, specific movements to the body. Hence, dance becomes an execution of a particular arrangement of pre-determined steps in which a teacher or defined style of dance dictates whether the movement is correct or not. This arrangement extends to social functions such as clubs, weddings and bar mitzvahs. In social settings participants aren't necessarily complying with an artistic aesthetic so much as they are subscribing to the status quo and what culture deems an appropriate social movement. Those that do not are often ridiculed.

This fear of dancing inappropriately is quite pervasive. In one episode of the sitcom *Seinfeld*, one of the main characters, Elaine, is ridiculed for dancing terribly at an office Christmas party. On the soap opera *Coronation Street*, the character Roy is so ashamed of his lack of rhythm that he secretly takes disco dancing lessons before going to a disco with his girlfriend. It is commonplace for adults to confess they can't dance when in social situations where dance is expected. On the contrary, a child's natural and innocent movement to music is considered dance whether they

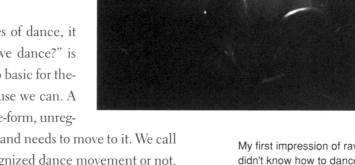

My first impression of rave was that I didn't know how to dance. My sister came up to me and said no one cares what you look like you know. And I was like oh OK and I started dancing like mad. **LITTLE ZERO, Toronto, ON, age 29, M, 7 yrs.**

[73]

Dancing is foremost a physical expression or representation of our music and the energy/emotion it invokes in its listeners. That's why in general people have different styles of dancing for techno/house/drum and bass, etc. When you are dancing you are showing what the music means to you, how it moves you and your personal (and for me very intimate) interpretation of the music. For me this alone makes dancing incredibly important to the scene. Also I believe it is a form of moving meditation and when done in unison with 1,000 [or] 20,000 people it can be a profound spiritual/emotional experience.

Alex Pitsirilos, New York, NY, age 22, M, 2 yrs.

understand it as such or not. Somewhere between infancy and adulthood the doors to free movement are closed. At raves these doors are opened again. Movement is suddenly liberated, and participants dance with reckless abandon much like children on their living room floor. All of a sudden the fear of social scrutiny and criticism is forgotten and, to borrow from Grace Jones, participants become slaves to the rhythm.

There is one important element absent from most accounts of rave. It is dancing that is the mainstay of the rave community, offering a variety of personal and individual meanings to those who participate. Dance is an outlet for self-expression and often a unifying experience in a highly stratified culture. Raves are a breeding ground for dance. They initiate it and maintain it for hours on end, until legs wear out or drugs wear off. Popular analyses of rave and its cultural meaning often omit the very root of rave's existence: that the participants have gathered communally in order to dance. The act of dancing itself is lost in repetitive critiques of the morals of drug use and of hedonism. By taking dance out of both its academic and regular club confines, raves help to establish dance as a meaningful, non-rational form of communication—an innate human activity.

Marginalization of Dance. Dance is often rationalized away and sometimes outright ignored in much sociological literature. It takes up little theoretical space in comparison to other cultural barometers such as music. This may be due in part to dance's transitory nature. In other arts such as painting and sculpture you are left with the artistic product. In poetry and literature you have the written word, and with music you have a musical score. The dancing body and the dance cannot be separated. Dance disappears into the air, leaving nothing tangible to be scrutinized and analyzed.

It has been suggested that dance first became marginalized in the West during the Middle Ages. During this period in Europe, the Catholic church condemned anything hedonistic. One's main purpose in life was to save one's soul. The body was seen as a hindrance to this goal. In order

to free the soul the body was ignored and punished. Natural behavior was seen as impolite and coarse. A similar situation existed in Puritan New England in the 17th century where amusement and idleness were condemned. Calvinistic doctrine prohibited any sort of play. Life was intended to be devoted to work. Dance was contrary to work and so it was forbidden. Dancing between men and women, in taverns, around maypoles and accompanied by feasting and drinking were all prohibited.

Dance is believed to be one of the oldest arts. In primitive cultures it was associated with various rites of passage. As cultures progressed and became more complex and bound by formality, dance lost importance and became less relevant. Perhaps it is this deep-seated Puritan view of dance along with Western culture's generally negative attitude toward the body that has slowed and limited dance's prevalence in cultural discourse. It could also be argued that dance, as a display of bodily emotions, has been marginalized because of Western culture's privileging of rationality over emotion. Western culture views the spoken word as most important in defining reality.

Rational vs. Non-rational Views of Dance. It is often the most obvious thing to attempt to rationalize dance. If we've forgotten what it feels like to spin in circles until we fall over in dizziness and laughter then we are likely to try and rationalize why one might do it. A child would simply say she did it because it was fun, but an adult feels the need to explain it as ritual or transcendentalism. If the same spinning action is part of a secular dance on a Western stage, the average dance critic will undoubtedly criticize it as being redundant and unimaginative. However, in the Turkish tradition of whirling dervishes, spinning is deemed meaningful because it is steeped in religious ritual. By understanding the volatile nature of dance, the ever-changing ways it is esteemed can be realized. To place all dance on a more equal critical footing, one must look at dance non-rationally.

MEANINGFUL MOVEMENTS

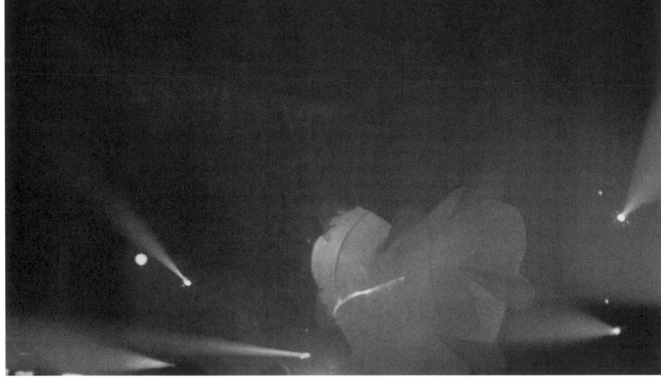

The dance becomes a mechanical configuration; it represents, as it were, the mechanization of the sexual impulse.
Geoff Mungham, *Youth in Pursuit of Itself*, 192

I like to express myself with my dancing and attract chicas. I've learned that girls really like a guy that dances!! I couldn't live without dancing!! Just go to dance and have a good time. That's all you need to do, leave your drugs at home little kids. **SETH, Las Vegas, NV, age 18, M, 3 yrs.**

For the most part, the Western idea of dance is a limited and polarized one. On one end of the spectrum dance is assumed to be high art, something only appreciated and enjoyed by an elite group. On the other end of the spectrum dance is seen as something enjoyed by a limited group hidden in the darkness of clubs where movement is sexualized and routinized for the purpose of mate-hunting. In this way dance is rationalized. It has a reasonable purpose: either to entertain or to aid in finding a mate. Like most art forms, some styles of dance have value ascribed to them and others do not. Western culture commonly esteems dance which exhibits specialized skill and training and which is performed on a proscenium stage in front of an audience. Ballet is the most highly recognized of this type of dance. We rationalize ballet's importance as a beautiful art form that reflects our societal values. Dance that doesn't take place on a proscenium stage typically has little value ascribed to it.

Understanding dance as either art, ritual or play sheds light on why some dance is deemed more meaningful than other dance. In many non-Western cultures such as African, dance is understood by sociologists as ritual: a codified, repetitive social practice encompassing symbolic actions and steps and adhering to the myths and ideologies making up that culture. In Western culture dance can be subdivided into art and play. Art is performed on stage and adheres to a set of artistic rules with the purpose of entertaining an audience. It is usually categorized by its degree of specialization. An art establishment consisting of critics, historians, schools and museums defines what is and is not dance.

Art establishments reflect the deeply rooted divisions and stratifications within any given culture. Dance that is understood as play is the dancing done at clubs, bars, raves and in living rooms, and is typically the type of dance that is demeaned or ignored. Play is understood to have very little meaning and importance. Western culture defines play for those other than children as negative. The culture deifies work, and play is deemed non-productive and not serious. More often than not, what surrounds the dance-as-play, including fashion, venue and illicit behavior, takes precedence, leaving the act of dance ignored.

In social dance arenas previous to rave culture, the event and the dancing itself were viewed primarily as pretexts for courtship, dating and sexual bargaining. Were the ordered and conformed proceedings on the dance floor simply a vehicle for sexual gratification, or were these couples actually enjoying dance for its own sake? That people chose a dance arena over other recreational outlets as a marriage meeting place would suggest the latter. In the 1970s the rise of the DJ and the decline of the live act were inadvertently altering the way people danced at social events. The continuation of music between tracks left no time for the ritualized search for a partner between songs. The dancing itself became a primary means of communication because of the absence of quiet moments in which to

What attracts me to raves is the fact that they are dance parties. You can do drugs and listen to music at home, but you can't have up to 5,000 people dancing in your living room! **SHLOOPY, Toronto ON, age 28, F, 6 yrs.**

If it hadn't been for the dances I went to every week I probably wouldn't have met my husband. The Beach Ballroom in Aberdeen, Scotland was a ballroom strictly for dances every weekend for teenagers mostly. They would have live bands mostly playing rock 'n' roll. The ballroom was completely round with a huge disco ball and wooden floors. A couple of times a night they would have a lady's choice where girls would ask the guys to dance. So I asked this good looking guy to dance with me. I was 15, he was 18. We dated for a few months and that New Year's Eve 1956, he proposed to me . . . at the same ballroom on the balcony that overlooked the dance floor. **COLLEEN McCALL, Scotland, age 59**

talk between songs. Dancing in groups as opposed to with one partner started to become the norm.

Body language arguably allows us to communicate with someone across the dance floor with much greater ease than having to shout over the music. Scenes such as disco and rave have helped give dance its own meaningful outcome.

Martha Graham, one of the century's most gifted and influential artists, offers a non-rational view into dance from a dancer's perspective. She speaks of dance in terms of personal expression and not cultural acceptance or entertainment. In her essay "I am a Dancer," Graham explains why dance has such an enduring quality: "I think the reason dance has held such an ageless magic for the world is that it has been the symbol of the performance of living." Her aim is to reveal something of herself every time she dances. "The essence of dance is the expression of man—the landscape of his soul."[4] Dancers at a rave may be revealing themselves in a similar manner to Martha Graham.

Dance as an Inscription of Social Values. Dance has a direct relationship with culture and is a reflection of that culture. The use of the individual body relates to a greater social body. A culture that is strictly controlled will reflect this control in its accepted body movements. (As an instructor of ballet, tap and jazz, my classes usually have no male students.) If boys do register they are often overwhelmed by the number of females and only attend a couple of classes before quitting. Male participants are consistently absent within dance. The majority of boys treat dance with disdain and embarrassment. It is mocked because these young skeptics see dance as gay men in tights doing twirls with their arms above their heads. The recent movie *Billy Elliot*, whose main character hides the fact that he is taking ballet lessons, attests to this view. Typically, expression through the body is a feminine ideal in North America.

Can you describe why and how dancing is important to you?

A. It helps me express the way I feel, the music just flowing liquid to the bottom of your soul and right back out again. **Charlie, Mobile, AL, age 22, M, 3 yrs.**

A. It is complete freedom. Your soul expressed physically. **Anonymous, Toronto, ON, age 23, M, 2 yrs.**

With this feminine ideal comes the stereotyping of male dancers being effeminate or homosexual. Even established male dancers are assumed to be gay, and the idea of masculine, straight, male dancers is beyond the Western world's comprehension. Society has instilled in us an image of dance that is feminine.

Ballet and its patriarchal plots explain how dance is a reflection of societal values. Simply put, ballet helps perpetuate myths that are rampant within Western society. Large or very tall women will never be accepted into the prestigious ballet schools just as Western society only worships, consumes and idealizes thin women. This reality is reflected not only in dance, but also in magazines, fashion runways, advertisements, music videos and television series. Most dance performed on stage reflects these archaic yet entrenched stereotypes of female and male. While it is true that a woman considered overweight can have the necessary muscle for balance and agility and still possess the gracefulness required for ballet, she will rarely be seen on stage or even encouraged to dance because she is too "fat."

Western culture promotes and consumes its ideal of the beautiful at whatever cost. An audience is innocently seduced by the beauty of art, leaving the ideology of art invisible. Classical ballet is one of the most accepted forms of dance internationally. It is controlled, conforming and unrealistic in its portrayal of stereotypes and gender roles. The dancing at raves is the opposite of this; it has no preferred body type, is unbridled in its movement, dismantles gender roles and for the most part is not codified. As a culture and a dance form, however, it is generally unaccepted.

African Dance. Unlike dance in Western culture, which is marginalized and enjoyed by an elite crowd, African dance is an essential component of life shared by old, young, female and male alike. The body movements in African dance generally imitate and symbolize aspects of life. African dance has been described as the site where body, mind and

How do we read against the grain of the patriarchal body? How does the fledgling ballerina vomiting in the school bathroom refuse her anorexia and recognize that the unattainable White Swan she is looking for in the mirror is an imaginary, fictional woman?
MARIANNE GOLDBERG, *Homogenized Ballerinas,* **307**

MEANINGFUL MOVEMENTS

Like the tree deeply rooted, which cannot survive without the earth, life without dance cannot exist. **JOHN KULLBALI, Cote D'Ivoire, 1961.**

soul unite. In anthropological terms, African dance is stereotyped as primitive while dance such as ballet is civilized. In laymen's terms, ballet is codified and controlled while African dance is free and innate.

The movements of African dance stand in stark contrast to ballet's courtly, controlled movements, quiet elegance and high art status. Loud and boisterous, African dance is low to the ground, uncontrolled and steeped in ritual as opposed to artistic regulations. Although there are a multitude of African dance performing troupes, the dance was not originally a means of aesthetic expression like ballet nor pure recreation like social dancing. African dance communicates everyday emotions associated with war, marriage, gods, harvests, birth and death. Dance is so integral in Africa that in Ghana, if a chief cannot dance according to the way of his people, he can be dethroned.

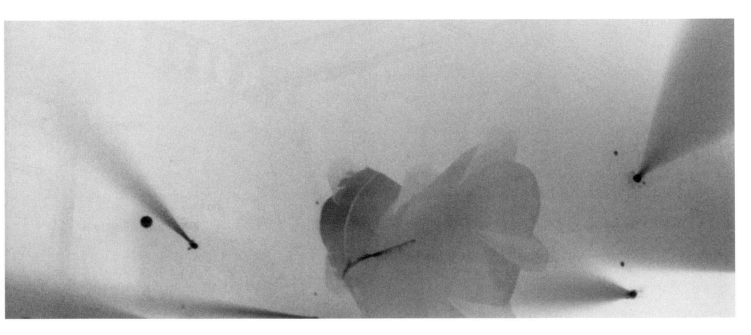

Just as the refined, upright and poised movements of ballet grew out of the highly refined, straight-spined, controlled movements evident in 17th-century European courts, African dance is an extension of its culture's general bodily movements. The more bent, relaxed and close to the ground movements of African dance are a continuation of everyday African activities such as farming. This is the main difference between Western dance forms such as ballet and modern, which are always performed on the ball of the foot with the body in an upright position, and African dance, which typically uses the whole of the foot pushed down into the ground with the body's centre of gravity much lower.

Dancing to me is a release. The world slips away when I'm in the music.
DJ Akommodate, Wichita, KS, age 19, M, 4 yrs.

African dance and drama are often used as a means through which people communicate with various deities. Dance itself is an act of worship. Ironically, this fact has been used by some Western critics of dance to disqualify African dance as art. If it's worship, this logic goes, then it can't be considered equal to ballet or other Western forms. European performance delights in the ideas of spectacle, decoration and limited audience participation. Contrarily, African dance is both ritualistic and functional, so the fragmentation between audience and performer disintegrates. Unlike in Western societies where dance is either frivolous play or art, appreciated by few and performed by fewer, dance in Africa is of central importance in everyday life, in which most people participate. In Gabon, for example, the stage is in a constant state of flux. It can span village streets to the bush in the outskirts. Dancers usually come and go during a performance and the

MEANINGFUL MOVEMENTS

Q. Can you describe why and how dancing is important to you?

A. It's an opportunity to move beyond the senses into the realm of the senseless; it's the letting go at the edge of the waterfall; it's having no body (I try to dance in such a way that my body collapses as I dance, continuously . . . I stop possessing the joints, and let my body do its thing); it's the best form of exercise... dancing is the sexiest way of being. **CAPTAIN NUTMEG, Vancouver, BC, age 26, M, 8 yrs.**

If you go to a circuit party the energy's . . . sexual, whereas if you go to a rave it's more about having fun . . . I don't think that raves have a very sexual energy at all. A lot of the popular rave-style dancing is very solo. It's your own experience or briefly shar[ed] experience with other people, whereas in the gay scene not everyone but a big group in the middle of the dance floor are all touching each other. It's not really dancing, it's more like swaying and they are in these tight groups, very close to each other and it is a group experience. Maybe because these people are at the center of the dance floor is what is making the whole party have this sexual energy. But I know a lot of popular places that mix gay and straight together like the Playground in Montréal and the Sound Factory in New York. A lot of these big world famous club nights have a very sexual energy. Maybe that is what attracts the straight people to it. This sensual energy, 'cause

audience participates by dancing, clapping, singing, talking and eating. The duration of the performance is dependent on the participants' energy levels.

Sociocultural change in Africa, including colonialism and the introduction of Christianity, has directly affected traditional customs and is responsible for the slow retreat of dance from its ritualistic ways. The recent infusion of pop culture also discourages traditional dance by opening up new contexts and forms of dance. As Africa becomes more aligned with Western culture, so too does dance, which now functions as mere recreation in many African cities. As African dance leaves the ground and takes to the stage, it marks a progression from ritual to performance art. As African dancers perfect and choreograph their once ritualized movements for an applauding crowd, the lines between ritual and performance get blurred.

Dance in the Rave Setting.
I'd forgotten the clarity I always achieve when I dance. Really dance. When it's dark enough that I'm not distracted by all those around me. When I'm swallowed up by rhythm so that I have no desire to yap to my friends. For that moment I'm free enough to think the thoughts I'm often afraid to. Free enough to feed off my own creativity. Inspired by the visions I have of my future and goals I see before me. Dancing at a rave is a reminder that you are alive. A reminder that you are not just a cog in the machine. That you have feelings, emotions and love for yourself and those around you.

So is dance at raves art, ritual or simply play? Possibly it is all three. Some events not only feel like a ritual, they blatantly tell you they're ritual. Toronto's Ritual promotion company is a case in point. So what sets rave dance apart from other social dancing such as that done at night clubs? What makes it a prime vehicle for self-reflection, expression and communication? The seamless, tribal-like drone of techno and its multitude of sub-genres makes trance-dancing possible. For the most part, electronic rave music is lyricless, it has no catchy melody to sing along with. Its repetitive rhythms can be highly consuming and enrapturing. In techno, emotion isn't spelled out in words as it is in pop music. It is measured by the emotion it strikes in dancers as it acts as a vehicle for losing one's self on the dance floor. For many, ecstasy is the catalyst that aids in this process. Rave also provides an optimum environment for music to work its tribal magic. Unlike clubs and bars where patrons are often there to pick up or be picked up, rave's often dirty, dark and sometimes painfully loud environment makes the pursuit of a mate seem futile. For most in attendance it is certainly not the primary intention.

Ritual. I'm at Ritual 10. It is sometime between 4 a.m. and 5 a.m. One of the bouncers opens the fire escape door to cool off. Suddenly there is that outside world. Seeing out onto the street that I almost forgot existed. I have been so sucked into the music's rapture that for a moment I forget that there is even a door over there. Staring out of the opening onto the street and seeing the Pizza Pizza sign I am jarred out of my trance . . . awoken from a dream that I didn't realize I was having.

I had been going to clubs since I was 13, but it wasn't until I went to my first few raves about eight years later that I truly understood what it meant to lose yourself in music. Going to raves taught me how I could meditate by dancing to the thundering drone of electronica. The music at raves is usually so loud that it actually penetrates you and reverberates in your chest. At a rave, music not only surrounds you, it envelops you until it has stolen your thoughts and taken you to a pure meditative or trance state without you even realizing it. The emotions you experience at this sacred spot can make you feel naked, exposed and vulnerable. But then you look around and realize that it's all OK because those around you are also baring their souls even if just for a short while.

it's not a scary thing, it's not going to break out into an orgy or anything. There is crazy stuff going on though, whether it be in the bathroom or on the dance floor, but I like crazy stuff going on! I think it adds a flavor. It gives a twist to your night and you [can] talk about it for a long time after. **JASON FORD, promoter**.

The thing I noticed was that it (rave) was the antithesis of the club scene. I had been so used to going to clubs where it is so about meeting the opposite sex, [and] you're around all these sweaty bodies pressed up against one another and it doesn't matter, you're not into that vibe at all, and that's so amazing. **GARTNER, Toronto, ON, age 30, M, 3 yrs.**

The rave offered a release from day-to-day realities, a temporary escapist disappearance like the weekend or holiday . . . A Dionysian ritual of dance and hedonism evolved, whereby the established self was undone. **HILLEGONDA RIETVELD, *Living the Dream*, 58.**

MEANINGFUL MOVEMENTS

Q. Can you describe why and how dancing is important to you?

A. I can think of only three activities in life that let me stop thinking: sex, listening to really good music and dancing. They are wonderful escapes and I'd have to say they are equally important to me. I can't imagine living without them. GARTNER, Toronto, ON, age 30, M, 3 yrs.

Unfortunately it is sometimes difficult for people to reach this space without the help of drugs. We live in a fast and noisy environment. Must of us haven't learned how to shut off, to focus on ourselves and feel our connection to the rest of the world. It's quite ironic that this peace, this inner solitude, is so easy to find in an environment that is loud, crazy and so completely intense. A disused, dank warehouse filled with music made with computers would seem the most unlikely place to communicate with the cosmos. A rave is indeed a strange urban oasis, the ultimate in controlled chaos.

DANCING IS THE BEST DRUG THERE IS!!!!
Anonymous, Seneca, PA, age 19, F, 2 yrs.

Mother earth gives so much energy to us [that] when I dance I give it back to her. It is like a tribal dance . . . I dance to mother earth. It is healthy to dance and it lets you release out all the bad energy so you don't stress about the everyday shit. I love to dance! CHRISTINA C. SNIDER, Royal Oak, MI, age 21, F, 3 yrs.

Derrick May and Kevin Saunderson are battling over four turntables sometime between 2 a.m. and 3 a.m. I have been dancing non-stop, sweat absolutely dripping off me, my eyes closed, or staring at the floor, or staring through the floor. And then I look up and realize that I haven't even noticed the DJs until now. These godfathers of techno aren't superstars, aren't pretentious, aren't there for themselves. They are there for us... they are playing the music we need and want. Twiddling frantically with knobs, grabbing the next record, all with lightning speed. They are working, working us . . . without us even realizing it. They are teaching us how to dance. The music they play in the sequence they decide to play it controls my movement, our movement. All of us together, at the same time, feeling the same euphoria, the same rhythm. This is vibe, and these DJs helped create it. Vibe hangs over the crowd like an invisible mist, it congeals mysteriously, it allows everyone in the room to feel safe, happy, welcomed . . .

free. Once again I have found my center, my focus, my meditative space at that point where music, color and energy thrust towards me while I swallow them whole, allowing them to become part of my inner motion. Purely losing myself in the soundscape.

Rave dancing would make much more sense in the African savannah than in a prestigious ballet or opera house. The movements associated with rave are liberated, lucid and typically beyond anyone's control. Feeling connected and in complete synch with hundreds of other people at a rave is the closest many urban youths will ever get to being part of a tribe. These are the moments that you start to truly understand what vibe is all about. The DJ seems so in tune with the crowd, and vice versa, it's as though everyone is predicting the music. People are helping each other dance without knowing it, feeding off the collective anticipation for that moment of synergy where it feels like utter madness: cheers, claps, whistles, hands in the air. Suddenly everyone is dancing in unison. During those intense moments of connectedness when you look around at a party and believe everyone else is feeling the same joy you are feeling, you feel like you belong. It's a belonging that is so unlike anything you've ever experienced before. It doesn't rely on any of the previous forms of communication you've come to know through your socialization. The purity of the connection is completely primal.

Play. The lack of attention paid to the dance component of rave in books, news segments and other journalism suggests how it is viewed by society: as play. Although there are ritualistic and artistic tendencies woven into the rave agenda, it is seen more or less as an arena for teens and young adults to play. A place to act out roles, to exhibit complete freedom, abandonment and expression. While such an opinion is largely born out by the facts, it does not take into consideration the importance of play

Q. How would you compare DJing at a large rave event as opposed to a small club?

A. Well, it's pros and cons, I mean the thing about . . . a lot of DJs, especially DJs who are really, really into their music and have a passionate love for music prefer probably smaller venues because they're more intimate. And you can relate more closely to your crowd. When you play at these big raves, it's like a lot of money involved. It's all about money, and I mean you lose a lot of intimacy. By the same token, you know, when you're playing on a big powerful sound system that is catering to a 10,000 or 15,000 people audience, you know there's a certain . . . power there. So, I have a good feeling also, I mean I played in big raves in France before, and in Germany, Scandinavia, you know . . . It's a good feeling, because you know you have the power. You're controlling [tens of] thousands [of] people all at one time. That's a hell of a feeling. **JUAN ATKINS**

MEANINGFUL MOVEMENTS

It was very spiritual. Some of those moments in the club were unbelievable. People literally went into trance states, including me. Not from the use of drugs, but through that music and the human energy that was going around . . . It happens on the plains of Africa and South America, but it's not something that's happened in Britain for centuries. **DANNY RAMPLING, quoted in** *Adventures in Wonderland,* **117**

Play is an open event. It's free. Little kids are like dogs. They run around, touch things, sing a song. Actors play like that and musicians too, and you dig watching someone play because that's the way people are supposed to be— free, like animals. **JIM MORRISON.**

Play seems senseless, admitting the very chaos and misrule that social structures are meant to control. **EMILY SHULTZ and ROBERT LAVENDA,** *Cultural Anthropolgy,* **175**

in the development of healthy people. As mentioned previously, acts of play are generally given little notice in sociological literature. It is little wonder that rave has experienced a lack of scholarly attention.

Rave dancing seems childlike in the dancers' faces and its freedom of movement. Radiant with smiles, ecstasy's amphetamine-like nature does more than just make you dance—it helps turn sexual feelings into sensual feelings. Guys on E don't necessarily want to pick-up and grope girls. The drug puts them in touch with their feminine side and allows them to feel love without the usual physical manifestations of love. This means a lot of hugging and loving at raves (even heterosexual guys hugging one another) without the pending doom of a one-night stand. In turn, girls are allowed to interact and dance more freely. Dancing is no longer limited to attracting attention. Rave dance functions as a means of moving past the need to watch and be watched. Rave clothing reflects this in its privileging of comfort and mobility over body-hugging fashions.

It was my birthday—Richie and Speedy j live with Mark Farina and Derrick Carter—E and acid-concoction . . . anyway, all night, this beautiful girl would grab my hand and run with me through pulsing crowds to get me some water—seemingly forever, up/down/in/out stairs, rips in paperwalls to the hidden room where they put the sink, oh my god this music is divine . . . dance . . . melt, and then my hand, grabbed again, being pulled toward a bunch of people who all gave me a crazy massage . . . . and then, ooze back into the groove, losing my shit to Derrick Carter, so high I can't remember what down looks like . . . dance, dance, dance, massive-spherical extra-sensory extra-bodily orgasm that rode through the room, just floating around for an unending amount of time . . . uuuuuhhhh . . . **Captain Nutmeg, Vancouver, BC, age 26, M, 8 yrs.**

Performance. A rave is in some ways akin to a concert with the focus primarily on the stage or wherever the DJ is set up. A majority of the lighting and sound also originates from around the stage, drawing participants forward like moths to a flame. With most participants dancing in one direction, the crowd often appears as though it is one live organism. Although there is definitely mingling and chitchat at a rave, the intense forward focus is more reminiscent of a concert environment than a club. Also similar to concerts is the typical clapping and cheering when a set is done or the night has ended. Unlike the typical concert with a band and singer, there isn't much to watch. A DJ spinning records can be interesting if you can get close enough to see what he's actually doing, or if you're a devoted trainspotter—a person who watches the record spin, desperate to know the name of the track so you can seek it out for yourself.

Q. Describe the best time you ever had at a party.

A. First one :) Awwwwww I was . . . 15 . . . [and] very nervous as it was the first time I'd been to a rave but I knew I was gonna love it just as soon as I started queuing as people were chatting away to me and everyone looked sweet. I wanted to do E, [but] I only did a half and after about one hour after getting in I was dancing away, loving it. I was with friends and meeting new ones. And seeing your friends from school in that situation was cool. Was one of the first happy hardcore raves too, Fusion 2 at the Farnborough (just outside London) Leisure and Arts Center. Was amazing. **DJ_S2C, South Coast, England, age 22, M, 8 yrs.**

Dancing was, for a long time, something I could vent all of my testosterone-driven anger into. In recent years though it has become a more technical and artistic expression. **FU MAN CHU, Eatontown, NJ, age 21, M, 7 yrs.**

MEANINGFUL MOVEMENTS

Q. Can you describe why and how dancing is important to you?

A. Dancing has helped me overcome my shyness. I dance like nobody's watching and really get into it, making up all sorts of cool moves. Then I realize that people are watching, but in admiration. **SYNAPSE, Toronto, ON, age 27, M, 8 yrs.**

Dancing can almost be described as my life. I live to dance every weekend. I'm always up for learning new moves. I go to bed thinking about what I can do tomorrow on the dance floor. **JERNET, North Carolina, age 17, F, 3 yrs.**

Dancing became increasingly important to me when I stopped doing drugs at parties. It's a whole new aspect of the scene that is really interesting. When you realize how many different dance styles there are and how amazing some liquid and popping dancers can be, it's inspiring. It makes me want to practice and really take dancing not just as a simple, instinctive thing but as a skill as well. **LAILA, New Jersey, age 18, F, 2 yrs.**

But it isn't the DJ that is as exciting to watch as the crowd. In some rave environments the dancers are so in sync with one another that the moves appear learned and highly skilled. To an outsider the motion can appear artistically choreographed and is delightful to watch. At some parties, participants will get completely decked out in boisterous clothes in an effort to invite onlookers. In this sense the audience at a rave is the performance.

[On ecstasy] it doesn't feel like dancing, it's like an art or something. **LIL'CHIC, Grant, AB, age 18, F, 0 yrs.**

Some events are so dark that it's difficult to see your own feet let alone someone else's. Usually people are so enraptured that they don't care what they look like, or who's watching them. Most like the fact that they're not being gawked at and judged like they might be at a club, while others openly admit to showing off their moves. As rave transgresses from its original path, movements have begun to become codified. Very often ravers dance with chemically-induced robot-like stamina, dancing with marathon endurance for countless hours. Some now argue that there is a particular way to dance to jungle as opposed to trance or house. Break dancing, for example, made its way out of the New York ghettos of the 1980s to find an additional home specifically at jungle events. It's not unusual to see a circle in the middle of the dance floor and break dancers taking turns in the limelight. Onlookers in the breaking circle's peripheries cheer and clap at the one-upmanship.

The feminine overtones associated with dancing are also diminished at raves where the men often outnumber the women. Men dance with as much vigor as women, and sometimes more. This is a contrast to clubs and bars where the majority of patrons, male and female, do the usual two-step, head bop or casual sway. Club dancing is usually controlled whereas rave dancing is individual and free. The friendly atmosphere at raves, which is arguably induced by ecstasy, awards people the freedom to move without the usual judgement from others. On ecstasy everyone is too content in their own private moment to be judging others. Ravers are suddenly children again, twirling on their living room floor.

"Free your ass and your mind will follow."
FUNKADELIC, 1970, Westbound Records, Bridgeport Music Inc.

While the scene could exist without the drugs and the music could evolve until it was unrecognizable, without the dancing, raves would certainly not exist. The primary function of a DJ and the music he chooses is to get participants dancing. A rave without dancing is devoid of vibe: the buzzword for rave's almost tangible, collective energy. Without the dance component a rave would simply be a boring concert, where the musicians do little to entertain visually. Raves provide a place to free your mind and therefore your body through dance. You can adopt a guise and be anyone else for the night. Raves allow you to become free enough to be a star even if it is for only a few hours. This alternate reality is attainable with the help of rave's darkness, outlandish costumes, pigtails, baby soothers, loose clothing and hair dye, all of which disguise gender and age. Raves are often viewed as utopian and anarchistic by their participants because drug use is welcomed, and social barriers are overcome. Rave companies and parties called Utopia, Liberty, and Promised Land substantiate these

London clubs had always been about people drinking, trying to chat up girls [and] looking good but not dancing. All of a sudden we completely changed that—you'd come down and you'd dance for six hours. The idea was, "If you're not into dancing, then don't come down." **PAUL OAKENFOLD, quoted in *Generation Ecstasy*, 59**

At times, the crowd seemed to transcend physical limits. They would literally climb up the walls. They would fall to the floor, legs thrashing in the air. **SHERYL GARRATT, *Adventures in Wonderland*, 41**

Q. What was the impetus behind 808 State?

A. I can only talk for myself, I just wanted to make music to dance to. I had no idea everyone else was tripping. I got off on dancing, so I would say my goal was to move people. **GUY CALLED GERALD**

Q. Describe the best time you ever had at a party.

A. The best time I ever had a party was at my first party. It was an incredible August night, the moon was shining, and there I was, in the middle of the woods, dancing like crazy. Never will I forget that first night where I had the chance to express my feelings and opinions through music and dancing. **ANONYMOUS, Montréal, QC, age 18, F, 1 yr.**

Dancing is so important because if you're so down and sad all you have to do is dance and it'll make you feel so good! **LESLEE CAROTHERS, Bloomington, MN, age 16, F, 0 yrs.**

ideals. Rave provides an outlet for urban youth to go outside their problems through dance.

Transcendance Productions' name epitomized rave for me: transcendence through the vehicle of dance. I wasn't alone in my affinity for these raves; a close friend of mine had the Transcendance logo tattooed on the top of his back. He rationalized the permanent imprint that scars his spine by explaining that the people he met and the events themselves had such a profound impact on who he had become that the symbol representing fevered nights of dancing will be forever meaningful.

The Function of Dance. One rave participant rationalizes his disappearance from the scene claiming, "I stopped raving when I stopped dancing." Whether it was his distaste for the evolved rave music or the toll drugs were taking on his body, he could no longer dance, and without dance, raves became meaningless. Perhaps this is the truth for many others as they withdraw from the scene.

If we are to understand dance as a meaningful way to communicate our inner selves, we must start looking at dance in non-rationalist terms. Only then may we begin to see subcultures like rave as an arena of expression and an avenue of freedom, not simply a drug-haven.

When you dance you are creating for the moment. Once a dance has ended there is nothing left to grasp. If the dance is not on stage and not enjoyed by anyone except the dancer the meaning may be rather elusive. Non-theatrical dance appears to serve little function in society because it performs a highly personal inner function that others cannot see, feel or experience, unless they too are taking part.

Ballet communicates myths, fables and the dominant society's perception of gender. African dance communicates facets of everyday life from birth to death. Rave communicates emotions, freedom and individuality. In today's fast-paced, technology-driven world it's often difficult to see why an undirected outpouring of emotion is necessary.

When asked for a definition of dance, dancer Mary Wigman quite simply answers, "The dance is a language with which man is born, the ecstatic manifestation of his existence." When a member of the Bantu tribe was asked about his dance he answered, "What a man danced, that was his tribe, his social customs, his religion." [5]

Dance is a voiceless articulation of your existence at a particular point in time. It is the physical manifestation of a person's feelings toward a simple heartbeat, an African drum, a full orchestra or a thrashing 180 bpms of drum and bass. It is an innate language for the entire human race.

Ack, maybe I'm too skeptical and jaded for my own good sometimes. I've survived 44 turns of this stone around the sun. Brit girlfriend is same age also. Heh. But we try not to let it show too much . . . usually raving with people under half our age, and we're still among the last left dancing when the event turns us out. (:>) We're not the oldest we know either. Heh. It's all a great leveller. (;>~ And such fun! CAW! **PWL, Hampshire, England, age 44, M, 5 yrs.**

Music is essential to the rhythm of life and dance is the embodiment of music. When we dance together, we are as one together. **DJ VYB.**

H. Jackson Huang

DRUGS SATURATE ALL facets of Western civilization.

They are used to improve health, enhance relaxation, to assist in cultural rituals, gain enlightenment and for hedonistic purposes such as escapism. As much as drugs are sought after and even worshipped for curing ills and alleviating ailments, they are also feared and condemned. Western governments have been fighting a visible war against drugs over the past two decades. Historically it has been almost impossible for a music-based subculture to exist free from associated drug use.

> When you push yourself to an edge in that setting, when you do enough drugs that you're just so far removed from your normal function, you can discover yourself . . . So when you go back to it, you're much more comfortable with your natural form. It's like taking a vacation from your normal, conscious self.
>
> **Max, Toronto, ON, age 30, M, 10 yrs.**

06

GETTING HIGHER

Northern Soul and the mods had amphetamines, acid rock and hippies had LSD, disco had LSD then coke and hip-hop has pot. Rave culture wouldn't have been initiated had it not been for its own catalyst drug: M D M A .

MDMA alters the brain's electrical impulses, increases feelings of happiness, empathy and sociability and heightens the sensations related to touch. A normal dose of MDMA will last between three and six hours. On the other hand, ecstasy (aka MDMA, aka 3, 4-methylene-dioxymethamphetamine) causes the brain to release above normal quantities of serotonin, a neurotransmitter which is primarily responsible for our moods. Ecstasy offers people an instant outlet for self-expression in a highly stratified and repressive culture. It allows those who indulge in it to experience the freedom necessary to transcend insecurities and self-consciousness. One pill can erase, for up to four hours, the need to conform to normalized gender roles and the socially constructed rules of interaction. For some, as the drug wears off so does the insight. This leaves some ravers searching for more elation, often found only with more E.

Ecstasy. The history of acid house and ecstasy in Ibiza and later in England would suggest that the drug's coming of age took place overseas. In fact, experimentation with ecstasy was undoubtedly initiated in the U.S. Although MDMA wasn't in common use until the 1980s, and didn't become a Schedule 1 drug in the U.S. until July of 1985, its history dates further back than LSD. MDMA is a hallucinogenic amphetamine and is also classified as an empathogen. The term empathogen was coined by Dr. Ralph Metzner, Dean of the California Institute of Integral Studies in 1983, to describe a group of drugs known as phenethylamines such as MDA and MDMA. Metzner suggested this name because these drugs

produced feelings of empathy toward oneself and others. On the streets and in the media the drug has many names such as XTC, X, ecstasy, E, Adam, and the love drug, among others. Originally synthesized in Germany in 1912 as an appetite suppressant, it wasn't until 1977 that the first traces of underground batches appeared. Psychotherapists and psychiatrists started experimenting with the drug in the late 1970s and attempted to control dissemination of MDMA for fear that it would become a street drug and suffer a similar fate as LSD.

In the mid-1980s it became obvious that MDMA was being used as more than just a psychotherapeutic tool. Bill Mandel published a notorious article entitled "The Yuppie Psychedelic" in the *San Francisco Chronicle* in 1984. Until this time MDMA had been legal, but by a month and a half after this article had been published the Drug Enforcement Administration (DEA) and the Food and Drug Administration (FDA) recommended that MDMA become a Schedule 1 synthetic. This classification made MDMA into a narcotic. By April 1985 *Newsweek* had a full-page article with the headline "Getting High on 'Ecstasy'." The article discussed not only the spiritual insights brought on by MDMA but its use as a recreational, campus drug. That year MDMA was a topic of discussion on the *Phil Donahue Show*. It was reported that a lab in Texas had been creating MDMA at a rate of 30,000 doses a month. In gay clubs in Austin and Dallas, ecstasy could be bought at the bar as legally as beer. Initially part of the gay scene, ecstasy use crossed over to include college kids who had the money to buy multiple pills at a time.

In May of 1985 the DEA held a news conference in Washington and announced that it considered MDMA a serious health threat and that abuse was now a national problem. The DEA placed an emergency ban on the drug with the view to making it a permanent ban within a year. Classifying MDMA as a Schedule 1 drug made it as controlled as heroin or cocaine. The Schedule 1 classification would hinder further research on MDMA and completely curb its use as a psychotherapeutic tool. Dr. Ron Siegel of

A guy named Kelly called from S.M.U. in Texas . . . Over the summer [of 1984] S.M.U. had gone dry. But the student body had found something to replace liquor, Kelly said. The bars were full of people on a drug called Ecstasy. "I want to send you something that's going to change your life," he said. **"Experiencing Ecstasy," *New York Times Magazine*, Sunday January 21, 2001.**

[MDMA] is known as "the love drug" on college campuses where it is considered to be an aphrodisiac, but users who were interviewed said it precipitates emotional, not sexual feelings . . . "You can't sleaze with it," said student Jeff Manning, who has taken the drug several times for the "experience." "Our true emotions come out . . ." **"Psychiatrists Defend new Street Drug for Therapy," *Los Angeles Times*, Monday May 27, 1985.**

All the evidence the DEA has received shows that MDMA abuse has become a nationwide problem and it poses a serious health threat. This emergency action is a stopgap measure to curb MDMA abuse until the administrative process can be completed . . . Officials of the drug agency said their intention was to replace the emergency ban on MDMA with a permanent ban within one year. **JOHN C. LAWN, in an Associated Press dispatch, *New York Times*, June 1 1985, as quoted in *Ecstasy: The MDMA Story*, 15**

GETTING HIGHER

On May 19, 1985, John Flinn published an article in the *San Francisco Examiner* where the DEA assistant administrator Gene Haslip announced, "We're going to ban Ecstasy within the next several months . . . By next fall, Ecstasy will be as rigidly controlled as heroin. It's extremely dangerous."

"The New Drug They Call Ecstasy: Is it Too Much to Swallow?," published in *New York* magazine by Joe Klein in 1985, quotes Ron Siegel from the UCLA School of Medicine: "We're getting people who claimed to have taken this drug who are disoriented for days on end . . . We've had people locked in fetal positions for as long as 72 hours. We had a psychotherapist that took it, disappeared, and turned up a week later directing traffic."
as quoted in *Ecstasy: The MDMA Story*, pg. 22

The Trouble with Ecstasy
The drug is seductive, controversial, dangerous—and now illegal.
***Life* magazine, August 1985**

The mission of the Drug Enforcement Administration is to enforce the controlled substances laws and regulations of the United States and bring to the criminal and civil justice system of the United States, or any other competent jurisdiction, those organizations and principal members of organizations, involved in the growing, manufacture, or distribution of controlled substances appearing in or destined for illicit traffic in the United States.

(1) SCHEDULE 1.
(A) The drug or other substance has a high potential for abuse.
(B) The drug or other substance has no currently accepted medical use in treatment in the United States.
(C) There is a lack of accepted safety for use of the drug or other substance under medical supervision.

www.usdoj.gov/dea/

the UCLA School of Medicine acted as a witness for the DEA in its study of recreational MDMA use. Siegel suggested that MDMA's effects were similar to those of mescaline. He also noted that street level use caused hallucinations, psychotic episodes and disorientation. This opinion did not take into consideration that dealers may have introduced any number of additives or different drugs to any given MDMA pill. The users that Siegel spoke of may also have been taking any number of doses.

In 1986 MDMA was officially a Schedule 1 drug and the moral panic associated with it was slowly subsiding. Although the media exposé

surrounding ecstasy faded, its use certainly did not. Ecstasy had already made its way over to Britain with the help of people in the music business. In 1988 in the U.K., ecstasy use had reached a plateau. Thousands were becoming enraptured by the drug's effects when coupled with house music and the burgeoning scene that was unfolding around this drug/music symbiosis. MDMA was in the media limelight again, this time in England. In its new home of raves and tabloid journalism, ecstasy was a reporter's dream.

LSD. Ecstasy and LSD have a similar history. Both had been synthesized well before the public or media became aware of widespread use. LSD was first utilized in the 1950s as a treatment for alcoholism and as a CIA interrogation tool. It is more familiarly known as the hippie drug, which helped bring upon its illegal classification. Similarly, ecstasy's first public use was in psychotherapy; once it became known as a yuppie and college drug it also became illegal. Today ecstasy is best known as the fuel for the rave generation, but LSD use at raves is also common.

In 1938 Dr. Albert Hoffman, a Swiss chemist in the Sandoz laboratories, first synthesized LSD 25 (lysergic acid diethylamide of the 25th compound), a compound he isolated from the fungus argot in an effort to cure headaches. Five years later he accidentally ingested a small dose of the compound and noted the experience as "an uninterrupted stream of fantastic images of extraordinary plasticity and vividness . . . accompanied by an intense kaleidoscopic play of colours."[6] Hoffman had synthesized one of the most powerful hallucinogens which came to be known as "acid" or "LSD."

LSD alters and expands human consciousness, increases bodily sensations, heightens awareness of color, distorts scenery and perception of space and time and initiates concern with philosophical, cosmological and religious questions which can lead, if the trip is positive, to an intensified interest in the self and the world. Psychedelics like LSD are some-

Q. If you do drugs at a party, what is your favorite drug or drug combination

A. LSD.

Q. How does this drug affect the way you listen to music?

A. That's like asking how the pen altered the way people write. **CAPTAIN NUTMEG, Vancouver, BC, age 26, M, 8 yrs.**

The first time I took two drops of acid with my friend, it was awesome. We met a lot of really nice people and saw "the glowstick god!" **BLUE, Milwaukee, WI, age16, F, 1 yr.**

Candy flipping! LSD mixed with MDMA. LSD makes the lights sparkle and the music sound great. MDMA makes the mood and heightens my empathic sensitivity. It makes you seem more friendly, but it's a shallow kind of friendly. There's something about it that just seems fake after a while. Maybe I'm just getting older. Personally, I don't take E anymore. I was getting emotional hangovers that would last up to three times longer than the high. But in our closed-off, selfish society, E can be a good catalyst to get people out of their shells and meet each other. Just don't mistake the map for the territory. **SYNAPSE, Toronto, ON, age 27, M, 8 yrs.**

Appendix 6.a
Common Recreational Drugs.

Note. This is not intended to be a complete listing, these are just the basics.

3,4-Methylenedioxymethamphetamine

MDMA
[also known as Ecstasy, E, or X]

Effects of the Drug
Produces a sensation of euphoria, physical stimulation and the feeling of increased emotional closeness to others. Side effects include dry mouth, loss of appetite, a rise in body temperature/blood pressure, nausea and muscle cramp, especially in the jaw.

How it works
Stimulates the brain to produce increased levels of serotonin, a neurotransmitter that affects mood.

Origins
Patented in Germany in 1912 by Merck as a diet pill, but was never marketed. Rumored to have been tested by the U.S. military in the 1950s as a truth serum. Used by some psychologists in the 1970s and '80s as an aid in therapy. Illegal in the U.K. since 1977 and since 1985 in the U.S.

Associated Problems
Many deaths associated with MDMA have been traced to dehydration, which can happen more easily when a user is dancing for hours in a hot room without drinking enough water. Some studies point to long-term problems with depression related to depletion of serotonin as well as memory loss. Another major concern, as with many drugs, is that pills containing other substances are often sold as MDMA.

2-[2-Chlorophenyl]-2-[methylamino]- cyclohexanonec

KETAMINE
[K, Special K, or Vitamin K]

Effects of the Drug
Ketamine is a dissociative drug with effects ranging from mild disorientation to out of body or near-death experiences, depending on dosage.

How it works
Blocks nerve pathways without causing circulatory or respiratory failure, which makes it useful as an anaesthetic.

Origins
A common anaesthetic (usually for veterinary purposes) generally sold under the names Ketaset and Ketalar. Made a controlled substance in the U.S. in 1999.

Associated Problems
Normal situations such as crossing the street can be dangerous to an individual who is experiencing a dissociative state. Studies have shown that frequent and/or high doses can cause permanent brain damage. Ketamine is also sometimes given to the unconsenting as a date rape drug.

Gamma Hydroxybutyrate

GHB
[Liquid X, Georgia Home Boy, Goop, Gamma-oh, or Grievous Bodily Harm . . .]

Effects of the Drug
A central nervous system depressant used for its ability to produce a state of mild euphoria. Also taken as a sleep aid and for its ability to stimulate muscle growth.

How it works
Stimulates the creation of dopamine in the brain, yet inhibits its proper transmission. Effects are felt when the stored up dopamine is released. Also affects the pituitary gland which gives the drug its muscle building properties.

Origins
Originally considered a safe and "natural" food supplement for muscle growth and insomnia and was sold in health food stores. After health concerns emerged, it was made illegal in the U.S. outside of a physician's care in March of 2000.

Associated Problems
GHB is physically addictive and can produce drowsiness, dizziness, nausea, unconsciousness, seizures, severe respiratory depression and coma. GHB is especially dangerous when combined with alcohol. There are also cases of it being used as a date rape drug in higher doses.

Phencyclidine

PCP

[Angel dust, Supergrass, Killer Weed, Embalming Fluid, or Rocket Fuel]

Effects of the Drug

Wide ranging effects depending on dosage and the individual, including dissociation, a sense of invulnerability, auditory hallucinations, or visual distortions. Side effects can include slurred speech, paranoia, violent behavior, or anxiety. Popularity of PCP has gone down since the 1970s due to its reputation as a high-risk drug

How it works

Research is under way to explain the biological actions of PCP, which has been found to block the receptor that responds to glutamate, a normal chemical messenger in the brain.

Origins

Investigated as an anaesthetic in the 1950s but its development for human medical use was discontinued due to side effects. Used as a veterinary anaesthetic in the 1960s, but its manufacture was banned in the U.S. in 1978 due to abuse.

Associated Problems

Frequent use can cause chromosomal damage that can be passed along to offspring as well as a mood disorder similar to schizophrenia. Improper synthesis can create related substances that produce unpredictable effects or even death.

Lysergic Acid Diethylamide

LSD

[Blotter, Boomers, Cubes, Microdot, Sugar, Tabs, Yellow Sunshines, etc.]

Effects of the Drug

The LSD high (known as a "trip") can cause changes in mood, and distortions in perception of time, space and self. Physical effects can include dilated pupils, increased body temperature, loss of appetite, sleeplessness, dry mouth and tremors. Effects can last up to 12 hours.

How it works

The way LSD works is not yet completely understood by scientists, but most theories involve the brain treating it as a neurotransmitter. Some claim that it travels to unused portions of the brain, thus creating new perceptions

Origins

Dr. Albert Hoffman first synthesized LSD in 1938 and accidentally consumed it in 1943, discovering its hallucinogenic properties. It was made popular in the mid-60s due to "acid gurus" like Timothy Leary and was legal in the U.S. until 1966.

Associated Problems

Some users experience "bad trips" in which they feel amplification of emotional problems or unpleasant physical stimuli. "Flashbacks" in which some of the effects of the drug can recur in the future without warning are possible as well. High or frequent doses have been documented to cause a schizophrenia-like condition sometimes known as "LSD psychosis." effects or even death.

Methamphetamine

METH-
AMPHETAMINE

[Crystal, Speed, Meth, Chalk, Hitler's drug, Yaba, or Ice . . .]

Effects of the Drug

Causes a heightened sense of alertness, euphoria, confidence, energy and physical stamina. Larger doses can cause hallucinations. Some possible side effects are sweating, insomnia, anxiety and tooth grinding.

How it works

Releases high levels of the neurotransmitter dopamine, which stimulates brain cells, enhancing mood and body movement.

Origins

Discovered in Japan in 1919, and rumored to have been used by Hitler's soldiers to fight fatigue. Currently has some (very restricted) accepted medical use for weight loss in the U.S. Illegal trafficking in North America is often tied to motorcycle gangs.

Associated Problems

Methamphetamine is highly addictive and heavy use can cause a variety of problems including damaging brain cells that contain dopamine and serotonin, strokes, respiratory problems, irregular heartbeat and anorexia.

Cannabis

MARIJUANA
[Mary Jane, Reefer, Pot, Herb, Chronic, Gangster . . .]

Effects of the Drug
Causes mood lift, relaxation and deeper sensory awareness. Hallucinogenic at higher doses. Medically, it can be used for nausea and pain relief. Side effects can include hunger, slowed reflexes, blood shot eyes, dry mouth, concentration problems and fatigue.

How it works
THC changes the way in which sensory information gets into and is processed by the hippocampus, a component of the brain's limbic system that is crucial for learning, memory and the integration of sensory experiences with emotions and motivations.

Origins
Hemp has been grown for fiber, medicine, and food by a variety of cultures around the world for over 3,000 years. In India it is associated with Shiva and is seen as sacred. In China, it is mentioned in the earliest medical texts. Grown extensively in North America from colonial times on, it was made illegal in the U.S. in 1937 officially for "public health" reasons, though other reasons are often cited, such as pressure from the cotton and lumber industries (hemp can be made into clothing or paper.)

Associated Problems
Chronic use can cause long-term problems with attention, memory and learning. Causes the same kinds of lung problems as smoking tobacco.

Cocaine Hydrochloride

COCAINE
[Blow, Snow, Crack, Charlie]

Effects of the Drug
Users feel increased energy, confidence, euphoria, clearer thinking, improved athletic performance and sexual desire. Side effects can include increased blood pressure, teeth grinding, restlessness, paranoia and insomnia. The peak from snorting cocaine lasts about 30 minutes, while the peak for smoking crack is much more intense and lasts for 3-5 minutes.

How it works
Cocaine is a strong central nervous system stimulant that interferes with the reabsorption process of dopamine, a chemical messenger associated with pleasure and movement.

Origins
The natives of South America have harvested the coca leaf for medicinal, religious and nutritional purposes for thousands of years. Cocaine was first isolated and extracted from coca leaves around 1855. Freud published his book *On Coca* in 1884 in which he promoted its use. Touted as a cure-all, cocaine was an ingredient in many medicinal and food products, including most famously in the first formula for Coca-Cola. Banned in the U.S. in 1914 after 5,000 cocaine-related deaths in one year were reported. The more potent, smokable "crack" cocaine was introduced in the 1970s.

Associated Problems
After effects can be unpleasant, such as mood swings and lethargy. Cocaine can be extremely addictive and a tolerance develops over time that makes the highs harder to achieve and the after effects worse. Withdrawal symptoms include irritability, apathy, intense cravings, loss of sex drive and sleeplessness. Cocaine is also expensive and an addiction can mean financial ruin.

Dextromethorphan

DXM

Effects of the Drug
Similar to alcohol at low doses, at higher doses it can cause dissociative and psychedelic experiences. Side effects can include skin irritation, nausea, sexual dysfunction and hangovers.

How it works
DXM's reaction with the brain is complex and is not completely understood. Believed to affect receptors of dopamine and NMDA (a chemical linked to schizophrenia and addiction.)

Origins
DXM is a cough suppressant available in a huge number of over-the-counter cold medicines. It has been used recreationally since the 1960s, but this has only started to become well known.

Associated Problems
People using DXM recreationally are taking much higher doses than would be used to suppress a cough. Many of these products also contain other ingredients that can be very dangerous at high doses. DXM can also create bad reactions when combined with alcohol or other drugs, especially prescription anti-depressants. High or frequent doses can cause brain damage or death.

QUAALUDES
[Sopors or Ludes]

Effects of the Drug
Smaller doses relieve tension, larger doses can cause feelings of warmth, euphoria, and sedation. Side effects can include disorientation, slowed reflexes and blurred vision.

How it works
Slows down the central nervous system as well as respiratory and cardiac functions.

Origins
First synthesized in India in 1955 by M.L. Gujral. Widely prescribed as a sleeping aid and anti-anxiety drug in the 1960s. Production stopped in most countries after it was discovered to be addictive and often lethal in overdose.

Associated Problems
Can become highly addictive, tolerance builds up quickly and overdoses can cause coma or death. Seizure is sometimes a symptom of withdrawal. More dangerous when combined with alcohol.

Psilocybin / Psylocin

PSYCHEDELIC MUSHROOMS
[Magic Mushrooms, Shrooms, Fungus, Cardboard, Simple Simon]

Effects of the Drug
At lower doses causes mood and sensory enhancement, in higher doses causes hallucinations, dissociation from the body and a feeling of connection to the Universe. These sensations can be negative or positive depending on the state of mind of the individual.

How it works
Believed to inhibit the release of the neurotransmitter serotonin.

Origins
Used by cultures all over the world including Africa, Siberia, and South/Central America since ancient times. Became part of the 1960s psychedelic movement after it was written about by several ethno-biologists studying their religious use in Mexico.

Associated Problems
The main danger is in the possibility of accidentally consuming the wrong kind of mushroom, which can be fatal.

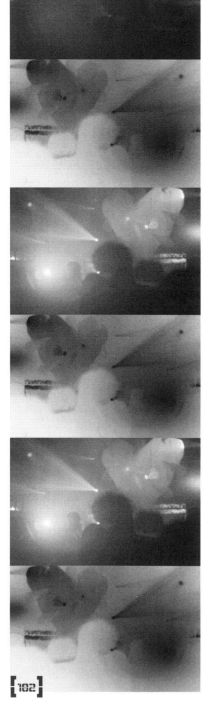

times disorienting by allowing one to access different thought processes. This disorientation is amplified by the complete sensory overload at raves. On acid everything seems a little more: lights are brighter, colors are more intense, sound has more depth. Although not for everyone, feeling slightly off-balance in an environment where there is no judgment can be liberating. It forces you to find structure and control in a beat and a rhythm. Many ravers combine ecstasy and LSD. This is known as candy-flipping. In this combination, LSD curbs some of the overly touchy-feely effects of ecstasy while the ecstasy maintains your ability to dance.

Hippies Reincarnated? The Levi's advertisement below certainly wasn't the first to suggest that the hippie was a precursor to the raver. Twenty-one years after the original Summer of Love in 1967, English youth danced in remote fields and concealed warehouses. It was coined by many as the reincarnated Summer of Love. Once again the media discovered white, middle class youth embracing new music, a new awareness and a new drug. Or were they new? Was the birth of rave a 1990s version of the 1960s hippie era, or was this something completely different?

LSD and MDMA were relatively new to the public sphere when introduced as the fuel for these two subcultures. LSD was banned in 1966 just prior to the height of public consumption, while MDMA was banned in the U.S. in 1985 after an American media frenzy over street use of the drug. In trying to decipher whether the drugs led to the scene or whether the scene led to the drugs, the inherent symbiosis becomes evident. As hippie culture became more accepted, so too did media and public discussion of LSD quietly subside. A similar development has occurred in Britain with rave. As rave proliferates globally and becomes more acceptably mainstream, public fears of MDMA slowly lessen.

Hippies and ravers alike claim that drugs offer the possibility of adding new dimensions and depth to their music. One commonality between the two cultures is the idea of "seeing" music. In hippie culture

there was a hierarchy in the type of drugs used in music appreciation, with acid usually considered the most influential and mind-altering. The space held open by drug induction ("spaced-out") allowed for greater differentiation of sound reception and hearing manipulation. In particular, drug use allowed listeners to simultaneously follow the lines and sounds of different instruments, which was impossible for "straight" people to do. In some cases, acid helped listeners go inside the music: groups like Frank Zappa, Pink Floyd and guitarist Jimi Hendrix claimed that their music could only be understood through drug-induced listening.

There is no doubt that the initiating element, the sacrament, the symbolic centre, the source of group identity in hippie lives was the psychedelic drug trip. **JAMES BAKALAR and LESTER GRINSPOON,** *Psychedelic Drugs Reconsidered,* **70**

[On E] I can feel the music running in and out of my body, like music is coming out of my fingers and toes! **ANONYMOUS, age 16, F, 0 yrs.**

Teach your eyes to hear and teach your ears to see, then only will you understand our culture. **ANONYMOUS**.

"Hippies—The original blueprint for ravers."
Levi's jeans advertisement.

Like the progressive rock of the 1960s, the aesthetics of techno are conducive to drug-induced listening and dancing. Because techno uses very repetitive drum and bass loops, some find it too grating or monotonous to tolerate while "straight." Specific genres such as trance use intensely high frequencies, layered sounds and intense climaxes to accentuate a psychedelic drug trip. Inversely, the drug trip accentuates the music. The use of samples sometimes alludes to drugs: The Shamen's "Ebeneezer Goode" (translation: Es are good), Josh Wink's "Higher State of Consciousness" and Ashley's "Dope Makes You Feel All Right" are only a few examples.

Different Drugs for Different Times. Understanding the parallels between hippie culture and LSD and rave culture and MDMA, one begins to comprehend a key relationship between the hippie ideology of self-discovery, and the hedonistic rave ideology of collective empathy. Rave has given birth to what has come to be known as the E generation: a culture synonymous with drug consumption. Just as we can

I am instantly more connected with the music, and have recently discovered that I can DJ much more effectively while slightly "on" than "off." E can allow you to differentiate tracks more effectively, as well as have a better intuition about what the tracks are then capable of doing together. Now, it's worth mentioning that a little pot can do so much fantastic stuff to one's acoustic perceptions, that it can spread out and separate different sounds—it really adds another dimension to listening to music. **MAX, Toronto, ON, age 30, M, 10 yrs.**

When I did E, I started seeing everyone coming together and wide-eyed. I got home and realized that everything had changed. Everything was different. This has changed my life. **LITTLE ZERO, Toronto, ON, age 29, M, 7 yrs**

As psychologists have known for ages, [ecstasy] breaks down some of our interaction "walls" and gives us the freedom to . . . be really honest about things. On or off of the dance floor, this can be really fun! People find their dancing groove and you can see people really start to physically manifest tracks like never before . . . Interaction is far freer, more open and easy. Back in the day when the whole room was all doing the same stuff at the same time, you could feel connected, relaxed and happy with everyone in the room! (I miss those days.) **MAX, Toronto, ON, age 30, M, 10 yrs.**

On E skin becomes an erogenous zone. Being touched and caressed by your lover, by a stranger, by the same sex or by your sibling is freeing, beautiful, open, and sensual as opposed to sexual. Skin on skin feels tingly, electrifying, ecstatic. Males are often liberated from heterosexist models of same sex interaction; women may be liberated from the need to dress up and [wear] make up to be sexy and accepted.

ask whether hippie culture was a reflection of middle America rediscovering itself, or discovering a new drug, a similar question surrounds rave. These sub-cultural evolutions were dependent on new drug experimentation and it is doubtful whether either scene would have developed in isolation from a surrounding drug culture.

Many would argue that ecstasy is the ultimate club and dance drug. Not only does it increase a taker's ability to feel music, it also makes those who wouldn't normally dance uninhibited enough to do so. MDMA emphasizes the physicality of music and mysteriously begs those on it to move. Initiating feelings of self-love, MDMA boosts confidence but not necessarily ego. It increases communication, collective awareness and empathy, making the dance floor a more electric, inviting environment. If the 1980s club environment with cocaine as the fuel was the "me" generation, the 1990s with MDMA as its fuel is the "we" generation. Generation X has been accused of being alienated and disenfranchised. Yet this generation didn't choose an ego-based, self-empowering drug such as coke; it chose a drug that would help people love one another, even if for only a few hours.

BOY GEORGE: THE QUEEN'S OWN DJ
The former Culture Club singer turned disc jockey visits Bosnia with the hope that his gigs will get Serb, Muslim and Croatian kids dancing together. *The London Times Magazine, Saturday June 9, 2001.*

The combined effects of ecstasy and acid house are remarkably obvious. Sexual, racial and class stereotypes and barriers are being challenged, while reservations and feelings of intimidation have been eased. Some have even argued that ecstasy was the catalyst in dissolving disputes between Protestant and Catholic ravers in Northern Ireland who united in the rave arena every weekend. Others have suggested that ecstasy has eased hostility between soccer hooligans. MDMA also seems to deplete sexual aggression, allowing dance to free itself of sexuality and participants to exhibit sexual indifference. The atmosphere initiated by E stands in contrast to the codified environment of most clubs. Ecstasy assists in the elimination of perceived social barriers and allows partakers to believe they can talk to anyone and love everyone. The drug helps to foster an environment that is open and non-discriminatory. Much like the disco scene a decade previous, gays are welcomed and are often prominent within the scene.

Acid house and ecstasy allow people to disappear from daily, mundane rituals. By inducing a more empathetic state, the drug permits participants to feel comfortable and free enough with their surroundings to express emotions to strangers. Straight males can feel uninhibited enough to hug and massage one another openly without fear of public scrutiny, while for females ecstasy creates an environment so unfettered by ritualized gender roles that they can hug males and even take off their shirts without worrying about being objectified and solicited for dates. The touching and feeling that MDMA initiates has given it the inaccurate reputation as an aphrodisiac. The drug actually increases the sensitivity of touch but decreases the libido and is therefore instrumental in re-introducing males and females as friends and not just possible sexual partners.

Q. If you do drugs at a party, what is your favorite drug or drug combination and why?

A. When I was more into it, my favorite was E—I love the effect, the closeness, the feeling, the bond you have with others around you, the way the music sounds, the lights look, everything . . . you just feel so happy and in love with everything. Combo? I'd take half a speed before that—it tends to cut out the nausea that I typically get from the E if it's too strong. **MESSYCAT, Montréal, QC, age 24, F, 2 yrs.**

People just become less inhibited and more sensitive to other people's needs and moods. Makes it easier to get on with people excatly for that reason. People tend to appear to be more outgoing than usual although E can't make you like this, it can only enhance what you're already feeling so it tends to bring under-confident people out of themselves . . . to interact in a way they would like. Personally, I like people on E (in sensible doses) although when I'm straight and talking to them, they tend to be a little harder to deal with (or maybe I'm just jealous?) **FLUFFY, London, England, age 22, F, 2 yrs.**

. . . a hug from a fellow raver is not usually a sexual advance as much as a show of platonic affection, much like grade-schoolers holding hands. **LORI TOMLINSON, *This Ain't No Disco*, 200.**

Kick Ass!!!! I could dance all night !!! And feel FREE like a bird. But I got over that and now I know that I can do it without that magik pill . . . and have just as much fun and truly take it all in. **ANONYMOUS, Trafford, PA, age 17, F, 0 yrs.**

I don't take drugs. I never have tried it or been under the influence of it, just . . . because I never was interested. I like to be able to say to myself in the morning after a party that I had a great night without taking a drug. It makes me proud that I have not fallen into those rave stereotypes. Hehe. I also love seeing the faces of shock when people find out I have never taken drugs, being a raver [and] a DJ. ;) **DJ QT, Sydney, Australia, age 24, F, 8 yrs.**

Depends on the strength of the E in question. Usually, a feeling of light-headedness [and] I become more sociable, I smile more, am less annoyed at various unpleasantries or people and my legs weaken. If it's stronger, my stare becomes blank as my brain [which] proceeds to interpret my surroundings in weird but positive ways. I usually sit down and stare at nothing specific with a big fat grin on my face. Communication becomes difficult as ideas are easily lost and forgotten. I feel overjoyed and my worries are gone for a short while. **DJ PSONYK, Montréal, QC, age 30, M, 8 yrs.**

Resonance. It was the first time everything came together for me. I'm chillin' out against a wall, waiting for my E to take hold, listening, chatting with my pals. Suddenly, everything becomes soft and chewy. The music is coming from everywhere, the floor, the ceiling, the darkness. It's deep inside me, a force I can't escape. I find myself moving like I've never moved before—feet, legs, arms [and] hands all finding their own way, guided by the beat. And everyone around is moving with me, the room a mass of energy locked into a perfect vibe. It's amazing, the best thing I've ever experienced in my life! Someone taps me on the shoulder and says "Dude, I really like your hat, dude!" and we smile and laugh. Then his friend says "Hi" and grabs my shoulders and she starts giving me a massage and I have to close my eyes and I must be on my way to heaven, it's so good. When I open them a girl is dancing on the bass bins in front of me and god she's so beautiful I think I'm gonna cry. I look around and everyone is there with me, old friends, new friends, smiling, waving, laughing [and] loving. It's a perfect moment and I know my life has changed forever. **GARTNER, Toronto, ON, age 30, M, 3 yrs.**

The best time I ever had at a party was the first party I went to sober. I realized what . . . all that [was] and I now go sober to every party . . . After researching each drug you will find out how they affect you in the long term and it's not worth it. **PriNcEsS LiNdZy, Little Rock, AR, age 17, F, 2 yrs.**

I don't do drugs at a party because I want to enjoy dancing to the music, seeing friends. And plus I'm just a big sXe kid. **LITE BRITE, Las Vegas, NV, age 15, 2 yrs.**

If you're really desperate, push on your eyes for a few seconds and you'll start to see weird colors. Pretend that everyone in the room is your best friend and feel the love rush . . . I think that we, as ravers, are more able to play with reality and interpret it in ways other than what we've been provided with our whole lives. Whether this is through drugs or not doesn't really matter, as long as we remain healthy and courteous. Keep shinin'. **STAN, Lafayette, IN, 23, M, 5 yrs.**

Having packed enough food for the weekend, checked over our camping gear, and acquired enough drugs to get 10 people high, two friends and myself set out on the highway with a tray of hash brownies under the passenger seat and sparked up a joint. This would be a weekend to remember I thought to myself as I pushed a tape into the deck and waited for the beat to hit.

As we neared the campgrounds several joints and two hours later, we were met by a police checkpoint. A police officer appeared at my window asking if we had any alcohol or illegal substances in the car. Filled with fear I looked the officer in the eyes and responded "No." He glanced at my two companions and waved us through. My heart began to beat again and I decided to eat a hash brownie to celebrate our arrival. We grabbed our gear and jumped on a ferry to get across to the island campsite. Once again we were searched, this time by security guards who were willing to overlook the bag of pot they found on me.

While we set up camp the bass was echoing in the distance, filling me up with anticipation. The three of us decided it was time to consume our drugs of choice for the night and find our way to the party. Washing the foul taste of mushrooms out of my mouth I walked in time with the beat that now seemed to be calling my name. As I emerged from the moonlit beach I was consumed by a mass of people celebrating and rejoicing. There was a sense of community and openness that was intoxicating. As the music moved me I found myself rising higher and higher and soon I was lost in the moment within an ocean of people.

The next morning I woke up in a puddle of mud completely confused. I had pushed myself to the limit the night before! I washed myself in Georgian Bay and cleansed myself of the night before. I stumbled across a friend I had met at a rave a year before [and] he gifted me with the biggest mushroom I'd seen in my life. I began to chew on this huge stalk and wandered some more while the sky seemed to turn an intoxicating blue . . .

I stumbled upon a drummer friend of mine who was drumming on his African Jambe in the water. We went back to my campsite [and] smoked a hash joint. We busted into a jam, him with his Jambe [and] me with a big jug of water as my drum. When we stopped, applause echoed from the surrounding tents as fellow ravers cried out for more.

At 12 a.m. I was shaken awake by one of my friends. I had passed out in the sun in a chair in front of my tent. Night two was ready to begin. As we drew closer to the main stage we stopped to admire the moon, smoked a joint and popped our Es. Dancing the night away I met countless people—a few of whom I still have the pleasure to call friends. It was a night to share. Joy filled my limbs as I danced. I was no longer a fragmented, alienated white male, who worked at the Gap to pay my bills while I was at school. I was alive and capable of manifesting my dreams, even if only for a night.

As the day broke I danced feverishly knowing that my hours of celebration would soon come to an end. During the night I had been busted by the Reserve Native Police who had caught me rolling a hash joint. I gave them all the drugs I had in my tent and they were kind enough not to turn me in to the OPP. The confiscated drugs didn't matter. What mattered was being able to express and share my passion for life.

It was 3 or 4 p.m. by the time I had packed up camp. Wearing my favorite Hawaiian shirt I set out to catch the ferry back to civilization. Noticing a few locals had docked their boats near by I asked if we could charter a boat to get home. Myself and seven others jumped aboard for a $5 ride. The owner of the boat invited me to sit on the bow with him. "I love your shirt," he said, "Can I buy it?"

"Sorry, it's my favorite shirt, I can't part with it," I said. As the owner pointed out cloud masses and storm fronts that were off in the distance, I became aware that my raving days were done. It was time for me to return to Earth and start living for more than just the moment. As I stepped off the boat I turned to the man who had given us the boat ride and handed him the shirt off my back. **PSYCHEDELIC PhD, Toronto, ON, 25, 6 yrs.**

World Electronic Music Festival, August 1998

Apparently it was a dosing of crystal and coke, and his heart literally exploded. He was dead for a long time at the rave."

Anonymous

A 16-year-old boy had speedballed with his friends who danced around him while he died. They were either too scared to report it or too messed up on drugs themselves to realize he was dying. Rigor mortis was setting in as the bass continued its rumble, the lights flashed and feet trampled in ecstatic bliss all around the stiffening body. That same night someone reported an attempted rape in the bathroom.

I will not do that hit of E,
Thank you but it's not for me.

I will not do it at a pub,
I will not do it at a club.

I will not do it while I'm dancing,
I will not do it while romancing.

I will not chew that little pill,
It's bitter taste just makes me ill.

I would not could not during sex,
I will not do that hit of X.

I will not do it with a trick,
not if I need to use my dick.

Even with a bump of K,
I would not do it anyway.

I do not like it when I roll,
Not one bit, one bit at all.

I will not do a "Mitsubishi,"
I told you no just let me be.

I will not do a "Calvin Klein,"
what's yours is yours,
what's mine is mine.

I will not do a double-stack,
It makes no sense, that is a fact.

I cannot bring myself to trip,
Not at a rave, or after it.

I will not do a microdot,
They're fine for you,
for me they're not.

I refuse to do any since the day,
Ecstasy stopped being made with
pure MDMA!!!

-from group e-mail thread, source unknown

THE HONEYMOON IS OVER

07

While our parents thought E was one step down from heroin, we thought it was one step up from beer. **BILL BREWSTER and FRANK BROUGHTON,** *Last Night a DJ Saved My Life,* **369**

The "chemical generation" passed through the doors of perception into a world where drugs were not only acceptable, but all-consumingly glorious. **MATTHEW COLLIN,** *Altered State,* **281**

In the initial days we were the ones who supplied all our friends. We got some loose MDMA powder from my dealer. We had asked for about 16 hits worth of loose powder. We dumped the powder out on a table and when I saw the mound of white powder à la Scarface I realized that we were in it pretty deep. We had no scales—we just filled up the caps until it looked like enough, and put a little extra in the caps that would be ours! **ANONYMOUS.**

Ecstasy—bad for your health, good for your soul. **GARTNER, Toronto, ON, age 30, M, 3 yrs.**

The number of deaths mentioned in frantic British tabloids and American TV news magazines were often rationalized by participants as being extremely low considering the amount of raves and users of ecstasy. Are raves to be blamed for the validation and naturalization of such extremist behavior? How does rave transgress from hugs, smiles and feel-good vibes to attempted rapes and overdoses of cocaine and crystal methamphetamine?

Ecstasy's Not a Drug. Ecstasy wasn't the type of drug that you bought off a seedy dealer in a back alley. It was a drug that you bought from a friend who had bought 10 extra hits from another friend who happened to know a dealer. Nothing about ecstasy and how it was initially distributed and bought seemed comparable to drugs like heroin or cocaine. You didn't have to shove it up your nose, inject it into your veins or even smoke it. All you had to do was swallow a capsule or a pill that had a cute name. It would perhaps be a pretty color such as pink or blue with an embossed character on it. It was as easy as taking your Flinstones vitamins in the morning.

Describe the best time you ever had at a party. A. Having my girlfriend tell me she loved me as soon as my E was kicking in. **Anonymous, Toronto, age 23, M, 2 yrs.**

One of the effects of rave culture was to alter participants' opinion of illegal drug use. In some large cities ecstasy became a rite of passage for club going youth, almost as innocent as having an experimental drag of a cigarette. It was a drug for teens that didn't do drugs. It had the reputation

Describe the worst time you ever had at a party. A. Getting dumped by your girlfriend 'cause she tells you she's a lesbian while tripping. **2E, Sydney, Australia, age 18, M, 2 yrs.**

of having low toxicity and few physiological effects. MDMA didn't alter your ability to go to work or school like more addictive drugs such as heroin or crack. It didn't make you aggressive or forgetful like alcohol. It didn't make you arrogant or egotistical like cocaine was known to do. Instead, MDMA made you warm, friendly and huggable. It made you feel love. How could something that made everything so positive and beautiful be bad for you? Raves were a never-never-land of all that was good and happy, making it difficult to see if there was anything criminal going on. MDMA came with a package of pretty lights, colorful fashion, and its own sound-track; to its millions of takers, ecstasy seemed innocent.

Physiological Effects of Ecstasy. The come-down from ecstasy happens within about four hours of taking the pill, depending on the dosage. There will be no more serotonin left in your brain to be released. Taking more ecstasy at this point won't work because it's the release of serotonin in your brain that causes the happy E feelings. Unless the dosage is lower than normal, ingesting more MDMA at this point will give you the amphetamine effects but not the desirable empathetic feelings. In some instances if the dose or doses have been strong enough, so much serotonin will have been depleted that you will have less than you had in your normal state. Some users will then experience a come-down that puts them in a lower mood than they were in before they took the pill. It causes them to feel depressed, irritable and anti-social—the very opposite of the ecstasy experience.

Well a nice clean dose of MDMA fairly early on with perhaps a little bit of an energy boost from something (ephedrine or an energy drink) to keep me energized for the night. I was excited about the implications of taking Prozac shortly after the MDMA to help protect the old neurons in your head, as well as the idea of taking 5-HTP both a few hours before and a few hours after to help keep the serotonin levels up, as well as taking vitamin C to help further prevent neurotoxicity. **MAX, Toronto, ON, age 30, M, 10 yrs.**

but don't drink too much water.

There have been a few deaths reported from people drinking too much water while at a rave. This is extremely rare. However, drinking 2-4 cups an hour when dancing is about the right amount. You should also try and eat something salty (not always easy if you've taken a stimulant drug) or drink fruit juice or a sports drink like Gatorade. Remember, water is an antidote to dehydration, not ecstasy. **www.dancesafe.org**

[111]

THE HONEYMOON IS OVER

The substance that made the scene so special also contained the means of its destruction. **MATTHEW COLLIN,** *Altered State,* **159**

The first time I did mushrooms, I didn't know how much to take. The only reference I had to compare it with was Ecstasy . . . when I didn't start feeling it, I just kept munching more of them. God knows how much I took. The night went from hilarious to beautiful, to really, really ugly. It was at the first WEMF and it was pouring rain the first night when I took the shrooms. I just sat in the car and watched the rain morphing its way down the windshield. By the morning as I walked into the drenched tent area everyone looked positively hideous . . . I was so used to everyone looking beautiful when I was on E it was jarring to see ravers that looked so fucked up on drugs . . . it just seemed like a circus with really awful clowns! **BUNNY, age 27, F, 6 yrs.**

Your body heals from drug use, but an open mind is hard to close. **ANONYMOUS.**

The serotonin may take up to two weeks to be completely replenished depending on the dosage of MDMA. This is why many people notice that they don't get as much of a rush when they do E two weeks in a row, especially if they do it two nights in a row. They will get the speedy effects but not much else. Frequent users notice periods of depression if they keep doing ecstasy without giving themselves enough time to replenish their serotonin levels. This may result in below normal levels of serotonin in day-to-day functioning. Some users have begun taking 5-htp supplements. 5-Hydroxy Trytophan is an amino acid that is a catalyst in serotonin production.

A number of ecstasy-related deaths have now taken place throughout the world. The primary reason is heatstroke. Ecstasy causes a rise in body temperature. This fact coupled with the often high temperatures at raves can contribute to heatstroke. Dancing, especially in a hot environment, will raise the body's temperature even more. Ecstasy users must make sure they replenish the fluid they are losing through sweating. Heatstroke can happen on even a low dosage of MDMA, depending on the surrounding environment, the level of physical exertion and water replenishment.

Heaven-on-Earth Too Many Times. In one episode of the British mystery series *Inspector Morse,* the Inspector is investigating the mysterious suicides of three young adults. The only thing that links the three deaths is the fact that the deceased all raved and had been known to take an experimental, fictitious drug. This euphoria-inducing drug created such a heaven-on-earth for its takers that there was nothing left for them to live for. I'm not sure if raving has inadvertently caused any suicides, but the idea may not be completely far-fetched. If you've been a raver and then stopped you may agree that there is definitely an intangible void. After partying for a few years the desire to indulge in the excesses of the rave world may decrease, but there is often nothing that will immediately replace the wonders that the scene provided.

Rave itself can be seen to function as a drug. Those who attend raves are forever in anticipation of that initial high—that first party that blew your mind. Attainment of this is rare, for in most cases, it is the newness of the experience and the spectacle that creates the high. Inevitably, the come-down from E and the rave experience means drifting back to reality, an often disheartening feeling. Herein lies the tragedy of raving. Touching heaven-on-earth so many times is just too consuming to endure for any prolonged length of time. Ecstasy's returns eventually diminish. Those who can't easily slip back into reality simply deny it with more drugs until the rave dream becomes their whole world. Some become casualties, sucked into the dark underbelly of rave excess, while others withdraw completely from the scene because they no longer desire the drugs and are unable to divorce the rave experience from the ecstasy experience.

A repeating cycle within rave scenes starts with a honeymoon period where new recruits see only the positive effects of E, followed by the come-down, when the drug offers diminishing returns and usage either slows, stops or turns into excess and abuse. There is an inherent duality built into rave culture. On the one hand it can be a spiritual experience, a heaven-on-earth exuding a beautiful, happy, asexual love. On the other hand rave has a dark side of potential drug abuse. The rave lifestyle of partying every week usually means a weekly roller coaster of emotions. In the late week there is intense anticipation for Saturday night. Sunday is then used to recover from the sleeplessness and exhaustion of the night before or sometimes the party will continue into Sunday afternoon. Sometimes it will take all of Monday and Tuesday to get over the excessive serotonin depletion and the psychological depression of having to come back to reality; a reality which may seem a little less meaningful than before.

Q. **If you do drugs at a party, what is your favorite drug or drug combination and why?**

A. I don't do drugs because I realized how much of an idiot I looked like on drugs . . . I don't mean to speak badly about people under 18 being that I am one myself. But I see more and more irresponsible kids e-tarded out on the floor. You know it when you see it. Blatant drug use is starting to get out of hand. It's like we went through a honeymoon period where the drugs were OK and rave wasn't as huge here. It would be less likely that I would've been at the parties back then [because] I couldn't drive, but back then there definitely weren't as many people on drugs who couldn't handle their shit. Now it's just blatant. And it's just wrong. **JERNET, North Carolina, age 17, F, 3 yrs.**

The machine is demanding, exacting a heavy toll on its human software: post-rush comedown and midweek ver-out . . . ravers turn into man-machine contraptions gone haywire, teeth grinding, twitching, gurning . . . this regime of bliss wreaks a terrible attrition on the flesh-and-blood components of rave's orgasmotron. **SIMON REYNOLDS,** *British Rave,* **56**

I don't take drugs anymore. I've read too much about the future effects. Very bad things. And I've also noticed a huge difference the day after when you do or don't take drugs. If I do, I'm incapacitated for a few days—just really exhausted and my head is not all there. If I don't, I may be tired the next day, maybe the day after, but that's it. It's much better that way since typically I have to work at 9 a.m. I can function much better when I haven't taken anything the night before. My brain isn't freaking out. **MESSYCAT, Montréal, QC, age 24, F, 2 yrs.**

Q. What kinds of changes have you noticed in your scene?

A. Mentality has radically changed. To quote a track's name by an electronic group called Prototype 909, "The kids don't care." Raving has gotten to be casual . . . the magic is gone. Back then, raves were scarce and far between. We counted the days till the next party. Today, raves are held every week so there is nothing magical about attending a rave anymore. It wasn't so long ago that people . . . would see you as some sort of an underground hero if you mentioned you attended raves and walked around in phat pants. Now, phat pants can be found at Wal-Mart and when you mention the word "rave," people go "Oh yeah, those things." **DJ PSONYK, Montréal, QC, age 30, M, 8 yrs.**

It can't change your life every time. The buzz gets weaker, the insight it offers more banal. **SHERYL GARRATT, *Adventures in Wonderland*, 314**

Initially parties were few and far between. Even if you wanted to go every week there was just nowhere to go. It was difficult to get addicted to the rave experience; there simply weren't enough events to attend. Now in most large cities there is guaranteed to be at least one large event a week plus smaller rave-oriented club nights. With so much to choose from it's easy to go to raves every week. For some, however, raving simply consumes too much bodily and mental energy to endure for any extended period of time without experiencing burnout.

Polydrug Use. No matter how great a drug is, it's bound to get boring some time. The high just gets too predictable. Soon you need five pills to equal the same effect. Even then, you can't replicate the sense of wonderment that your virgin E experience provided. So you try something else, perhaps a little cheaper, or perhaps something that will last a little longer. You hope for more bang for your buck. At $20 a night you rationalized that an ecstasy pill was cheaper than a night of drinking, and by all accounts a lot more fun. You could remember everything the next day and instead of embarrassing yourself you had embraced yourself. But justifying $20 times two or even three was a little more difficult to do. Meth's a little cheaper and hey, it lasts three times as long. Or perhaps you just want a different buzz altogether and opt for some K. And before you know it, you're too fucked to even dance. Sitting in a K-hole, you've convinced yourself you're dancing but it's just the movement in your head.

Regardless of how wonderful a drug feels, the effects eventually become benign. As some users become bored with the usual E experience they try new, faster ways of getting the rush. Some extreme users inject ecstasy, others try inserting it anally, while many snort it out of sheer impatience for the rush. More frightening than alternate methods of usage is the lack of purity in what is being pawned off as E. Drug dealers have been known to put everything from vitamin C to PCP in ecstasy tablets. The effect of this is noticeable on the dance floor. The drug that once made you move like an angel eventually slows you to a halt. Additives such as trace amounts of heroin literally slow dancers down. Some complain of being too mashed-out to dance. They simply stand or sit, close their eyes and become enveloped by the music. Sometimes too much speed in a tablet simply constricts your muscles so much that your body feels too heavy to dance.

One of the latest additives to MDMA has been DXM (dextromethorphan), a cough suppressant that has a drying effect on the lungs. High doses raise body temperature and prevent sweating by drying out the skin. This inability to sweat inhibits the body's natural cooling system and increases the risk of heatstroke. Hallucinations and itchy skin are indications that what was supposed to be MDMA is either laced with or is largely DXM. Another extremely dangerous additive found in ecstasy is PMA (Para-methoxy-amphetamine, 4-MA). This powerful stimulant is dangerous and has caused a number of deaths in the U.S. and abroad. It is more easily manufactured than MDMA and is less expensive to produce.

Crystal. It's sad, how cute and energetic meth makes its teenage users. The first time I noticed the effects of meth was in a girl in a bathroom at a small rave. She had given herself the job of clean-up person because she was so speedy she needed a project to keep her occupied. In a strange way she seemed very focused, almost like a child on Ritalin, but at the same time extremely chatty and antsy. Energy was just pouring out of her.

Taking more and more ecstasy will not help maintain the same high. The effects are totally reliant on the amount of serotonin available in the brain. The only effect gained will be the speed. Knowing this, it's

Last month, paramethoxyamphetamine (PMA) disguised as Ecstasy hit American shores after killing several users in Europe. Like X, PMA raises blood pressure. Unlike X, there's no limit to how high PMA can raise it—the more pills ingested, the higher the pressure. Two Chicago area ravers died from the drug. One of them had taken a staggering five doses. **"Ecstasy without Fear,"** *LA Weekly*, **Friday June 9, 2000.**

Q. Worst time you ever had at a party?

A. I took some bad drugs and had a seizure. **LIL'CHIC, Grant, AL, age 18, F, 0 yrs.**

A Chicago Drug Enforcement Agency spokesperson called the difference between MDMA and PMA "like making angel-food cake and coming up with chocolate-chip cookies." **"Taking the E Train,"** *Shepherd Express*, **Thursday December 21, 2000.**

E used to be the drug of choice although not anymore . . . it got to [be too] much and then the evil crystal took over my life. Now I'm just down with smoking a joint here and there . . . all natural! **ANONYMOUS, Kelowna, BC.**

Speed (methamphetamines in tablet form) is the undisputable king of mega parties. And they are happily supplied by local biker gangs for ridiculous prices. **ANONYMOUS, Montréal, QC.**

Now all I see is a bunch of little kids tweaking on crystal meth, x'ing their ass off so hard they can't dance, and the whole thing has turned into a big drug fest . . . a lot of people don't even care who is on the tables, or anything about the music; as long as they are high off their asses. Crystal meth and too much x is killing the scene near my neck of da'-woods. **"Letters to Lotus,"** *Lotus* magazine, **Issue 12**

It was my first party and when we first got there I was confronted with hugs and friendly introductions. I was outside of the club waiting for the doors to open, and all my friends and I were hitting the balloons filled with nitrous. After a while we went inside of the club and I made friends with these three candy raver chicks. They were all rolling, and asked me if I was. I said "no," and they felt so bad for me that they pitched in all their money and bought me a bean. I sat on this stool, and my friend Valery came up and began massaging my back. The rest of the night I went around learning how to dance, getting back massages, and Vicks blown in my face. Ever since that night I have been a raver. ***STAR*, Covina, CA, age 18, F, 3 yrs.**

I think drugs can teach us things, but that after we have learned the things, we should let them go . . . Try them. Learn. Put them down. Smile from thereafter. My $.02. **GNAT, Philadelphia, PA, age 19, M, 4 yrs.**

little wonder that many turn to straight amphetamine or methamphetamine, otherwise known as crystal, to create a similar speedy effect at a much lower cost. Early on in the rave scene crystal meth was taboo; little signs on flyers stating "No Crystal" confirmed this. Within a couple of years, it was impossible to keep the drug out. One Canadian participant voiced his concern in *Lotus* magazine: "Why is it that these mindless pricks are constantly asking me if I want to buy some crystal? Meth brings out bad vibes, as well as non-social behavior. It's ruining our scene. Wake up!"[7] In some cities crystal became almost as commonplace as ecstasy, and in some cases it was difficult to find ecstasy without some trace of crystal. It became the secret ingredient that would make ecstasy pills last for eight to twelve hours instead of three to four, but the after effects were harsher and much more addictive. The allure of crystal over pure MDMA was its reduced cost and its lasting effect. After doing crystal, some ravers would have bouts of insomnia for days. As one raver explains, "I lost control of my whole life. I wouldn't go to sleep all weekend, and was literally sleeping on my break time at work."

Drug use had turned into polydrug use. Chemicals such as ketamine, nitrous oxide, GHB and crystal methamphetamine were coming into prominence. Nitrous oxide, more commonly known as laughing gas, is a dissocative anaesthetic. Its use at raves began on the West Coast and eventually spread to the rest of the U.S. and some parts of Canada. The balloons fit the childhood nature of rave, and at $5 a hit the price was right. Dealers with one tank could fill up over 200 balloons. Inhaling nitrous oxide causes a dissociative, dreamlike effect that lasts about a minute.

Ketamine, also called special K or just K, is another dissociative anaesthetic that is usually used in veterinary medicine. Starting as a liquid, ketamine is usually cooked and then sold by dealers as a powder to be snorted. It has been found in E. Mild effects of K are similar to the dreamy feeling of nitrous oxide. In higher doses ketamine becomes hallucinogenic and extremely dissociative. Users will often find it difficult to move in this state, which ravers call a "K-hole," where mind and body feel separated. It has been described by some as a spiritual, near-death experience.

BREAK-INS FOR RAVE DRUG TROUBLE VETERINARIANS

For the first 14 years of his veterinary practice, Steve Kromka says no would-be thief even so much as smudged the clinic's glass. In the past six weeks, his practice has been broken into twice. Ketamine, an animal tranquilizer and now a popular drug used at raves, is the likely reason for the increase, he said.

Denver Post, Thursday November 16, 2000.

GHB was inaccurately called liquid E for a time because of its mild euphoric effect. It then became known in the media as the date rape drug because it could be mixed undetected into drinks. When mixed with alcohol GHB is likely to cause a user to pass out. It is difficult to know what dosage of GHB will cause an overdose, especially when taken with a depressant such as alcohol.

Can you believe that hardly anyone dances out here? In a crowd of 15,000 people, I'd say only 100-200 people dance . . . the poor kids are too drugged out on cat tranquilizers, heroin and speed to do anything, even smile. **"Feedback," Fix Magazine, November 1995**

It was a 2000 New Year's party and I had the pleasure of watching three people OD and go into convulsions. It was terrible. **KID*NASA, Milwaukee, WI, age 17, M, 2 yrs.**

Phryl party at the Masonic Temple in Toronto. My best friend and I split some acid and pot. I'm dancing away having a good time and suddenly the music turns dark and evil. I'm hearing things that aren't there. Horrible screaming. Guns firing. Trains roaring by. Lions roaring. Babies crying. I'm trying to tell my pal what I'm hearing but I can't speak. I'm able to form coherent thoughts, sentences in my mind, but in the process of moving them to my tongue everything is garbled, and I can't make an intelligible sound. Four of the most frustrating hours of my life. **GARTNER, Toronto, ON, age 30, M, 3 yrs.**

Two years ago some dude got into a fight outside the venue and started shooting up the place, everyone was running around like useless pigs. Especially when the cops showed up. Since then Wichita hasn't had a problem. **DJ AKOMMODATE, Wichita, KS, age 19, M, 4 yrs.**

Accidentally head-butted (I was throwing myself forward when he was leaning back or somethin') a massive "rude bwoy" at World Dance in the London Docklands. He was wearing a red jacket and grabbed me and shoved me into all his mates and they told me I was a dead man. On four pills and a gram of Base that's not what you wanted to be hearing. LOL. **DJ_S2C, South Coast, England, age 22, M, 8 yrs.**

It is arguably this polydrug use that depletes vibe, the wonderfully congealing component of an event that mysteriously unifies all rave elements and participants. A variety of drugs creates a multitude of headspaces as opposed to the unifying headspace created by the mass use of ecstasy. Kids on a polydrug trip will often lie in the hallways of clubs because they are too out of it to stand up. Ravers have begun to use terms such as "tweaking" and "sketching" to describe polydrug highs.

Effects on Attitude. After attending countless parties over numerous years, why was my mom only now concerned about me attending a rave? It surely wasn't a coincidence that this had been the week that raves once again garnered an influx of media attention. This time though, it wasn't a drug overdose, it was a homicide. Two raver twins, Lucky and Chucky, who were apparently quite well known in the local rave circuit, had stabbed another raver.

At a party around the same time I had a friend admit to me that he had just swallowed his own puke because he didn't want to lose the Es he'd taken. I thought: Wow, you're going to swallow the regurgitated drug that made you vomit in the first place! What on earth is happening here?

In some rave scenes, ecstasy's smiley face reputation has disappeared to reveal rave's ugly drug-based underbelly. Regardless of the "love and hugs" reputation of E and the circuit of friendly drug dealers who were also ravers, there were inevitably people in the scene who were only there for the drugs, deals and huge profits. In Montréal, biker gangs started controlling certain aspects of rave's drug scene, knowing full well there was a huge market to be exploited. Likewise in Toronto, there was a growing amount of violence in some after-hours clubs and at a couple of raves, undoubtedly related to drugs. Knowledge of drug use and fear of violence led to increased police presence at raves and extremely tight security. Each cuddly-looking raver was subject to a full body frisk with metal detectors. Even legal drugs such as aspirin would have to be hidden now for fear that they would get you thrown out of an event.

Many aspects of the traditional rave scene have now become meaningless: drug use has become more rampant, the age of ravers has become progressively younger and many participants don't even seem to know or care which DJ they are listening to. It is now rare to find a posting of the DJ lineup at any event. The atmosphere of clubs and raves has deteriorated as dead souls wander the dance floor, haggard and out of it. The blissful effects of E have faded, leaving only the twitching and jittering after effects of amphetamines. Many young ravers are addicted to crystal and psychologically addicted to ecstasy years before they can legally drink wine.

As a drug dealer, raving is quite a different experience. As you enter a party, the security almost always searches everyone. They check pockets, arm sleeves, pant legs, bags, bras . . . But, they hardly ever check crotches (although, I've heard of guys getting their balls grabbed at by security.) So, my panties were usually stuffed full of E, speed, weed, and other mind-altering substances that I had for sale. Sometimes it was difficult to walk, because I had a plastic package the size of four super maxi pads between my legs. Once, my friends [and I] traveled to a three-day Destiny outdoor festival rave. I was driving my father's station wagon, and as we exited the off ramp to the location, there suddenly appeared about 10 security guards poised to search our car for substances. Well, inside the car there was quite a sight to see: my friends and I moved so fast! All of us were scrambling for our "stashes" of drugs (which were located in several bags throughout the car!), and when we found them, we all had to quickly jam copious amounts of drugs down our pants! Luckily we made it into the party without hassle, because they were actually searching the car for alcohol. **SHLOOPY, Toronto, ON, age 28, F, 6 yrs.**

There is growing concern over the safety of doormen in urban nightclubs. As a result, weapons are the priority for friskers. Second on the agenda is outside alcohol and "hard" drugs. Any pot that we might confiscate will be consumed by staff members later that evening. **ILAM NEBRANN, Club/Rave security guard for 6 years.**

Vigil. Toronto.
Sometime in 2000.

A friend of mine presented me with a flyer for a huge warehouse party complete with big name DJs and high ticket prices and suggested that a group of us all dress like candy kids and head out to the party. The stereotypical raver costume consists of huge baggy pants that drag on the ground, pacifiers, baby tees, fun fur, dozens of plastic bracelets on each arm and cutesy Powerpuff Girls or Teletubbies backpacks. I hadn't had a pacifier in my mouth since I was an infant, but decided to go for it anyway.

Most of the parties I attend have no more than a few hundred people, and everyone there is a friend of a friend of the DJ's or promoter's. I do however sometimes enjoy the vibe of a huge party as there's something energizing about being among thousands of people all dancing together. The lineup for this particular party was enormous, and most of the attendees were definitely not of legal drinking age. Being in my late 20s, I worried a bit that I looked like a narc. When I got carded at the door I breathed a little easier realizing that though I didn't look 15, I would probably fit in just fine, especially in dim lighting.

The party was divided into two large rooms, one playing trance and the other full of manic chipmunks on speed: happy hardcore, definitely not my thing (I won't take the crystal meth or speed that is needed to enjoy it properly) so I spent most of my time in the trance area. I danced all night, hugged my friends and immersed myself in the teenagers offering me lollipops and wanting me to sign their books. It was not the kind of party I wanted to attend every weekend and I felt like a bit of a tourist, but the music was good and it was a fun experience in a costume party kind of way.

A few months later, the same promoters were throwing another party at the same venue. Those of us who went to the first party encouraged others to come along this time to experience the silliness with us. An even bigger crew showed up for the second party and on the cab ride over, I briefed some of them on what to expect.

I headed straight for the trance area when I arrived and danced to maybe two tracks when I heard a scuffle going on behind me. Two men were fighting and everyone backed away. I turned to look for my friends, and when I looked back there was blood stretched 10 feet across the floor. At one end there was a man lying on the ground soaked in it. A few seconds later, a stretcher rolled in and hauled him away. Security staff roped off the area and told everyone in the trance room to go into the happy hardcore area.

The happy hardcore room was packed after they closed off the bloodied trance area. The music was frenetic and not particularly soothing after seeing something so evil. My friend Al, who had witnessed the attack, was holding onto me tightly, feeling extremely overwhelmed. His panic triggered a caretaker instinct in me. Some friends of mine were working at a special information booth at the party intended to provide services related to drugs and safe partying. They were able to provide us a place to sit away from the pressing crowds. I held Al's hand and he told me that he could sense that the victim had died. We had no news, but I feared he was right.

Most of the people at the party didn't see what had happened and kept on dancing. The crime scene was blocked from sight, and rumours started circulating about what had happened. Almost everyone just kept on dancing. I wanted to leave right away, but the coat check was on the other side of the trance room and we weren't allowed to go there for a few hours.

I stayed with Al and kept a lookout for my other friends, a few of whom had never been to a real rave before. Some of them saw what had happened, some didn't, but none were impressed. When we were finally able to get our coats, we had to walk through the crime scene with the blood still on the floor and lights turned up bright. I invited everyone to come to my place to hang out together, since none of us really felt like being alone. We stayed up most of the night talking about what we had seen. I had trouble wiping the images away from my mind.

The next day on the news we heard about what had happened. The graduation picture of the victim was in the paper; he was a bright, promising A+ student who had died protecting a friend from the attacker. Attaching the image of a smiling high school student to the body I had seen lying on the floor brought me to tears. A few days later I read that the attacker had been caught, which brought a sense of justice, but not of comfort.

A vigil was held for the victim a few weeks later in a park. It was cold and rainy, but about 30 people showed up, plus several members of the media. His family would not attend, as they blamed the rave scene for his death. Though violent fights are commonplace at nightclubs, when it happens at a rave the media is often quick to blame the scene instead of just a rogue attacker acting alone. A reporter commented that none of the people at the vigil actually knew the victim and wondered why we were there. I commented that we were mourning more than just the loss of one person's life

I don't go to big parties much anymore. With larger numbers comes more risk that some of the partiers don't subscribe to PLUR. Although the term is now an often-mocked old raver cliché, it's really what it's all about.

Margaret, Toronto, ON, 29, 4yrs

CYBERSPACE IS A labyrinth of ideas, voices, words, subcultures, counter-cultures and various elements of mainstream culture. The Net has created countless virtual spaces for like-minded individuals to congregate. Madonna fans, porn-seekers, techno music enthusiasts and stamp collectors all have sites on the Net where they can question, flame, compliment and socialize with one another. Every website advertises other individuals, corporations, ideas and cultures, and opens doors and windows to other websites, ad infinitum. Cyberspace is a labyrinth with varying points of entry and exit, and endless parameters that expand and contract each day.

08

CYBERAVE

OFFICIALS CANCEL PARTY AFTER WEBSITE BILLS IT AS A RAVE

Washington County Fair Park officials have canceled a contract for a New Year's Eve party after learning that it was being advertised as a rave party on the Internet.

Milwaukee Journal Sentitnel, Thursday December 28, 2000

Everyone is a star, you are the future. You've got to believe in yourself, your god within, as we jam hand in hand . . . celebrating another loving year of the planet family . . . of global chillage. **—copy for a 1995 New Year's Eve rave in Los Angeles called Circa '96**

At their best, clubs are places where the marginalized can feel at home, where we can experiment with new identities, new ways of being. They are places where cultures collide, where people dance alongside each other and then, when they meet again in the real world outside, understand each other a little better. **SHERYL GARRATT, _Adventures in Wonderland,_ 321**

One subculture with a strong Internet presence is rave culture. Some have even suggested that rave and the Internet go hand in hand. In a 1997 article entitled "Parents urged to be wary," the _Toronto Star_ quotes Ray Pidzamecky, founder of a parent watch program, as saying, "Parents should start looking for signs like their kids leaving for the night with knapsacks, or an interest in the Internet on Thursday or Friday."[8] According to the article these signs may point to a child who is raving. The assumption that ravers always dance with knapsacks and have a close affinity towards the Net is grossly overstated, but not entirely invalid.

Community. Historically, the definition of community has relied heavily on spatial parameters. In this sense, a community may share real estate but little else. As predicted, the Internet has been instrumental in the creation of communities that obliterate borders. This can also be said of rave. American raves often attract attendees from numerous states, as any scan of a parking lot outside an event will attest. These ravers congregate not because of a common location, but because of a common interest—the love of dance, music and rave.

The rave functions like the Internet. Some raves are hidden in the most unlikely places and some remain secret until the last possible minute. Raves carry on through the night hours with no one knowing, sometimes not even cops or parents of participants. In the morning the only evidence that remains is the empty water bottles and the mess. Perhaps the rave is more "virtual" than one may suspect. Raves create communities that are as virtual as those on-line. They build communities that last only for a night. Mass sound and light systems are put up in a matter of hours and disappear after the party is over. After partying with like-minded individuals for up to 10 hours, it is almost impossible to come away without new friends, or at least to have shared smiles, candies or hugs. The Internet also builds mini-communities with its various listservs, newsgroups, chatlines and message boards within the larger confines of cyberspace. In some ways the Net helps homogenize otherwise disparate communities, and has created global communities. Although different cities may have affinities to specific music styles, fashion and rituals, rave culture is most definitely global. Rave experiences shared over the Internet are similar whether one is in South Africa or Toronto. One raver explained the similarities between a desert rave in Los Angeles with his previous Canadian rave experiences: "It's funny—you see all the same faces, all the same types of people no matter where you go. It really could have been any outdoor rave in Ontario. It felt the same, with the exception of the nitrous oxide ballons. People here call ecstasy 'X' instead of 'E'."

The Net functions as a free-form anarchistic community, without rules or confines. It allows underground factions that are not readily accepted in the mainstream to thrive. Raves also have an air of anarchy; they are, or were at one time, pseudo-secret events, taking place during the night, often illegally, away from mainstream culture in warehouses, fields and a plethora of imaginative spaces. Just as governments have tried to control information on the Internet only to have individuals find inventive ways around this control, so too have rave promoters found ways of bypassing the laws by finding more obscure locales and keeping them secret. They have also successfully brought their culture into legal venues to overcome restrictions.

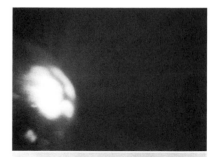

The Internet has allowed ravers to feel that they are truly part of a relevant subculture— rather than just a party scene— [that] transcends borders and distance to communicate. We know that there are hundreds of people like us out there, and that gives credence to our ideals. **LITTLE ZERO, Toronto, ON, age 29, M, 7 yrs.**

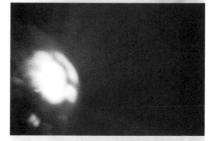

We are extraordinarily social beings yet we impose upon ourselves rules that limit our social interactions. At raves, these social laws are not as readily applicable . . . we are finally allowed to express ourselves freely without fear of retribution. **ANONYMOUS, Winnipeg.**

Raves are a place where any human being can go and feel totally comfortable. They know they will be accepted no matter age, race, religion, sex or any other minor detail that so many get criticized for everyday. To all happy ravers out there, keep the scene safe and real. **NAH-TANHA BORLAND, Seneca, PA, age 19, F, 2 yrs.**

What I was attracted to raves for was that I could be whoever I wanted, there was no bullshit or false pretenses. I think that's what raves really allow people to do, to get past the socialization and let them be whoever they want. **PSYCHEDELIC PHD, Toronto, ON, age 25, M, 6 yrs.**

Virtual rave sites on the Net exist in tandem with rave culture. Do ravers create these virtual spaces to compliment and extend their real rave experiences? Or do these virtual spaces create new audiences and participants in more remote parts of the world? Either way, without actually attending a rave, the on-line subculture helps you step into the culture without ever putting your dancing shoes on. The Net allows ravers to connect with one another, hear samples of techno music and even provides recipes for MDMA. By nature a rave is a gathering of real people and in this sense the on-line rave community cannot simulate the experience. It functions instead as a means of spreading rave discourse to like-minded individuals in remote places. Some raves are broadcast on the Web, while others have satellite link-ups to other events. In March 1996, Dose held its first linked event with a satellite feed in Toronto, Denver, Vancouver and Los Angeles. It was appropriately named "Two nations four cities one groove." This event spanned three time zones and was broadcast over the Internet, allowing four cities and those on the Web to party together virtually.

Freedom of Expression. Sometimes you will see the most unlikely characters at a rave. On occasion I've seen what appears to be a raving grandpa or grandma. I've been to outdoor events where people have brought their children. At one rave I saw a man who looked disheveled. He was wearing track pants tucked into his socks, circling around people and clapping his hands off-beat.

On the Internet you can be yourself without fear of retribution. You can also hide behind a facade such as a new name, stolen gender or false age. This can also be said of a rave, which typically serves as a place in which to be yourself without the often pretentious aura and restrictions of a nightclub. The darkness at raves, the sometimes outlandish costumes and childlike accessories, all help to disguise gender and age. Unlike bars and clubs, raves are places where dancing alone is socially acceptable, talking to strangers is inevitable and women are not usually the object of the male gaze. The Internet and rave are public spheres where you can be yourself or somebody else—the choice is yours.

> Computer games don't affect kids. I mean, if Pacman affected us as kids, we'd all run around in a darkened room munching pills and listening to repetitive music.
> **from group email thread, source unknown.**

Techno-logy. Generation X grew up with video games and as the first generation to use computers in the classroom. The bleeps of Pac Man and Frogger have been subconsciously etched into our psyches. We watched music videos take over our TVs. We idolized and endured all the electronica the eighties had to offer, moments that were simultaneously groundbreaking and plain awful. Rave music was a logical progression in the computerized world we had come to know.

Rave's relationship with technology spreads much further than the Internet. With its inherent relation to digitization and computers, electronica is not only the anthem of rave, but is often equated with a wider cyber aesthetic. Techno, house and their countless offspring are the music styles that bind the rave community. Their faceless, voiceless, ubiquitous presence within rave culture has united dancers worldwide. In some respects this music epitomizes the new information society we live in. It is fast paced, often solitary yet mysteriously global and continually evolving. The beats are repetitive, consistent, voiceless and often alienating. Yet ironically, the worldwide rave community has been built around electronica and is one of the first music subcultures to be connected globally through the Web.

The Internet and techno music are closely linked, mainly in spirit. They are both electronic and both global. They both symbolize the new global electronic connectivity. They both link all the people of the world in an uncensored, no-rules manner. Like the Internet, it is all about individual, yet faceless expression. **ZIMA, Los Angeles, CA, age 30, M, 6 yrs.**

Q. What has been the most important piece of technology in your music making career?

A. My computer, simply because I compose a lot of music tracks and have a tendency to have a lot of ideas simultaneously. The computer serves as an extension of my own memory as I would never remember all of the ideas that come. **LARRY HEARD**

Like the Internet that has democratized the dissemination of information, techno and house producers have helped initiate democratization in music making. Techno has been the catalyst for a change in the conventional meaning of instruments, musicians, musical aesthetics, how music is delivered and who makes it. Music is no longer limited to the historical confines of a five-piece band and a recording studio. An individual with some sequencers, mixers and a computer could be a musician. Decreasing prices in music making equipment such as mixers and sequencers have opened the doors for producers. Electronica has helped obliterate the conventional parameters of music making and distribution. Juan Atkins is one of many who exemplifies this. He started making techno in a makeshift basement studio in West Detroit in his late teens.

> Knowing that there are people all around the world raving is important to the spirit of a rave. It's about dancing for yourself, all together. It is about knowing that people all around the world are grooving to the same music you are.
>
> **Zima, Los Angeles, CA, age 30, M, 6 yrs**

You no longer need an agent, an expensive studio and a face or image that sells. Tracks can now be made by anyone with a computer and simple sequencing programs such as Reason. New technologies have helped give rise to the idea of virtual musicians. These are groups of musicians around the globe who communicate through email and the Internet. The rise of MP3 technology allows musicians to distribute their music without even making a tape or CD. Electronic music can be made, stored, shared and advertised via email, listservs and newsgroups, all on a personal computer.

Perhaps it is electronic music's lack of lyricism or voice orientation that allows it to flow so easily over borders. Unlike other music, electronica is not limited by language. As one raver puts it, "It is tribal in nature. It pulls you in, no matter who you are. As lyrics are for the most part simply textual, part of the aural landscape, the music reads the same no matter where you are, what your background is." Facelessness is also a contributing factor in electronica's success in transcending borders. Producers and DJs are known more by their signature sound than their face. Unlike pop music that heavily relies on videos, techno seldom has accompanying music videos. The few techno videos that are produced rely on computer-generated images, animation and graphics more than faces and star power.

Hardcore and jungle weren't getting airplay on commercial radio while they were breaking in Britain. Instead it was pirate radio that was instrumental in disseminating these new forms of music. In 1993 in London and the surrounding South East of England, there were at least 40 pirate stations, some of which had weekend audiences exceeding 30,000 listeners. Pirate radio, like the Internet, was free of licensing and operating laws. Anyone could set up a pirate radio station and play whatever they wanted to. Pirate radio was also instrumental in advertising rave in England when it was still an illegal, outlawed culture. Cell phones and more advanced messaging systems helped keep events secret and free from police busts.

Web sites. As part of their inherent ideology, raves promote themselves as egalitarian. The irony of this is that raves have historically been reserved for those in the know. A few years ago, unless you knew where to get rave flyers from techno record shops or rave clothing stores, the likelihood of finding a party would have been slim. The Internet altered this by making it easier to find links to the culture, people and party locations. Rave culture is apparent on the Internet in a variety of venues such

newsgroup postings to alt.drugs.ecstacy

>I had my first roll last Friday night . . . and even though I have done a lot of research on the Net I am not sure what the effects SHOULD be. I had the euphoric feeling but I also had some VERY mild hallucinations . . . I have read conflicting reports on whether it is possible to hallucinate on just MDMA. Can anyone give me some insight? **ANONYMOUS**

>>There are many different types of X. One is MDMA, another is MDA. MDA is often passed off as X [and] has very similar effects as MDMA, except you don't feel quite as "loved up," and you get mild hallucinations. All of the pikachu pills I have found have been MDA; personally I prefer it to MDMA. This is probably what was in the pill you took. Just my opinion. **ANONYMOUS**

>>>I don't know about that . . . I took two kaleidoscopes (mid Alabama), and they knocked my ass on the floor. I'd much rather lose a little bit of the "loved up" for good hallucinations any day of the week. But that's just me I guess. **ANONYMOUS**

CYBERAVE

as newsgroups, listservs, on-line magazines and Web sites. These venues act as a means of disseminating chat about the culture, advertising upcoming events, meeting ravers throughout the world and distributing rave music. One rave regular from Victoria, British Columbia, explained how he acts as a rave tourguide to foreign ravers traveling to B.C. They meet over the Net before traveling and then meet in person before attending the rave. He then helps to break the ice by introducing them to the Victoria scene and people.

Although there are a number of rave- and techno-related newsgroups on the Internet, *alt.rave* has the largest number of subscribers, reaching over 10,000 people per week. It acts as a gathering place and forum for people on the search for raves when traveling and people looking to discuss upcoming or past events or new music releases. Some

>I know this is probably an overdone post (or perhaps not) so please forgive me, but I'm looking for a site somewhere to teach me to glowstick/liquid dance. Are there any good sites that describe it well or videos anywhere that I can learn from? Anything at all? **ANONYMOUS**

>>Nope. Tee Hee. Actually mate, as I do this stuff a bit, one of the fundamental things with my thing is to not try too hard and just flow :) But keep your hands like, um following each other and like make shapes and keep your hands moving the same distance away from each other but doing all the above. Hard to explain. Maybe watch a video and see if you can spot a few dancing peepz you like. But no, there isn't like classes or stuff like that ;) Best I can do M8. **DJ S2C**

Raving exploded just as the Internet was finally starting to take off, so meeting at a party and keeping in touch with people was a simple thing to do. One could also meet over email and then meet up at a party. List-servs subdivide the on-line rave culture because they are generally place- or music-specific: they allow members to receive information on news, events, reviews and music.

UNDER London Bridge

New Years 1998.

Blacksheep did it again: every time I go to one of their events, I reckon it to be the very best rave I've ever been to. New Years Eve 1998 was no exception. Arrived early and found parking spaces close by, in a weird tunnel . . . opposite a grilled-off entrance to the main dance floor . . . as we later ascertained by peering behind a drape from inside. The whole area is a sort [of] underground complex of carparks and warehousing. We can hear the sound of the party while parking: maybe it's just the soundcheck, but it rocks already! Now we just need to wait for it to open. (:>) A few people slope off to find a pub, but our vanload prefer to lurk . . . in our tunnel, which has good photographic opportunities. We greet lots of other lost soul strangers that are arriving; a few of them are looking for another party that is also happening close by. The significance of this becomes apparent much later. Hehe.

Ah well, looks like [it's] starting now: people are queuing at another grille a hundred paces away. We scoot over, and by our good fortune arrive at the same time as the pub-escapees. As they still have all the tickets which they arranged, this is what I call good timing. (:>) It's going to be a good party. Greet the gate guards cheerily, especially as I recognize most of them from previous Blacksheep events. We get checked over anyway, but lightly and politely, while sharing a bit of banter about the sort of contraband people might want to bring in.

Inside now, and it is all beautiful Victorian brickwork, arched passages, with walls decked over with swathes of bright fabric. There is a lot of fabric everywhere too: not just around the dance floor areas. Even the row of portaloos, tucked out of the main thoroughfare among more arches, is a little partyzone of its own. Someone's been quite enthusiastic and lavish with the decor budget then! Through to the main dance floor, a huge area with a high ceiling arching away into the distance, PA stacks at the far end. Eh, but you can feel the sheer dB-power of it! Playing solid techno, but I'm not really ready for that yet. Only a few people in here this early, and we are a little cold. Duck through to the right, and a large chill-out zone: nicely heated though so we congregate around a heater for a while, chatting with others [who have] arrived before us, and the steadily growing influx of new arrivals. Soaking up the warmth and the atmosphere. It's becoming a good party already. The tea-stand is here and the bar for bottled water. Nice strong coffee. I go for a little wander on my own, get my bearings before the place gets busy. Find the second dance floor, much smaller and more intimate, and with a heater in there. Playing some wondrous trancey-stuff, and I get distracted by this and just have to have a little dance to get going. After a while I remember the friends I arrived with, and go and fetch the few that I can still find in the chill-out. They also think this dance floor [is] to their taste.

The main room is starting to get warm and lively, so I have to go and help that along too. (:>) It gets so warm and lively that I need to go and sit down after a bit of jumping about; have another coffee, get more water before any more dancing. Watching the internal security guards cruising about, discreet but alert for any sign of trouble. Say hello to them. I always chat with the security people at raves. Part of my wicked campaign to get at least a smile and a nod from every soul at a party. (:>) Ah, but these ones are easier than most, which I take as a good sign: they know the difference between punters and trouble. Of course, there won't be any trouble here anyway. This is a very fine party, people are polite and smiling fluffy-like. See someone bump another's drink, and it is just an apologetic gesture, with a grin in return. But one guard did tell me they have to be alert to gatecrashers and unwelcome unfluffy ones who might want to spoil things: they'd caught a few trying to force a back firedoor already. But the gentle nightdancers need not know nor care about any of this. (:>)

Most of the next few hours become a little blurry in retrospect, but there were some damned-fine choons going down on both dance floors; to the point that whichever floor I'm on, I have to keep checking the other. Difficult to choose between them, as both are so good in their own different ways that I don't want to miss anything. Heh. A lot of serious bouncing up and down with a friendly bunch of strangers: but not really strangers, for in the dance we are all there. Occasionally I see people I vaguely know, or think I know, so a cheery wave to them, and a hug if I'm lucky too. (:>) It's definitely a great party!

Midnight comes and goes, with a great deal of cheering on the main floor. The house is really rocking, and pretty packed everywhere, but still with enough room to dance, or make one's way around the place without undue difficulty. More coffee, more water, go sit in the chill-out area and chatter some more. I've been using a little Pentax point-and-shoot camera to grab a few, simple pictures most of the evening, but now I reckon time to get the SLR and tripod from outside. It has got cold condensation on the glassware now, so I leave it to warm up as it will, and go and dance some more.

Well, it's about 5 a.m. by now: the dance floors are thinning out a little, and I'm dancing a bit slower too. But that means a bit more space, and gentler dancing around with those remaining: these are the dance-dedicated, and more inclined to play "see if you can follow my moves" sort [of] games, which I rather enjoy. Heh, I reckon I can keep up with most. (:>) Good fun, and mutual congratulations if we meet in the chill-out while queuing for water or coffee. A few more fluffy hugs. This is a great bunch. Quite a few have never been to a Blacksheep-do before: came because a friend insisted or whatever. But all I spoke to said they were having an absolutely brilliant time of it. I'd agree with that sentiment.

Then I realize there is a sort [of] extra space leading out near the back of the chill-out area. Hey! What's this! Sure it wasn't there before! Hraark? Someone tells me it is the way to "the other party next door." Wow. Apparently, by mutual agreement of both sets of organizers, a dividing grille has been opened. People from both parties are wandering in both directions, looking completely bemused. What a wondrous idea! I have to see this: follow through a cavernous car-parking area, another doorway . . . and suddenly I'm in that other party next door—the Pie & Mash "Reclaim the Beats"-do. CAW! It's kicking too! I don't know where I summon the energy from, but I have to indulge in some very hectic jumping up and down again. An odd feeling of deja-vu: I sort [of] recognize some of the DJ's set, and there are more familiar faces than I can account for from the party I've just come from. Ummh. Then I realize: this is mostly from the Trancentral-do I went to a month or two ago! CAW! Brilliant! Wave and grin at a few faces, halfremembered from that other bunch. Okay, that's two damned-fine parties I'm at tonight then! Greetings to anyone from the Slimelight venue I might vaguely know then. And thanks to the kind people that said they recognized me with a nod or hug. And apologies to DJ Orange, I think we just missed you. Eh, another time then.

Ah well, back to the place I was before. Being an unashamed caffeine junkie, it was great to find the tea-stall open all night. I think I grabbed the last coffee of the party, while the building was being cleared at about 9 a.m. Bleary-eyed but cheerful. It was a great party. Eh, I'm up for the next NYE, please put me down for tickets!

Pwl, Hampshire, England, age 44, M, 5yrs.

UNLIKE THE EXTROVERTED politics of hippie culture that fought against the Vietnam War or the angst-ridden, anarchistic nature of punk, rave culture's politics are for the most part internal, personal and invisible to outsiders.

Rave has been accused by many of being apolitical, meaningless and hedonistic. No one can argue against the celebratory intent behind raving, but perhaps it is rave's sheer hedonism that is meaningful and political. Western society demeans the importance of celebration unless it is wrapped in the commercialized package of a greeting card holiday.

09

THE POLITICS OF PARTYING

In the movie *Footloose* Kevin Bacon tells us that dancing is often an outlawed activity; a Fundamentalist minister has banned dancing in a small American town.

The rave scene seems to be more of a deflection. Instead of saying, "Fuck your world!" it's saying, "This is our world." Instead of an explosion, it's a shield. I like that. I like the feeling that, as a group, we're respecting the worldview of other subcultures and culture at large. We're not saying that they're all wrong, just that we've found what's right for us and we're not going to let it go.
STAN, Lafayette, IN, age 23, M, 5 yrs

In 1997 New York Mayor Rudi Giuliani started closing down bars that were allowing patrons to dance without a cabaret license. Many bars at this time were forced to put up "No Dancing" signs.

Our culture dictates that individuals must work, pay their way and function in a manner recognized by the goverment and the economy. Normal people sleep between the hours of midnight and 8 am, they work between nine and five, enjoy the occasional alcoholic drink after a hard day's work, they take prescription drugs to make them well, hornier, help their hair grow, lessen depression, help them sleep easier and calm their unruly children. Ravers, on the other hand, rebel against what is defined as good and normal. They dance while others sleep, celebrate simply for the sake of celebration and take drugs for enlightenment and entertainment. Herein lies the politics of rave. It marks a refusal to conform to socialized gender roles or established codes of interaction and personal conduct.

Reactionary Politics vs. the Politics of Partying.

Many people have suggested that rave culture is a fusion of 1960s idealism and 1990s technocracy. Many within the scene like to adopt this belief as well. Is it incorrect to define ravers as flower power wannabes? Most of these comparisons are based purely on each culture's aesthetics rather than its ideologies or politics. The smiles that ecstasy created on the faces of its users made the late 1980s acid house smiley face mascot exceedingly appropriate, regardless of its previous adoption in the hippie era. Perhaps it was the hippie remnants in Ibiza where acid house was born that encouraged its originators to adopt an idealized sixties simulation.

There was a scene in England that did manage to bridge hippie elements with rave culture. A number of free outdoor festivals in the early 1990s brought together ravers and crusties who were essentially nomadic hippies that roamed England's countryside. Spiral Tribe was part of a new breed of renegade promoters who had been doing free parties with a more anarchistic, hippie edge. In May of 1992 Spiral Tribe was involved with the Avon Free Festival at Castlemorton Common in the Worcestershire countryside. It was one of the biggest illegal raves in history with an estimated attendance between 20,000 and 40,000. This huge festival had no sanitation and many urban ravers weren't prepared with the necessary shovels as were the crusties. In total, 13 members of Spiral Tribe were arrested, sound systems were impounded and the government soon passed a new bill, the Criminal Justice and Public Order Act (1994), in an effort to demolish this massive free party scene.

Although hippie culture was steeped in protests against reactionary politics that led to events such as the Vietnam War, the principal ideology surrounding hippie culture was a sense of spirituality related to self-awareness. The quest within hippie philosophy was for transcendence, and what better vehicle to attain this than LSD. LSD and marijuana were viewed by many hippies as the sacraments of their religion. Hippies opposed the plasticity of American society by living simply in communes and ghettos. Hippie ideology was not only a statement, it was a way of living. Hippies were stridently opposed to technology, reacting against its manifestations such as nuclear power, war and corporate America.

Contrarily, rave culture is built out of new technologies. Rave culture utilizes all things technological from computerized phone links to update party locations, the Internet for dissemination of information, computerized lighting and projections at events, to flyers created by computer graphics. Techno music and its counterparts are created solely by computers,

Let's see—in the sixties there were international demonstrations against the international power and wars of capitalism . . . for the rights of workers across Europe . . . In the late eighties and early nineties a few disparate groups of British youth come together to demonstrate for the right to carry on getting out of their heads and dancing to weird music at weekends. Are these really so glibly comparable? **GEORGE McKAY,** *Evereeebodeee's Freee; Or, Causing a Public New Sense?,* **118**

Q. What was it about the scene that sucked you in?

A. The music, the drugs (at least the milder/more intellectual ones), the community, the sense of belonging to something hidden and distant. The whole darn trippy and wacky nature of it all . . . since the meaning [of rave] has changed for other people (such as fellow partiers, city officials and space owners) using the word would make communication difficult. Therefore, I try to eliminate it from my vocabulary. **IAN GUTHRIE, promoter.**

drum machines, electronic keyboards and samplers. The use of white label or independent singles by DJs and relatively cheap computers and samplers put music making in the hands of individuals and posed a huge challenge to major record labels. The only non-democratic thing about electronica and DJ culture has been the lack of female DJs and producers. Whether the electronic music world has been less desirable to women than men or whether this male-dominated business has been hard to break into for women is difficult to confirm.

Rave was built on notions of community and unity and this is apparent at most events. Rave ideology is provided on flyers and album liner notes where blatant references to egalitarianism are made, suggesting that raves are events without door policies where people from all walks of life unite and become one under a hypnotic beat. The names of promoters such as Utopia, Better Days and United Dance are obvious examples. As uniting as these slogans seem, in her book *Club Cultures*, Sarah Thornton points to the irony that "only those 'in the know' could hear of and locate the party—moreover black and gay youth tended to see rave culture as a straight, white affair."[9] The hypocrisy of rave is that although techno music has Black roots, rave is predominantly a white middle class phenomenon, much like hippie culture.

A magazine advertisement for a rave called Zencentricity held in London in 1996 hints at efforts to ensure a psychedelic experience: "much has been done to recreate the meaningful relationship between both the musical and visual elements of the bona fide psychedelic experience." As the advertisement suggests, the rave is the epitomy of a psychedelic spectacle. But in many ways rave only looks like a hippie gathering. The sixties scene was built by university students, artists and writers steeped in psychology and Eastern mysticism who championed the civil rights movement. Contrary to the mind-expanding drug taking in the 1960s, rave culture and its associated drug, ecstasy, are like taking a holiday for the night and disengaging from all that is political.

Although there were hippie rituals such as the music festival, live concerts and nightly rap sessions, the hippie arena was life itself. Most hippies came from middle and upper class families, but chose to live in self-imposed poverty in slums, ghettos and communes. While hippie culture embraced public lifestyle displays, rave embraces the opposite: it has until recently attempted to remain hidden. Along with rave culture's nocturnal existence, details of events have always been secretive and limited to word of mouth and flyers in order to avoid police raids. Whereas hippie-ness is a lifestyle, raving is primarily a weekend event. This allows participants to be anything they want during the week and be a raver on the weekends. Roger Beard, a DJ in London, qualifies this observation in Mathew Collin's book *Altered State*: "The problem with the scene was that it only really existed for the time that you were in a club, whereas the sixties was a much more all-encompassing thing."[10] Although it is true that some ravers live for the weekends and attend raves almost religiously, one can only be called a raver when actually attending raves. Hippies, on the other hand, were still hippies whether they went to a Grateful Dead show or to Woodstock or not; it was inherent in their way of life, not in the events they attended. Hippie began as a lifestyle and as it experienced mainstream incorporation, it arguably became a weekend event for the second wave that only attended festivals and hung out in hippie locales. Rave, on the other hand, started as a weekend event and has for some become an all-consuming lifestyle.

Unlike hippie culture that embraced a grassroots way of living stressing environmental concerns, some rave communities are arguably symptomatic of a 1990s anti-environmental mentality. Any snapshot of a rave space after an event is evidence of the culture's wasteful nature. The floor is strewn with empty water bottles and flyers, soon to be tossed in the garbage rather than the recycling bin. Even at outdoor parties, it is typically the promoters who are left to deal with the carnage that patrons leave behind because they were too high to care where they littered.

Q. What kinds of changes have you noticed in your scene?

A. It used to be a bit of a freak show, and it was the subversive, artistic crowd that would attend raves. We were all in on a big secret. Now it's so popular that Joe Average, his girlfriend Plain Jane and their six billion clones are attending. Our magical, special scene has been diluted and the big parties feel more like rock concerts. **SYNAPSE, Toronto, ON, age 27, M, 8 yrs.**

I go raving every weekend, where there is [a] mass of drugs and other illegal activity. I won't stop . . . no one else will . . . why would we worry about laws, they can't stop us . . . we are too many!!!
MON, Sydney, Australia, age 17, F, 2 yrs.

Are today's ravers naive in that they have no cause, or have they unearthed the tribal secret in the power of communal dance? Is it accurate to compare the English ravers who held political demonstrations with the slogan "Freedom for the right to party" to demonstrations in the 1960s by student protesters in the U.S., against the Vietnam war? The rave phenomenon points to a global youth culture that lacks uniform ideologies. Perhaps the comparison of hippie politics and rave politics is glib, because it is impossible to quantify the politics of rave's collective yet subconscious social activism. For ravers, dance is political simply because it rejects society's rules and the status quo. Even the style surrounding the scene started to reflect this freedom from socialized barricades. Rave not only welcomes but encourages outlandish outfits as well as behaviors. The initial rave style of comfort, mobility and anti-fashion marked a resistance to the highly codified wardrobes of the club world. It was simply too difficult to dance for six hours in high heels and a tight skirt. It was also unnecessary, since the night's goal was simply to dance, not to pick up. The infantile uniforms that later developed such as lollipops, teddy bears, baggy clothes, hooded sweatshirts, baseball caps and visors have all became synonymous with rave. This style has helped to disintegrate the distinguishing marks of male and female, giving way to an androgynous aura.

Rave fashion and culture have not only given rise to androgyny, they have helped break down assumptions of gender interaction. Most rave bathrooms will attest to this. When raves moved into venues that actually had bathrooms as opposed to porta-potties, males and females mingled freely together. Women at raves just didn't seem to care that men were peeing in the stall beside them. In a public bathroom in a mall this would be an outrage—at a rave it is the norm. A bathroom at a rave is actually one of the best places to chat, because it's actually light enough to see and quiet enough to hear. On E it's practically impossible to be standing beside someone for more than a couple minutes without at least saying hi, and this becomes apparent in the bathroom line. No one thinks it odd that you're being overly friendly, in fact it would be odd if you weren't friendly. Imagine being on a subway car squished together with strangers and everyone suddenly starting to chat and mingle. How strange would that be? Now you've imagined a rave bathroom. Why shouldn't it be that way? Society has taught us to be wary of strangers, especially if we're from a big city.

Rave Laws. Rave began in England and in large U.S. cities like New York by breaking laws. Many warehouses for events were claimed through breaking in or trespassing. In the early 1990s in Los Angeles, Daven-the-mad-hatter-Michaels held a rave called LSD (Love, Sex, Dance). He outsmarted police and other promoters by securing a building and claiming it was for an afterparty for Madonna's concert that night. Jay Pender of World Dance in England once outwitted police with the argument that his party was for members only, and that to be a member people payed £15 and provided their addresses.

Rave has slowly become less of a renegade culture. It has been absorbed by the institutions it fought against; DJs have become stars and small white labels have been bought and distributed by large corporations. The more codified rave became in its fashion and ritualized behavior, the more media attention it garnered. Paradoxically, the less political and subversive rave is internally because of its incorporation into the mainstream, the more political rave has become externally through media exposure. This increased attention and awareness fueled the need for governments and municipalities to restrict and control rave. In the 1960s, hippies were political because they protested against the government. In the 1990s rave has become political because the government has reacted against it.

Police units and laws to support their actions have been set up in England and Canada to deal specifically with what some politicians see

I think there was a society-wide increase in ecstasy use. By no means limited to ravers or even nightclubs. Still, this increase will get the attention of the DEA. But, I do think it goes a little deeper than that too. I think raves are as offensive to certain policy makers and members of the DEA as gay bathhouses were in the 1980s. Furthermore, they see the club drug epidemic as an epidemic like AIDS—one spread through promiscuity and drug use. These members are a minority of these organizations, but many are policy makers for those groups. I imagine that when no cameras are around, they are discussing the "War on Clubs" with phrases like "by any means necesary."
WILL PATTERSON EM:DEF (Electronic Music Defense and Education Fund).

Any gathering of four or more people can now be legally broken up by the police if it's thought to be causing a disturbance, plotting to kill the Queen (or something). Whatever happened to our right to free association?
FLUFFY, London, England, age 22, F, 2 yrs.

The tourist board markets our clubs as a vibrant attraction even as laws are being passed to close them. **SHERYL GARRATT,** *Adventures in Wonderland,* **319**

as the pending rave problem. The first law associated with raves was enacted in 1990 in England. The Bright Act allowed for promoters to receive six months in jail and a fine up to £20,000 for throwing an unlicensed party. The Act was responsible for the biggest mass arrest in English history at that time. The police hauled away 836 clubbers in Leeds at an unlicensed warehouse party. A total of 17 were charged and the DJ was sent to jail for three months. Four years later the government created a more extreme law that was not only directed at raves but at a particular type of music. The Criminal Justice and Public Order Act was passed in 1994 and defined raves as outdoor gatherings of over a hundred people with music that was characterized by a succession of repetitive beats. This Act gave the police power to order away promoters if they believed they were going to hold a rave, ravers who were waiting for an event as well as ravers who were at an event. Anyone not obeying these rules was liable to a fine of £2,500, or three months in jail. The Act also gave police the power to turn away anyone on their way to a rave within a radius of five miles; the fine for non-compliance was £1,000.

In Canada in early 2000, Ontario's consumer and commercial relations minister headed a summit in an effort to strategize an end to raves. Another summit was held on March 14 of that year at Toronto's police headquarters in an effort to create a rave task force. The city's mayor initiated Operation Strike Force and proposed bylaws were pending that would award police and fire marshals greater control in stopping rave events. A few weeks later the city council passed a temporary ban on raves on city-owned property, arguably the safest places to hold them. These two provincial summits in Toronto set the stage for proposed bylaws which would inevitably help push sections of the rave scene back underground. Only promoters large enough to afford the appropriate permits and fees for spaces that maintain fire code regulations would survive.

In an effort to protect the Toronto rave scene the Toronto Dance Safety Committee (TDSC) was set up by a group of city councillors, staff from various city departments, promoters, security providers, ravers and lawyers. After a number of rave-related deaths in the city, there was a coroner's inquest into the death that generated the most media attention. The jury recommendations included ensuring unlimited drinking water at events, restricting raves to those over 16 and advertising guidelines for raves that would forbid explicit depiction of drugs or their use. The jury had more than likely been shown rave flyers such as MDMA (Most Deranged Musical Atmosphere) and On-One Productions which had photos of ecstasy pills all over them. Rave locations now had to be printed on tickets and events had to be drug-free including a 50-cent surtax added to the price of admission to be awarded to community-based harm reduction projects.

POLICE THOUGHT DRUGS WOULD BE SOLD AT RAVE

When police raided a Halifax rave last month, they expected to find 200 vials of the date rape drug GHB hidden in the dance-hall ceiling . . . Many of those searched—some of whom were in their early teens—have publicly said they felt "violated" by police because they were forced to strip.

Halifax Daily News, Friday, February 11, 2000.

RAVE KIDS AREN'T CRIMINALS

Pat Duncan, a lawyer specializing in police matters, compared the search to an armed suspect being searched in a crack house . . . Kids dance. Some get high. Parents, policing your kids is your responsibility. Raise your kids better, so the police don't feel obligated to strip them of their dignity.

Halifax Daily News, Saturday February 12, 2000.

Q. Have there been any bylaws set up in the city to curb events?

A. Aparently there have been now— "Swirl" was cancelled because the city decided to refuse to give out any more permits for this type of thing. I don't know what the laws are like but I have been to parties that have been broken up by the cops before. **MESSYCAT, Montréal, QC, age 24, F, 2 yrs.**

THE POLITICS OF PARTYING

Q. Do you know of any laws in your city/country that are directly related to raves and trying to stop or control them?

A. Council and police approval, entertainment licenses [and] permits [are]
needed; raves need to be legal now
mostly because people are sick and
tired of shut downs. **DJ QT, Sydney, Australia, age 24, F, 8 yrs.**

With the recommendations from the coroner's jury, the TDSC created the Recommendations Regarding the Regulation and Licensing of
Raves, a document which outlines recommendations and requirements for
safe raves such as proper ventilation, unlimited drinking water and ade-
quate security and police presence. Meanwhile, the Ontario Rave Act 2000
is a provincial law to regulate raves by enforcing promoters' obligation to
obtain a permit for an event. The Act requires promoters to ensure,
through force if necessary, that anyone with an unlawful purpose leaves the
event. It gives police the power to enter a rave that doesn't have a permit
and vacate the premises if they believe a violation of the Act or any by-law
is taking place. Corporations can be fined up to $50,000 for violating the
Act, and attendees can be fined $5,000 if they refuse to vacate the premises.

Vancouver also has a set of regulations for what it calls "Alcohol-Free
Late Night Dance Events." These regulations state that all promoters obtain
a permit that will cost up to $200 for any event with a capacity of less than
350 people, and up to $800 for any event with a capacity of 2,000 or more
people. A permit must be obtained six weeks in advance. The city may limit
the number of events and ensure that events are held where there is ade-
quate parking and access to public transit. Regulations such as these help
quash any underground spirit that may have been left in rave culture; they
also ensure that governments are getting a piece of the rave profit pie.

Despite all the efforts made by various governments to stamp out
raves, there is little evidence of ravers forming a united front to defend their
culture. Ravers have been accused of demonstrating a lack of social collectivity. In England in 1989 as the Bright Act was being prepared, Sunrise
promoter Tony Colsten Hayter along with other major promoters, formed
the Freedom to Party campaign. Rallies were not well attended and faded
after only a few attempts. As unifying as the rave scene may appear, it
encompasses a variety of disparate groups that often don't communicate
outside of a rave venue. Many rave communities are split between musical tastes, age and promoter loyalty. While Ontario's rave scene was under

close scrutiny by the government, the Toronto Dance Safety Committee pleaded for support to hire a lawyer to defend rave culture's interests at a coroner's inquest into a rave-related death. Sadly, the bulk of funds came not from rave participants but from the city's largest promoter, who obviously had the most at stake. Furthermore, only a small number of ravers were actually present at the inquest. The same week a benefit called Rave Against Rage was held at a small Toronto club and it was almost empty.

Perhaps this raver apathy is changing. On August 1, 2000, Toronto ravers finally seemed to notice that their culture was under fire. A number of rave-related organizations and promoters organized I Dance, a free rave and rally that took place on the grounds of Toronto's City Hall. The rave rally's slogan was "It's about Freedom to Dance." The response was overwhelming with an estimated attendance between 15,000 and 20,000. As techno ricocheted off surrounding downtown buildings, young and old ravers stated their cause by dancing, cheering and carrying placards such as "Raves are fun" and "Raves = Jobs."

The most extreme use of the law against rave culture took place in New Orleans, Louisiana in January of 2001. Attorney Eddie Jordan used a 1986 statute that was intended to persecute crack houses against a rave promoter and the managers of the State Palace Theater where raves were being held. The crack house law was intended to curb the use of inner-city buildings and homes as places to sell and consume crack. Section 856 of the U.S. Penal Code states that it is a felony "to knowingly open or maintain any place for the purpose of manufacturing, distributing, or using any controlled substance or to knowingly and intentionally rent . . . the building, room, or enclosure for the purpose of unlawfully manufacturing, storing, distributing or using a controlled substance." Violators can be sentenced to up to 20 years imprisonment or fined between $500,000 and $2,000,000. With attempts failing at curbing the supposed ecstasy problem, the use of the crack house law was the latest attempt at persecuting rave promoters. The attorney's argument was that many ravers go

Q. What do you feel is the future of your scene?

A. We are going to get shut down and this makes me sad. Here in Pittsburgh they are trying to do everything in their power to shut it down . . . it's not fair. **NICOLE BRINZA, Trafford, PA, age 17, F.**

Q. What kinds of changes have you noticed in your scene?

A. It's gone downhill—the city has been comin' down and breakin' up all the parties here in Vegas. And a lot of the partyers are young and still in high school—not that it's bad—just annoying sometimes. **ORION, Las Vegas, NV, age 20, M, 2 yrs.**

THE POLITICS OF PARTYING

The scene here will rise if the justice system would stay off our ass. I would like to address the issue in New Orleans. Two men are being held on trial for supposedly running a crack house. All they were doing is holding raves in their venue. Now they are facing 25 years to life in prison. This is straight up bullshit. **DJ AKOMMODATE, Wichita, KS, age 19, M, 4 yrs.**

Since I have been raving I have noticed that the drugs in the party have declined a good amount. Also the pacifiers and Vicks have been banned from some of our parties. Also T-shirts that represent anything that could be considered drug-related have been banned. I think the crack house law is going to shut down the major rave scene and it's probably going to go underground as it once was before. It is the future of music, and no matter how hard the government or any type of officials try to stop it, [rave] is going to survive. **MAJIC MYK, North Little Rock, AR, age 20, M, 2 yrs.**

Alicia Downard of Dallas thought it was "typical drug-war absurdity to equate ecstasy with crack. When was the last time you read about a drug-addicted mother who spent her welfare check on ecstasy?" **Letters section, *Time* magazine, April 30, 2001.**

SELL A GLOWSTICK, GO TO PRISON
Witness the humble glowstick . . . popular at Britney Spears concerts, Mardi Gras parades and summer street fairs. But because glowsticks are also commonly found at raves . . . they have become a curious casualty of the government's war on drugs. ***Salon.com*, June 20, 2001.**

to events with the intention of consuming drugs, and since promoters are aware of this fact they are violating the crack house law. Jordan argued that simply calling an event a rave violated the law.

Most shocking about the use of the crack house law was the ability of law enforcement agents to search premises based on the presence of what was considered drug paraphernalia: soothers, glowsticks and water. The fact that promoters were openly selling high-priced bottled water and rave accessories such as glowsticks now became proof in this attorney's eyes that promoters were advocating and encouraging drug use. In the eyes of the law, something as benign as water was now considered drug paraphernalia because of its association as a method of temperature control while on MDMA. Glowsticks that were once used as flashlights for camping were now more about dance and fashion and were assumed automatically to indicate drug use. The fact that glowsticks were now so common that even eight-year-old girls at 'N Sync concerts had them, had no bearing on their association with MDMA. Instead of true crack paraphernalia like blackened spoons and knives and crack pipes, this law stigmatized baby soothers and bottles of water. This was as ludicrous as suggesting that someone wearing a peace symbol was going to smoke pot

The search warrant for the State Palace Theater explained the rationale for considering these rave accessories as paraphernalia in the following way. Pacifiers were used to alleviate the tooth grinding and jaw tightening

caused by MDMA. Glowsticks were used to enhance the heightened sensory perception also caused by MDMA. Water was used to retain body temperature and hydration while on MDMA. The search warrant also suggested that it was common for rave promoters to allow participants to inhale Vicks Vapo Rub and similar inhalants to enhance olfactory sensations while on MDMA. One of the final points cited in the warrant was that it was common for rave promoters to allow patrons to massage and touch one another to heighten the sensation of touch while on MDMA. One of the most beautiful things about raves was their breaking down of socialized limitations on communal touching. The fact that ravers were massaging one another was indeed subversive in the eyes of the law.

Although the case against the State Palace Theater has been withdrawn for the time being, it poses a real threat to the rave community which is in essence being told that if it calls an event a rave it will more than likely be persecuted. The case also suggested to the media and the public that rave antics, rituals and fashion were now political. An *ABC-News.com* article on April 2, 2001 with the headline "Party Wear or Paraphernalia?" outlined the story of a Utah high school that had banned glowsticks, pacifiers, raver beads and dust masks because of their supposed signification of drug use. Just as kids weren't allowed to wear marijuana T-shirts or have bongs at school, pacifiers had now been branded as drug paraphernalia.

I never knew I could feel so accepted! So friendly, I can never have as much fun as I do at a party! So many people that just wanna give you a bracelet and a hug! I remember when security took my binkie and I was sad! So many people were just like, are you OK, hon? It was great to know that you have people around you that care for you even though they don't know you! The security is so much more tight! I mean they take away my binkie, my chapstick and my glitter—god, what's next? **LESLEE CAROTHERS, Bloomington, MN, age 16, F, 0 yrs.**

THE DARK SIDE OF ECSTASY
It is impossible to become physically addicted to the party drug ecstasy. It will kill you first. "It's such a toxic drug, you can't produce dependance," said David V. Gauvin, drug science specialist with the Drug Enforcement Administration… Often the drug is taken at raves, which Gauvin calls "nothing more than a crack house with music." . . . There have been reports of the people scratching themselves until they bleed because they need to be touched so badly . . . *Naperville Sun,* **Friday 20 October, 2000.**

Electronic music is art, and I think it's dangerous when any form of art is singled out because of a drug association the government suspects. Obviously the music won't completely disappear, though it could become less popular if nightclubs start disappearing, but the real danger is that when nightclubs disappear, they don't reappear. Getting permits to open a club is almost impossible today. I think the real danger is that our places of assembly are at risk of being lost forever. **WILL PATTERSON EM:DEF (Electronic Music Defense and Education Fund)**

THE MEDIA ATTENTION that rave culture generated was not unlike previous moral panics of the 20th century. Drug myths within rave discourse have origins previous to the 1990s. Headlines and stories associated with marijuana in the 1930s and LSD in the 1960s, all suggest a similar fear through the use of various symbols of deviance. The thirty-year span between each deviance discourse hints at a cycle of seemingly necessary social control and perhaps, social discontent. The media generally notices spectacular subcultures because they break established societal codes, either by their appearance, activities or more importantly, connection to illicit substances. Currently, one of the most poignant drug fears is ecstasy, which has come to be synonymous in the media with rave culture.

10

DON'T BELIEVE THE HYPE?

1930S—POT: It must be stopped. You and all the school parent groups about the country, you must stand united on this and stamp out this frightful assassin of our youth. **Reefer Madness, 1936**

1990S—ECSTASY: We need to stop the raves, it's not a dance, it's not a safe place for your kids. **ABC news 20/20, January 24, 1997**

Every subculture breeds its own moral panic [and] every moral panic is stereotyped by its own devil drug. *i-D magazine* **as quoted in** *Adventures in Wonderland,* **134**

1930s—Pot: New drug menace . . . destroying the youth of America. *Reefer Madness,* **1936**

1960s—LSD: New menace to youth. *UNESCO Courier,* **May 1968**

1930s—Pot: Youth gone loco. *The Christian Century,* **June 29, 1938**

1990s—Ecstasy: Spaced Out! 11,000 youngsters go drug crazy at Britain's biggest-ever Acid party. *The Sun* **(London) June 26, 1989**

1960s—LSD: The dangers of LSD. *Time* **magazine, April 22, 1966**

1990s—Ecstasy: Danger Parties. *Toronto Star,* **March 22, 1997**

In the 1930s Reefer Madness was a campaign to warn parents of the evils of marijuana: "It must be stopped. You and all the school parent groups about the country, you must stand united on this and stamp out this frightful assassin of our youth."[11] Articles in the 1960s like "My Son Is on LSD" had a similar message with a different drug. The idea was to reassure parents: "It's not the lack of a perfect home that drives children to run away to the hippie scene."[12] With rave culture in the 1990s the rhetorical structures from earlier decades remained intact with a similar message to parents in the U.S.: "We need to stop the raves . . . it's not a safe place for your kids."[13] Similarly the front page of Canada's major news magazine *Maclean's* warned on April 24, 2000 that "the drugs can kill—what parents need to know."[14] The formulaic fears of drug-mongering pied pipers have remained intact for decades: threat to family life, drugs for hedonistic purposes and dangers for youth.

With the influx of acid house clubs and the inevitable increase in young people dancing all night long and indulging in controlled substances, the media began to take notice. Being under surveillance by police and the media often helps in the creation of a subculture. Acid house and raves enraged the authorities in England from the onset. The more raves tried to hide from the downtown cores, seeking refuge in unused warehouses and obscure countryside locales, the more watchful the police and media became. Public outrage and media exposés helped entice new participants as each news article helped advertise the scene.

The majority of media discourse around subcultural drug consumption plays off one of these themes: that drugs are killing our youth, infecting our veins and dirtying our streets. The media plays an important role in helping to both uphold and create society's moral parameters. By recycling the attitudes and stories that situate drugs as evil and by creating moral panic, the media helps maintain a degree of social order. News stories generally frame drugs and the places they are found in as the villain while the teenagers that encounter them are victims. For the most part it is the rave that is framed as drug pusher; the teenage drug taker is not necessarily seen as delinquent but as an innocent, beguiled victim.

Society positions deviants against the status quo as a constant reminder of what not to be. By bringing hippies, ravers, drug takers and delinquents into the public's eye and hitting the panic button, the media inadvertently acts as a moral referee. The existence of deviants within society provides a vehicle for public fear. It allows those in power to take control via policing, laws and rules in an effort to free society of these deviants.

Q. How do you feel about the media's reaction to raves?

A. They will always take a perspective that appeals to the family community, so the drugs and youth aspect of the culture will always be a target. The only opinion I really have about it at this point is that they have their story and we have ours. **LEET, Toronto, ON, age 25, M, 8 yrs.**

In turning youth into news, the tabloids both frame subcultures as major events and also disseminate them. **SARAH THORNTON,** *Club Cultures,* **132**

DON'T BELIEVE THE HYPE?

The deviant is a bogeyman who helps control a populace by inadvertently outlining the essential basis for right and wrong and what is normal.

The discourses surrounding rave in the U.S., Canada and the U.K. are virtually interchangeable. In each territory, the rave space was immediately denounced as being the arena for evil drug consumption of the new and dangerous drug: ecstasy.

The media discourse surrounding rave subculture is impregnated with myth. Rave symbols such as the baby's soother are ripped from their regular context and re-signified. This re-signification by the media would have you believe that a teen who wears big beads or a baby soother in the 1990s likes to rave all night and ingest controlled substances. Instead of myth being read as a system of values, it is inaccurately read as a system of facts. What the media fails to recognize is that rave and its symbols have long passed the time when an easy correlation could be made between these symbols and drug use. Today, rave symbols are commodified and fashionable. They are available at your local mall. Kids who have never considered taking ecstasy are wearing rave-inspired clothes. Is this enough reason to brand them as drug takers?

A news story or magazine article doesn't stand by itself; it is one node in a network growing out of an accumulation of prior opinions and journalism. Anything written or broadcast about rave culture and drugs is necessarily implicated by default with other drug cultures from the past and every negative association of that past drug culture. There are meanings and significations lying beneath the surface of even the most fair-minded and journalistic of statements. For example, if an article outlines the case of a child who dies while on ecstasy, it inherently says much more than the details of that isolated tragedy. Giving one death prominence outlines to parents the dangers involved in drug taking and, by implication, raves.

Within much of the discourse that surrounds illegal drug consumption there is evidence of poor research and inaccuracies. That is not to say, however, that all news stories are based on lies and bad reporting.

A reader should understand the origins of the story, the time restraints behind the publication of the article and the framing provided by the writer/reporter. In addition to scrutinizing the statements that are made, one should ask, what statements are not made and why not?

Drugs for Hedonism. Is it drugs that are condemned in our society, or only drugs that are used for purposes other than medicinal? Could it be that only drugs that relate to societal productivity are culturally accepted? Drugs that calm and relax after a hard day's work such as alcohol and tobacco are non-threatening to productivity. A soldier who ingests an amphetamine tablet to optimize alertness is in fact conforming. Yet when a teenager ingests the same amphetamine tablet in order to have amplified fun at a party, the act is seen as deviant. Recent news reports have concluded that teenagers are increasingly using Ritalin, the prescription drug to control Attention Deficit Disorder, recreationally.

This recreational use is framed in the media as bad while the constant use of the identical drug by young children as a means of controlling hyperactivity is often framed as good or necessary. These cases show that it is not always the drug that is deviant but its use taken out of its intended context that is unacceptable. Some have even claimed that the most damaging drugs are those that are culturally accepted such as alcohol and tobacco. Whether drugs that are "bad" become illegal, or whether drugs that are illegal become "bad," is an unsolvable dispute.

Media Hysteria. The media discourse surrounding the drug ecstasy has been couched in slightly different terms than the drug discourse of the 1930s and 1960s. A distinctly recognizable youth culture was non-existent in the 1930s, which may explain why marijuana wasn't symbolically linked to any phenomenon or youth culture at the time. By the 1960s, Timothy Leary helped bring LSD into the public eye, thus aligning most news stories on acid with the "Tune in, Turn on, Drop out" college hippie movement. The

The predominant American view of mind- and mood-changing drugs has always been paradoxical. On the one hand, Americans drink more alcohol and down more pep and sleeping pills per capita than any other people in the world. On the other hand, anything that smacks of mystical changes or visions or lack of complete mind control is as anti-American as Communism . . . Madness was selling for $5 a dose. The headlines were big and black. Everybody hit the panic button at once. **JOHN CASHMAN,** *The LSD Story,* 115

Ritalin being used for inappropriate purposes harms everybody . . . It harms the patient who actually needs to use it, and it harms the person who isn't supposed to be using it. **"Ritalin Abuse May be a Problem,"** *Oregon Daily Emerald,* **April 27, 1998**

DON'T BELIEVE THE HYPE?

drug use of these two eras was not hidden, confined or aligned to a specific social arena. Although a subculture, and arguably a lifestyle, the drug use synonymous with rave culture only happens on the weekend. Unlike the two preceding drug cultures, ecstasy use as it relates to rave provided the media with a physical space to denounce. Not only was the drug itself blacklisted, but by implication so too were raves. It is a rave's seemingly secret, underworld nature that helps fuel investigation and fear. Like marijuana and LSD, ecstasy was not new when it first appeared in public discourse. Extreme cases of death opened the public's eyes to this seemingly new youth killer. Rave contained the ingredients for a tabloid dream story: youth, sexuality, after-hours activity, secrecy and illicit substances, all wrapped up in a pictorial spectacle of lights and music.

The articles first written about ecstasy were published long before raves ever existed. Contrary to what North American media will tell you about ecstasy use starting with raves in England, its use and abuse actually peaked in the early to mid-1980s in the southern U.S. Then it was identifiable as a yuppie drug and also a gay and college drug because of its supposed aphrodisiac effects. In articles in Britain and the U.S., ecstasy was misunderstood from the onset. It seems that journalists misunderstood the public openness, massaging and touching at raves and assumed that sweaty kids who had taken some of their clothes off were rampant sex fiends. In a 1989 article in the British tabloid the *Sun*, ecstasy was incorrectly described as an "opium-based" drug that could "boost sex-drive"[15] while another article cited ecstasy as "an aphrodisiac capable of transforming staid wall-flowers into sex fiends."[16]

Typically, rave stories in the news have centered on the most obvious symbols of deviance. Like most dance subcultures, the actual subject of dance is more often than not secondary to the music and drug taking which accompanies it. Only one sub-cultural magazine, *Lotus*, addresses rave participants for what they really are: dancers. Unfortunately most journalists pop into a rave for a couple of hours and only witness what they view as rave's criminal exterior. The majority of these media treatments uncovered so-called rampant drug taking. That participants were often traveling huge distances to dance was ignored.

RAVE DEPRAVED?
Drugs, Topless Cartoon Character on Flyer

Organizers of tonight's huge rave at a venue owned by the City of Toronto have been promoting the party at area schools with slick ads featuring drugs and a topless cartoon character.
Toronto Sun, April 22, 2001.

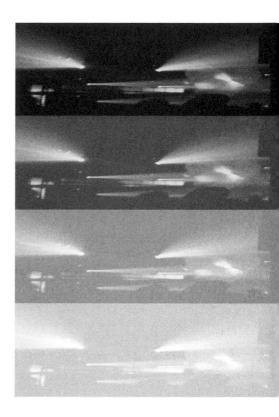

The media not only distorts subcultural activity, it creates the subculture as it names, describes and places discursive parameters around it. This development can be attributed not only to mass media such as newspapers, TV and tabloids but also to niche media such as the music and style press. Media involvement with acid house certainly began with the niche press, such as *i-D* magazine's December/January issue of 1987-88. The cover was a big yellow happy face with one eye as a hyphen, indicating a wink. The headline read "Get up get happy." This cover helped brand the acid house scene in England while it was in its earliest stage. John Godfrey's article, also in *i-D* magazine in June of 1988, brought the Shoom world to the public, with his exposé of what he called "smiley cul-

It's all about drugs to the media and getting ratings. Shit, why can't they just leave us alone and let us dance all night—we're not hurting anyone. But shit, I guess we could go get drunk somewhere and cruise around the city looking for fights. **SETH, Las Vegas, NV, age 18, M, 3 yrs.**

DON'T BELIEVE THE HYPE?

Q. How do you feel about the media's reaction to raves?

A. Hey Barbara Walters and all you other sensationalists out there—guess what? If you keep doing these stories depicting raves as drug havens you're making the situation . . . worse. You're giving ecstasy and all the other drugs the best advertising campaign dealers could ever ask for. Thanks to you, kids know that if they want drugs, all they have to do is go to a rave. That's not only going to hurt our scene, but our youth because now you're letting [everyone] know where to get these media-hyped drugs. This whole generation . . . has been created by the media . . . great job. **LAILA, New Jersey, age 18, F, 2 yrs.**

ture." The article included words like "peace," "love" and of course "acid." It is exposure of this kind in style- and music-based magazines that piqued interest in likely rave followers and began to initiate a movement. By the summer of 1988, not long after the scene had blossomed into larger venues, the tabloid press commenced an ongoing moral panic that often adorned the front pages.

The *Sun* tabloid discovered rave in its embryonic stages when the events were still named acid parties. The front page heralded the discovery: "Spaced Out! 11,000 youngsters go drug crazy at Britain's biggest-ever Acid party."[17] The caption under the picture of dancing youths read, "Night of Ecstasy . . . thrill-seeking youngsters in a dance frenzy at the secret party." The secret of rave had been disclosed and so had the new drug villain: ecstasy. Because of the mistaken assumption that acid house alluded to the drug LSD, the BBC banned any music with the word acid in it or identifiable as acid house.

Stories of moral panic help certify difference and legitimize subcultures, while media stories that speak positively about subcultures are the proverbial kiss of death. As soon as the press got hold of the smiley logo and the keyword "acid," both were dropped by the culture. This helps explain why acid house quietly morphed into rave after the media caught on to the term. Later rave would be dropped for the same reason, to become the more ambiguous term "party" or "event." Toronto promoter Beverly May alludes to the importance of being unaccepted by mainstream culture: "If your whole stance is anti and then you're accepted, what are you then?"[18] Once a culture has been accepted by the media and has been saturated by mainstream influences, it can no longer be called a subculture.

Subcultural participants usually condemn their own negative representation in the media but simultaneously enjoy the sensationalism and inaccuracies within stories. This misunderstanding by the media can be favorable and desirable for subcultural industries, as it helps advertise subcultures to new recruits who wish to be part of a defiant culture. To those who hadn't yet been to a rave, the media's exposé of all-night dancing and drug taking was enticement enough.

The Kid Next Door Starts to Rave. Deep inside this junglist's lair I saw a strangely out of place figure. He must have been 50 if he was a day. When I tried to talk to him he clearly thought I was on drugs and quickly dismissed me. I asked him if he was looking for someone and he told me he was there to find his son. Seeing the bewilderment and concern in this father's eyes I wasn't sure who I felt more sorry for. This dad subject to the onslaught of foreign noise and witness to teenagers engaged in what could be perceived as a marathon of ritualistic proportions, or his soon-to-be busted son, his safe haven uncovered.

Dissemination of rave and its description within the North American media has been relatively slow and arduous, but by the late 1990s the incessant beats were literally waking up the neighbors and causing a stir. One precursor to the full-fledged moral panic surrounding raves was the *Toronto Star's* full page article bearing the headline "Danger Parties" followed by the claim, "teens risk their lives at raves." In the article parents were "urged to be wary" and were alerted of the warning signs that their child was attending raves. The article suggested that "the entire community must come together to stop raves from taking place. It's going to take a fatality to make a change."[19]

Over two years later, a fatality did make a change. By 1999 raving was at its peak in Toronto, with events gathering record attendances of 10,000 to 20,000 people. Between July and October there were three rave-related deaths in the city, deepening the public's already apparent distaste for raves. After only a few articles and almost nine years of raving, news of

---

Q. How do you feel about the media's reaction to raves?

A. Betrayed. Not by the media—I expect them to be shallow and ignorant, but betrayed by the very idiots who stand up and believe they have the right to speak for the scene. Idiots like the random candy raver I see plastered on the news from time to time spewing out nonsense about raves and PLUR. I know the media purposely interviews them but at the same time I wish people had enough common sense to simply not talk to a reporter if they weren't absolutely sure about what was coming out of their mouths. Alas, that is the major downfall of a culture which attempts to accept everyone. In the end you get the low livers and the denizens of society.
FU MAN CHU, Eatontown, NJ, age 21, 7 yrs.

ECSTASY RULES RAVE SCENE IN VANCOUVER

Sarah's eyes bulge out like saucers and her smile is as constant as her chatter. "I'm really, really high right now," she says giggling on the floor and hugging people she hardly knows.
Vancouver Sun,
Tuesday January 2, 2001

DON'T BELIEVE THE HYPE?

the phenomenon hit the front page. In the *Toronto Sun* in September of 1999 the front page said it all: "Rave Scene: Drugs 'Too Easy'." Inside there is a picture of a police sergeant sitting with a mountain of seized rave drugs and money while readers are told that clubbers are "ecstatic about rave 'chemicals'."[20] Two months later raving appeared on the front page of the *Toronto Star*, the headline reading "Agonizing Over Ecstasy."[21]

It is difficult to surmise whether the moral panic spearheaded by the media and the Ontario government's task force to stop raves were due to the growing number of ecstasy-related deaths or to the fact that raves had grown in size over the last year. Although the two factors existed simultaneously, it could be argued that the deaths were partly due to the increase in the size of raves and therefore an increase in drug users. Promoter Beverly May suggests a reason why the media is only now so involved: "Now we have parties that have 15,000 people, the average youth's going, so of course the average mainstream media is going to be interested now, it's big news that Daddy's little favourite is exposed to these things."[22]

It is the averageness of participants that now, more than ever, makes rave newsworthy. If a delinquent, freak or drug addict dies it is not very newsworthy. However, if the average son, daughter or student with a promising future dies after ingesting the same controlled substance, it is definitely newsworthy because it provides the grounds for a crackdown on drugs. In the three most publicized ecstasy and rave-related deaths in the U.K., the U.S. and Canada, it was the normality and ordinariness of the deceased which was stressed. In the U.K., it was 18-year-old Leah Betts who became the poster child for the panic surrounding ecstasy. She lived in a remote farmhouse with her mother who was a nurse, and her father who was a retired police officer. Betts died after taking an ecstasy pill at her birthday party held in her home. It was her ordinariness that caused such a stir in the media. According to Sheryl Garratt, "a distressing, close-up picture of Leah in her hospital bed, tubes running from her nose and open mouth . . . was quickly turned into an anti-drug poster by the *Sun*."[23] The funeral was videotaped and permitted to be used in schools as a propaganda tool, while her picture could be seen everywhere on huge billboards.

In the U.S., panic was the order of the day on the nationally-broadcast ABC newsmagazine *20/20* in January 1997. The first segment was devoted to the uncovering of the the latest kid-craze, a craze that had ironically been occurring for almost a decade. The opening of the piece alerts parents, "Do you know where your teenagers are? This could be the night your child ventures into a secretive and potentially dangerous world. The world of the rave."[24] Out of a number of deaths, *20/20* concentrated on one case. Not unlike Leah Betts in England, Sandra Montessi was a regular, middle class, attractive college student whose mother pleaded that we "stop the raves. It's not a dance, it's not a safe place for your kids."[25] The reporter provided an analysis of what goes on at these "dangerous" raves, all in a 30-second mouthful: "It sounds innocent. But beneath the laser lights and loud music, America's youth are rebelling in a new and dangerous way. It's chaos fuelled by blatant, brazen drug taking. Raves are happening . . . anywhere that's away from adult supervision." The segment ended with a reassuring note to the audience that at least Americans "didn't start it." Just as Mexicans were earlier accused of bringing marijuana to the children of America, there is an "other" in the rave menace: the English. Somehow blaming the English relieved America of any guilt and instead portrayed American children as innocent victims who needed to be protected.

In Canada, the death most often mentioned is that of a 21-year-old Ryerson University student who was, according to one article, "just starting into third year in a field that promised a great future."[26] He was described in the same *Toronto Sun* article as a "polite young man who didn't act or dress outlandishly." Like in the U.S. and the U.K., the police tried to find a death in Toronto that would most appropriately validate their panic. Toronto's Deputy Chief Coroner Dr. Jim Cairns informed the public that "We're looking at which [Ecstasy-related death] would be best

Dear Ann Landers:
As the administrator of the Drug Enforcement Administration and the parent of three teenagers, I am concerned about the problem of Ecstasy and the look-alike killer drug PMA. Many parents are not familiar with the rave scene, where these drugs are readily available to their children. *Arizona Republic,* **May 7, 2001**

I wish a lot of the time that parents would go and experience a rave for themselves before they swallow everything that the media throws at them. They also need to keep in mind that their children are going to make their own decisions whether they want them to or not. It's also important to remember that every rave is different. And some people just have no business putting themselves into the situations they do having to do with the rave scene.
JERNET, North Carolina, age 17, F, 3 yrs.

suited to get the message across to the public, the perfect case that demonstrates our concern."[27] It had taken approximately ten ecstasy-related deaths over a decade for raves to be publicly denounced in the media. Toronto's police chief Julian Fantino led the onslaught against raves, suggesting they "provide a venue and willing customers for the drug dealers. [They are] mercenary merchants of death preying on kids who are out for a good time."[28]

A number of articles on rave seem to substantiate this claim. On May 5, 2000 the *Toronto Sun's* first page announced that the city's police chief had invited the Prime Minister to a rave to show him how "drug parties are 'threatening' youth."[29] The article includes a quote from the police chief who claims that raves are "threatening the very fabric of Canadian life." One week later city council made a decision to ban raves on public property. The mayor exacerbated fears and myths to panic proportions.

The condemnation of raves was not limited to print media. Toronto's *CityPulse* TV news also positioned mayor Mel Lastman as the unofficial guardian of the victims of rave culture. His government promised constituents that it would not tolerate "illegal after-hours clubs and raves . . . We will do everything in our power to shut them down . . . [we will] padlock these dens of drugs and guns."[30] The inaccurate linking of after-hours clubs with raves had the public believing that raves were a site of violence. Ironically, these news stories denouncing raves for their alleged violence and illegal activities did so over footage containing pretty lights, people smiling, waving into the cameras, hugging one another and dancing. In one *CityPulse* piece, a young man with sunglasses dances, a soother in his mouth and a brightly-colored woolen cap on his head, making the reporter's voice-over commentary about the veritable war against raves almost comic. The happy rave footage leaves the panicked rhetoric with little validity.

Another headline, "Celebrating Drug Abuse: The Rave Generation Tunes into LSD and Ecstasy," brings together a multitude of condemning discourses. According to the Alberta newspaper article which ran under this headline, not only is this generation doing drugs, they're celebrating it. Although a "new" drug and subculture have been added to the century-old list of menaces, the article repeats prejudices that date back to the 1960s and earlier. Just as the hippies were called "misfits" and "directionless,"[31] the drug users of the 1990s are accused in this article of being "lazy and bored."[32]

When people take this Ecstasy . . . they go nuts and you cannot control them. The cops cannot control them!

"COUNCIL BANS RAVE PARTIES,"
Toronto Sun, May 11, 2000

Mayor Mel, please educate yourself before passing judgment on our culture.

"MAYOR MEL, COME RAVE WITH ME,"
Toronto Star, Tuesday May 23, 2000

Media reaction to subcultures is often ambivalent. It is simultaneously fascinated and amused, terrified and outraged. It is a subculture's style that initially attracts media attention. As so-called deviant and anti-social acts are uncovered they are used to sensationalize the subculture's breaking of established codes. This is evident with rave and acid house

[Adults fear]… that their sons and daughters… are out of control and that the young people, by organizing and participating in these raves, have in fact started to take control over their own lack of control of society. **PHILIP TAGG,** *From Refrain to Rave,* **210-11**

Mayor Mel Lastman: Have you ever attended a rave? Because it really sounds as if you are positively misinformed and out of touch regarding the whole situation…I am a 20-year-old, intelligent university student, and, yes, I am a "raver." I am also extremely upset about the incorrect information now circulating regarding the rave culture… Mayor Mel, please educate yourself before passing judgment on our culture. **EMILY BALON,** *Toronto Star,* **May 23, 2000.**

DON'T BELIEVE THE HYPE?

Q. How do you feel about the media's reaction to raves?

A. They're always the last to know. So what they say is pretty skewed. I work in the media and was surprised to see the amount of opposition when I tried to do a story on the I Dance rally last year. The producers used every excuse they could to kill the story and get me busy on other things. **SYNAPSE, Toronto, ON, age 27, M, 8 yrs.**

Up till now it has been thought that the growth of the Christian myths during the Roman Empire was possible only because printing was not yet invented. Precisely the contrary. The daily press and the telegraph, which in a moment spread inventions over the whole earth, fabricate more myths . . . in one day than could have formerly been done in a century. **KARL MARX, as quoted in** *The Manufacture of News,* **5**

coverage in the British tabloid the *Sun*. The newspaper initially printed an acid house fashion guide calling the acid house style "cool and groovy." The *Sun* even sold its own version of the smiley T-shirt which had come to represent acid house. One week later as acid house's drug associations were uncovered, moral panic ensued and the *Sun* abruptly ended its T-shirt offer and started an anti-drug campaign accompanied by a smiley face with a frown. The situation was similar in the U.S. where *New York* magazine ran an article commenting on rave style and the outlandish, childlike nature of the fashion at the same time that the newsmagazine *20/20* denigrated raves for their drug play. In Toronto, there also seems to be an ambiguous relationship to raves, even within the same newspaper. In amongst a slew of condemning articles about rave in the *Toronto Star*, there appeared a two-page article devoted to rave flyer art with no mention of rave drugs and their side effects.

Journalists are taught to ask six integral questions about every news story they encounter: who, what, where, why, when, and how. Mysteriously, in journalistic discourse surrounding drug consumption, one of these questions is typically ignored: why? Youth have changed styles and changed drugs (or simply added to their menu) but what remains constant is the unanswered question of why kids consistently, generation after generation, are drawn to drugs. As an essay in the *New Republic* states, "Attacking society's minor symptoms, without recognizing society's major disease which causes them, is a fruitless pursuit."[33] Drugs have always been evidence of a much larger systemic problem at work.

In many of the articles condemning drug use in the 1930s, 1960s and 1990s, there is little differentiation made between drugs. Ecstasy was at one time considered an opium-based designer drug, then an amphetamine and even a hallucinogen. Society tells us all drugs that are neither prescribed nor government sanctioned are bad. All recreational drugs are considered bad because of the laws that ban their use. Marijuana, LSD and ecstasy are pharmacologically non-addictive and have been used medically during their life spans, but once aligned with the fear of a sub-culture, they become as ominous and frightful as crack or heroin.

The media helps perpetuate the quiet myths that are seemingly impossible to evade. Mathew Collin has written that "The dividing line between legal and illegal drugs is largely a social construct, reliant on tra-dition, morality and culture as much as science and logic."[34] One street drug becomes as evil as the next for some journalists, regardless of scien-tific evidence of non-addictive properties and few damaging physiological and psychological effects. These recycled myths become axiomatic in public opinion. A recent U.S. public service announcement spread dubi-ous fears that have been around for sixty years: "In a world this dangerous there's no such thing as a harmless drug: talk to your children about mar-ijuana." In a world this dangerous there's no such thing as a story without origin: talk to your children about myth.

I feel it is so important that the general public have access to the real scoop of what the rave movement and culture is all about; *Time* magazine and the like are doing a disservice to such a peace-ful mode of expression. I guess the pow-ers that be want us all hanging out in depressive bars downing gallons of toxic alcohol. At least that way they can moni-tor and tax our indulgences.
K. CHARPENTIER, Silicon Valley, CA, age 36, F.

E-COMMERCE

Once found almost exclu-sively at raves or in col-lege dorms, ecstasy is nearing the cultural ubiq-uity marijuana reached at the beginning of the sev-enties and cocaine achieved in the mid eighties. "It's sweeping through our society faster than crack," says Gary Murray, East Coast repre-sentative of the U.S. Cus-toms Ecstasy Task Force, "Everyone's doing it."
New York magazine,
Monday July 24, 2000

COUNTERSPIN, a current events TV program on CBC's News-world, devoted an episode to the impending rave problem after a city councillor got numerous noise complaints about an outdoor Halloween rave. Most interesting about this episode was not the formulaic platitudes about kids and drugs or the public nuisance of raves, but rather that the token rave panelist was addressed not as a raver or rave participant but as a "rave consumer." Even the media now saw rave culture as something that was bought or sold.

11
CASHING IN

How did the scene change?

A: Loss of secrecy and exclusivity of raves. When raves became "legal" (i.e. with proper city permits), it paved the way [for] money hungry promoters who saw a golden opportunity at . . . quick cash. Now, for some promoters, ravers are clients, raves an investment and a product that needs to be advertised and sold to the largest number of "clients" possible.

DJ Psonyk, Montréal, QC, age 30, M, 8 yrs.

They must have some pretty strong belts to hold those pants up. And the pacifiers . . . those have gotta go. Sure, I know they use it to keep their teeth from chattering when they're on E or whatever . . . but I think it's because they've done drugs that their minds have turned into mush. So basically, they've gone back to an infant state. Next thing ya know, ravers will [be] eating Gerber food products. **ANONYMOUS**

We dress this way because we want to look younger than we are. I want to feel younger than I am, because getting old in America is not much fun. **ANONYMOUS 21-YEAR-OLD RAVER as quoted in *Rave On*, pg. 43**

Media recognition and condemnation of rave acted essentially as publicity. The panic surrounding raves sold a lot of newspapers. This free publicity also increased business for promoters, drug dealers and the entire rave infrastructure such as record companies and stores, fashion designers, clothing stores and street-based youth and style magazines. Tony Colston-Hayter of the British rave company Sunrise admitted that his massive crowds were in part due to acid house being front page news. Undoubtedly, media attention and condemnation helps turn subcultures into big business.

Style. The look of rave was originally anti-style. The acid house dress code in Britain began as a parody of the tropical resort vacation. Shoomers were clad in baggy, Day-glo fluorescents and runners, rejecting the rigid London club style. The rave fashion protocol was dictated not only by the need to differ from clubbers but also by the exhausting nature of raves. Dancing for hours in combination with ecstasy made you sweat; so baggy, comfortable clothes, running shoes and little make up became almost a

necessity. Although this early acid house crowd looked more natural in the sense that they chose clothes and shoes that were comfortable, and the girls wore less make up, they actually stood in stark contrast to the typical club crowd of the time. In this sense their outfits were fabricated. These ravers deliberately dressed down while club goers dressed up. This anti-fashion statement was not only a rejection of fashion, it became its own style by coming to stand for ravers' marginalized identities. The style surrounding the scene began to reflect rave's freedom from social restrictions.

> A decade on, the key words did seem to have changed—from love and peace to investment and promotion, from music to marketing.
> **Matthew Collin, Altered State, 272**

As rave developed into a full-blown subculture and spread to North America, a distinctive style started to develop. Still adhering to the essentials of comfort rather than the dictates of fashion, rave style was now borrowing and altering elements from the loose-fitting styles of hip-hop, skater and snowboarding clothing. It was this bagginess that eventually became the style. Colorful, comfortable, baggy clothes made ravers look infantile, a subconscious refusal to enter the restrictive, rational adult world.

Bigger came to mean better and soon ravers were sewing panels into their loose jeans to make the bottoms wider. Phat pants would wipe along the wet floors like mops, sopping up sweat like sponges. It wasn't uncommon to see pants wet up to the knees. Huge sweatshirts and loose T-shirts gave ravers a pre-pubescent appearance, while plush teddy bears came to be a necessary rave accessory. Some ravers tried to look as outrageous as possible. They weren't trying to fit in; they were trying to stand out. Ravers

what is your favorite or typical rave outfit?

Once upon a time when we used to plan our outfits as if we were entering a pageant of sorts, I was partial to glow beads, pigtails and body glitter. **PEANUT71, Toronto, ON, age 29, F, 4 yrs.**

A small white tank top I have had forever and [a] pair of nylon silver drawstring pants. My shell-toed adidas and [a] white handkerchief on my head like Aunt Jaime. **PRINCESS NIKITTA, Cabot, AR, age 19, F, 2 yrs.**

Black T-shirt, black trousers, acupuncture trainers. **ALJI, Oxford, England, age 42, M, 24 yrs.**

Pair of trainers (Adidas, Nike, Reebok, etc.), a soccer shirt (Glasgow Rangers F.C., Scotland national team) or a polo shirt (Adidas normally), a pair of jogging trousers (Adidas 3-stripe, or Nike), and sometimes a Nike cap. **SCOTTISH RAVER, Glasgow, Scotland, age 15, M, 3 yrs.**

I used to dress like a typical candy kid—lots of beads, big fuzzy pants—but I guess I . . . moved away from that. Now I just wear BIG jeans and a shirt. **ORION, Las Vegas, NV, age 20, M, 2 yrs.**

Women's elastic bell bottom pants, vintage pink hawaiian shirt, leopard print beret, orange/blue Nikes. **PSYCHEDELIC PHD, Toronto, ON, age 25, M, 6 yrs.**

I just wear pants and a T-shirt and some sneakers. I used to be the queen of caffeine pants, but [now] I feel like everyone around me has them on as well. So I don't wear them unless they're really old ones and I know that only one other person could possibly show up with them on. I also really like wearing my gigantic shorts and boxers. I'm adamant about matching my shoes to my clothing as well. I'm a fashion whore but I'm not a scary candy kid. Even though I do appreciate some happy hardcore. **JERNET, North Carolina, age 17, F, 3 yrs.**

For me, it all starts with the hat . . . I base my outfit on the hat I'm in the mood to wear. Just like a lot of other ravers, my hats are my "thing." From there, I think comfort (think temperature, cleanliness of the venue, stuff like that . . .) A lot of choosing my outfit depends on how I feel. **HATGRRL, Detroit, MI, age 28, F, 2 yrs.**

were rebelling by looking cute and cuddly, in direct opposition to the mainstream club look of skimpy dresses and tight T-shirts. Soon ravers not only wanted to touch and cuddle teddy bears they wanted to look as teddy-like as possible. Enter fun fur. Ravers began making their own loose-fitting pants out of pastel fun fur. It wasn't uncommon in one faction of rave style to see a full-grown male dressed in pink or baby blue fun fur with a soother hanging around his neck. It is safe to say this style had erased all remnants of club machismo. Dressing up in outlandish homemade outfits showed you knew what rave was about. Your outward outrageousness was a symbol of your inner free spirit, your energy and enthusiasm towards the scene. Early ravers weren't buying style, they were creating it.

Rave-oriented labels weren't readily accessible in the early to mid-1990s, so ravers would make their own outfits. The metal wallet chains that had been a staple in skateboarding fashion were transformed by ravers into huge plastic chains, or baby toys stitched together hanging down to the knees. There were handmade necklaces made out of pom-poms, huge wooden beads and platform running shoes. Some ravers would add an extra layer of rubber onto their runners. There were wrap-around sunglasses, body stickers, Dr. Seuss hats, costume bug antennas and butterfly and angel wings from Halloween costumes. The rave aesthetic was a melding together of anything that was sequined, fluffy, colorful and tactile. It seems that the heightened sensitivity to touch caused by MDMA was the initiating influence behind the teddy bear craze and wardrobes that accentuated all that was pink and plush. Along with the teddy bear trend came candy ravers. These were young teenagers who not only supplied the much-needed sugar high by endlessly dispensing lollipops to those in need, they actually adorned themselves in candy—necklaces, bracelets and soothers that were suckers. Their oversized fluffy record bags were virtual treasure troves—not of records but of sugar.

Specific drugs also seemed to alter style and create new cultural signifiers. When amphetamines started to become more prominent in the scene, some ravers used baby soothers to stop the teeth grinding habit caused by excessive speed intake. This trend was soon adopted as rave style, regardless of whether the raver was consuming amphetamines or not. Suddenly soothers and other baby paraphernalia could be found in rave stores, not just drug stores. In *Subculture: The Meaning of Style*, Dick Hebdige notes a similar trend in punk, suggesting that the era boosted the sale of safety pins that were being used in a new, style-oriented context. Subcultural style not only initiates new trends but gives new meaning to old ones. Something like this occurred with Vicks Vapo Rub and Vicks inhalers. Both were stripped of their intended use as cold remedies to become instead a symbol of rave and more specifically, of ecstasy use. Increased olfactory sensations because of MDMA use made anything mentholated increase the buzz. The electronic band Altern8 appeared on *Top of the Pops* in England, and prominently displayed a jar of Vicks Vapo Rub. This was a clear signal of ecstasy use to those in the know. Displayed by a non-rave band, Vicks would perhaps signify only that a band member had a cold. In Britain so many inhalers were being sold to ravers that Vicks was forced to warn the public of misuse.

In time there were numerous people adhering to an aesthetic that became synonymous with rave. This look was primarily comprised of baggy pants, loose T-shirts, short often brightly colored hair, beaded necklaces, body sparkles, body stickers, ball caps, visors, safety chains, soothers, anything alien-oriented and children's television and cartoon character paraphernalia such as Winnie the Pooh and Teletubbies. Eventually with enough people copying, there were no longer individual rave styles. There was instead a new breed of ravers that began to consume what it believed the culture to be instead of helping to create the culture and continue its evolution. Similarly, ravers started copying each other's dance styles until certain movements became codified. Eventually some regions even acquired their own signature articulation of dance style. The original varied crowd that had defined rave eventually became a homogeneous mass

That's where my nickname comes from. I found this fabulous Washington Capitals Mike Gartner jersey from the late 70s at a Goodwill one day. $4. It's red, white and blue, with stars across the front and #11 Gartner on the back. It really stands out, and makes it much easier for my tripped-out friends to find me (which is the main reason I always wear it out). I hadn't thought about this in ages, but I've had hundreds of people come up to me at parties and say "fuckin' wicked jersey dude." Baggy pants to carry all my stuff, and of course, comfy running shoes for dancing. **GARTNER, Toronto, ON, age 30, M, 3 yrs.**

what kinds of changes have you noticed in your scene?

The vibe has basically gone to shit. There isn't talent like I used to see talent, and it's all about showing off what cool new phat pants you got and what color your glowstick is. **TAMARA ROSS, Kelowna, BC, age 16, F, 3 yrs.**

Not good ones: fake kids with Vicks and pills going for the light shows. They have no clue what it's all about. I don't have to get fucked to enjoy a party. **CHARLIE, Mobile, AB, age 22, M, 3 yrs.**

It is waaaay too commercial!!! Too many people [are] thinking that it is cool [to] go [to] a rave and get messed up . . . and they don't even care about the music. **ANOYMOUS, Redondo Beach, CA, age 14, 1 yr.**

There are a lot more kids going now. I mean 12, 13-year-olds. Don't get me wrong, that's great, but I think most of them go to look cool or just to do the drugs and that's not what it's all about. **KRAN, Newfoundland, age 22, M, 2 yrs.**

Rave has become another high school fad. It goes against the secret society aspect of rave to become yet another sub group such as mod, skater, punk, etc. **Ian Guthrie, *Transcendance Magazine*, Spring 1996**

It's falling apart. The new kids today have no respect . . . **RT, Tampa, FL, age 25, M, 11 yrs.**

More sleaziness, less positive vibes (a nervous, sketchy energy that I don't enjoy seems to be invading parties), more people who are more interested in being seen than seeing and hearing the DJ. **PEANUT71, Toronto, ON, 29, F, 4 yrs.**

There are so many people there that are just there because they think it is cool to go . . . and they really don't understand the true meaning [of] rave and it is giving us a bad reputation. I don't want to lose something that I love just because of these people that are trying to be cool. **NICOLE BRINZA, Trafford, PA, age 17, F.**

of phat pants dragging along the floor, dancing and sopping up rave dirt. Soon rave was nothing but a sweating, gyrating mass of androgynous fun fur.

Rave began as a rejection of mass culture, a transgression of gender roles and a dismantling of stereotypes. Unfortunately, many of the socialized norms once absent in rave culture are now evident. Fewer people talk openly to strangers and girls are often objectified in a similar manner to the club scene. Rave fashion is no longer about standing out, it's about looking the same. This has left some ravers complaining that the majority of those attending do not get it. The new ravers are accused of trying too hard at looking, dancing and acting a certain way. One raver, Psychedelic PhD, explains his early motivation to rave: "I wasn't going to be accepted, I was going to be someone who wasn't accepted, I was going to be someone who was different. I was inventing my fashion, I was inventing who I was." The majority of old school ravers positioned themselves against a homogenous mainstream that they were not a part of. So what happens when this heterogeneous rave crowd becomes homogeneous and in essence becomes the mainstream it was trying to escape? One raver, Little Zero, talks about stepping away from the scene when he noticed this happening: "I think that before rave was something I went to because I rejected and wanted to escape the mainstream. Now . . . the mainstream has brought its mentality and world views into it and pushed me out. It's become what I tried to escape."

It is sometimes difficult to separate the fact that today's ravers are consumers of rave culture, and the fact that consumers in the greater population have bought rave. In early 1999 the CBC's *Jonovision* television program devoted an entire episode to the underground world of raves and began the show by suggesting that the most important issue was what to wear. The segment continued by conducting three rave makeovers. Ironically, it had once been anti-style that defined rave, now rave had been reduced to a style itself.

Many people involved in the scene now changed their relationship to it by becoming DJs, promoters, drug dealers and graphic and fashion designers. By the mid-1990s there was an influx of Toronto-based clothing companies that became rave labels and brands. Companies like Snug created pants with special hidden dual purpose pockets that served as drug pouches. Snug was also the first label to have pants that unzipped into shorts, a perfect style for sweaty raves. In the spirit of Snug a number of other rave-inspired designers followed suit: Geek Boutique, Fiction, and Mod Robes have all enjoyed national and international success. These companies along with American labels such as Clobber, Freshjive, Liquid Sky, JNCO and Lush have come to be standard raver attire. Items such as overalls are still cool as long as they cost upwards of $100 and sport one of these brand names.

Before long it seemed that I couldn't attend a rave without watching at least a few of my necklaces on parade, along with a handful of homemade copies. My necklaces were seen on flyers, in a local magazine, in a Toronto-based music video, and around the necks of the pop group "Len." Standing behind stalls watching E-d out kids buying my wares was a totally new experience from dancing in the crowd. I was no longer just a participant at raves, I was participating in creating what was rave style. The final mark of my mainstream appeal was evident when CBC's *Jonovision* dedicated an episode to hip trends in fashion. Two models adorned the stage wearing my necklaces. This no longer represented rave fashion, this was simply fashion. SNUG

While newsmakers condemned raves, national retailers began thriving on its growing appeal. Chain stores were cashing in on the rave machine and were imitating many of the innovations of the above-mentioned street designers. The front window of Le Château, for

Rave culture has influenced us in many ways—[the] main reason [being] function and fit, but also in the way that we as designers are very much a part of it. Snug has been continuously growing on a level that makes one believe that we will become mainstream. However Snug's styles and customers will always remain underground due to our cutting edge designs and place within the scene. We are well known for creating new concepts as the rave scene progresses and incorporating the person's needs. Details include hidden pockets, designs with optional functions such as zip off pants/skirt/dress and removable pockets and other elements. **SNUG**

CASHING IN

Subcultural deviance is simultaneously rendered explicable and meaningless in the classrooms, courts and media at the same time as the 'secret' objects of subcultural style are put on display in every . . . record shop and chain-store boutique. Stripped of its unwholesome connotations, the style becomes fit for public consumption. **DICK HEBDIGE, *Subculture: The Meaning of Style,* 130**

RAVE SUCCESS SPAWNS PARTY FASHION STORE

If the phat ultra-flared pants, psychedelic tops, neon-colored platform shoes and plastic glow-sticks of various shades and sizes lining the shelves and racks of Richmond's Plastic Robot rave store aren't a dead giveaway, rave has become a big business.

***Richmond Review,*
September 13, 2000**

example, emulated a bathroom at a rave with flyers, empty water bottles and an empty drink container labeled "Rave" all littering the floor while rave fashions were draped on the mannequins. The venerable department store Eaton's was also keen to benefit from the rise in rave's popularity. In the youth section of the downtown Toronto store, a raver checklist was prominently displayed listing the necessary fashion components of rave. Around the same time Eaton's also created a candy store in amongst the rave-esque fashions of fluffy bags, baby tees and phat pants. Although chain stores marketed the rave look, the meaning behind the fashion had disappeared. Removed from the music, the crowd, the hedonism and the dance, the style was purely appearance. This neutralization is most evident when children as young as 12 are wearing phat pants looking as though they just came out of a rave. The only difference is that their pupils are not dilated from drugs, the bottoms of their pants are not filthy from rave dirt and they are not sweating from dancing. In rave culture the transition from authentic style to manufactured style happened very quickly. Style progressed from what was comfortable in the demanding, exhaustive arena of a rave to a specific commodity sold in chain stores. This commodification process will eventually limit the subculture's once rebellious nature. It has already happened to the punk and grunge styles, once symbols of defiance and later taken up by haute couture and modeled on Parisian fashion runways.

One of the newest Mattel Barbie™ dolls called "Happenin' Hair Barbie" sports her very own pair of phat pants with hair that changes into "funky" colors. It's impossible for phat pants to still be viewed as underground or resistant when they are being worn by Barbie.™ Similarily, pop icons such as Enrique Iglesias and Jennifer Lopez have both emulated rave-esque environments in their videos. Samsung, the electronics company, has advertised its MP3 player as a "portable rave scene." In October of 2001 Konami published a video game for the Sony Play Station™ called Dance Stage—Disney™ Mix. Gamenation.com advertised, "Turn your lounge room into a Disney™ Rave party . . . this rave is hosted by DJ Mickey Mouse™ . . . " Regardless of the fact that Mickey Mouse™ was now a rave DJ media panic would still have the public believe that attending raves is just about the most rebellious and underground act a teenager can participate in.

Music.
As technology keeps renewing itself and becoming cheaper, more music is being made. Music is more than ever fashionable and then just as quickly dated. Through the evolution of digital music technologies and their increased availability, a plethora of sub-genres have evolved out of techno since its debut in the late 1980s in Detroit. The effect of an increasing variety of rave music genres has been twofold. The rave scene has splintered in countless directions at the same time as it is more palatable to a larger cross section of the public. The music rave encompasses has widened, with some parties showcasing hip-hop stars as headliners. This hybridization of music genres has electronic dance music caught in a maze of semantics and classifications: acid house, house, techno, breakbeat house, handbag house, gabba, hardcore, happy hardcore, darkcore, jungle, ambient, ambient jungle, intelligent techno, trance, Goa trance, progressive house, garage and speed garage.

Slowly, the music that rave and its subsidiary scenes have undoubtedly helped sell to the masses has started to become part of our advertising wallpaper. Volkswagen used The Orb and Fluke. Mitsubishi used Groove Armada. Volvo used Mr. Scruff. Moby has been used in a Baileys ad. The Gap used Crystal Method. Video games like Wipeout had an entire soundtrack ranging from Future Sound of London to Photek. Commercials not only bought prominent electronica tracks they also created their own. Rave-stylized dance moves were popping up in the most unlikely of places, such as ads for Five Alive juice.

Inevitably as the role of rave music transformed so too did the music's primary deliverer, the DJ. Originally a faceless genre of music,

The music (house and techno) was everywhere: piped into the supermarkets, chiming in the chain clothing shops, blaring on the radio and the TV . . . where was the underground, the "vibe," the "scene" in this sea of corporate hype and beer-backed mega-events?
BEVERLY MAY, *Future Jazz,* **3**

The focus in the house scene is no longer on participation, no longer on the music itself, but on the deification of a personality—the DJ. In other words, it's rock 'n' roll all over again!
ANDREW RAWNSLEY, *XLR8R,* **Issue 19, 1995**

Q. How do you feel about the naming of a multitude of house/techno subgenres?

A. I think it's a ploy the industry uses via the press to fragment something too hot to handle. Could you imagine how much power dance would have if it was just one movement, independent and moving at speed through a very stagnant industry? That's why you get everything from deep house to tech rock . . . go figure . . . it's all in "my house."
GUY CALLED GERALD

CASHING IN

Q. Why do you feel underground music has historically been relatively faceless? Is this changing?

A. No . . . when house was underground it was't faceless. There were just a lot more darker faces.
GUY CALLED GERALD

Q. How have you adapted to the scene/music changes since the acid house craze in England?

A. Sometimes I think of that Adonis tune "Too Far Gone Ain't No Way Back," back then it was abstract stripped down funk, now it's dudes getting away with your money. 95% of all DJ/producers have everything but passion. I personally have never "adapted to the scene." I'm just getting down just for the funk of it. **GUY CALLED GERALD**

techno was born in clubs where the DJ was known by his music and not his sellable face. Because of this, artists and DJs were rarely seen, which helped give rise to a pyramid effect within the techno genre. Artists were placed at the bottom of this pyramid. Technology made producing techno easy and abundant, thus making the actual music groups/producers less important because of their somewhat transient nature. The record label lay in the middle because it was usually synonymous with a particular form or sub-genre of techno. Often people would know a particular record label because of compilations it produced representing different groups of a particular sound. The DJ was at the top of this pyramid: he/she was the collector and deliverer of a particular style of techno. DJs are typically the stars of raves, not live acts. The pyramid effect introduced by new technologies suggested changes in music's political hierarchy that were very much evident within the rave scene. Many ravers were more likely to know what DJ they liked than what groups or producers they liked.

Without the DJ, rave would cease to exist. While amphetamines help give ravers their all-night energy, it is the DJ who mysteriously manipulates it. Initially, techno and house DJs had little prominence: their faces remained unrecognizable to most. Eventually, despite electronica videos such as Future Sound of London which refused to show band members, CD packaging with graphics instead of faces, and the band Daft Punk who wore masks during an interview, house music yielded to the needs of marketing and publicity. Originally, DJs and electronica producers defied the usual parameters of authenticity and rock commodification because they couldn't play live as a typical four- or five-piece band does, and they made 12-inch singles on vinyl instead of full-length CDs. The music industry hadn't had much previous success marketing dance music because of the studio nature of its production methods, which stood in opposition to live dance bands. For the most part disco hits were produced on independent labels. By the early 1990s, however, record companies started making DJ compilations. The DJ was increasingly a good marketing tool, helping brand a particular music because of his rising success in the rave and club industries. Buying a mixed CD meant buying music from artists you probably didn't know simply because you knew and trusted the DJ that was endorsing them.

> The biggest difference for me would be that there was more sincerity about the music back in those days. A lot of good records get overlooked now if they don't have some hype or a brand-name producer or remixer's name plastered all over them. And, the people purchased more records than they do now. So much more time seems to be spent analyzing than just enjoying and purchasing in recent years. **Larry Heard**

More recently house and techno have begun to adhere to pop and rock music business standards. DJs' faces often adorn compilation packaging, their names have become recognizable and their booking fees reflect this. In addition to the usual 12-inch electronica singles, record labels now market CDs that prove more accessible than their vinyl counterparts. The DJ remix has become a standard, while compilations of generic trance, house and techno are marketed to a more general audience and can easily be found in chain retail music outlets and television advertising. Continuum records released a *This is Techno* compilation series, and the company's manager admitted, "We want our record to be the *Saturday Night Fever* of the 1990s. We're going after a wider audience, a suburban audience." 35 DJs who were once faceless are now revered

Q. What changes in the music industry have come about because of house and techno?

A. Sampling laws have been redefined, companies like Roland and Akai have had to change the way they manufacture instruments. The remix is now the standard. **GUY CALLED GERALD**

CASHING IN

Increasingly, I felt that what this culture had become was without hope. I had schmoozed with enough ego-drenched "stars." I had flyered at enough drug-driven, teenybopper, headache-inducing, multi-thousand person events.
BEVERLY MAY, *Future Jazz,* **9**

Why do big rave promoters still insist on booking too many "name" DJs for their parties, usually giving them a whopping [one]-hour set each? How many flyers have you seen that have 20 or more DJs on them? Precisely because of the pulling power of those names, and because of the star status which these DJs give to their parties.
ANDREW RAWNSLEY, *XLR8R,* **Issue 19, 1995**

with the same awe as pop stars. Some DJs have fans and groupies line up for their autographs. Many do tours just as any pop group would, performing in concert-type venues in smaller cities. In 1991, British DJ Sasha was called the "son of God" by *Mixmag* music magazine and was pictured on their cover. He was perhaps the first DJ pinup. Rave DJs and producers adorn magazine covers such as *URB* and *The Face.* Two magazines are completely devoted to DJing, *Mixer* and *DJ.* DJs who earned £50 a set ten years ago now get £1,000 an hour for spinning. For the millennium New Year's Eve some DJs were reputedly getting into the tens of thousands for a set. It was reported that a Japanese club had offered Junior Vasquez $150,000 to spin on New Year's 1999. Teenagers now want to be more like DJs than rock stars, while the most sought after teenage possession is more likely to be a turntable and a mixer rather than a guitar. In Japan turntables now regularly outsell guitars. Record bags have become stylish in homage to the DJ, regardless of whether a person owns records or not.

Clubs. Wednesday July 12, 2000. 1:30 a.m. Tonic nightclub with Detroit DJ Claude Young. After six years of raving and countless pages written towards insight, can any conclusion be drawn? The DJ clashes the sound of two records back and forth with almost violent precision. His rhythms are so syncopated that it confuses a lot of the dancers. The strobe lights are so repetitive I feel as though I'm constantly having my photo taken. I look around the assortment of people, trying to take my own mental photograph of the scene before me. There are a couple of guys in suits who look painfully out of place, not sure how to find their rhythm. Two couples in their late twenties are massaging one another, their bodies and actions a physical display of the drug they've ingested. They can only be new to ecstasy, their uncomfortable clothes and the looks of wonder on their faces are way too telling. I massage my boyfriend's neck, because he's tired from a long day of work.

A clubber makes the assumption that we're on E, smiles uncontrollably at us and waves glowsticks in front of our faces, thinking this will intensify our trip. It makes us both laugh. The odd raver wanders about with an air of nonchalance. Some are only dancing because they're in a dance club, not because they're inspired to. It's almost as if I can read their minds, "What is this techno stuff anyway?" I realize this club like many others is a melting pot for a number of disparate groups, probably reminiscent of early Toronto club raves. Regular people trying out what they believe to be new drugs for the first or second time. Old-school ravers coming to check out a particular DJ, others simply enjoying a few boers and a night on the town. There are moments at this club when we seem to synergize, whistles are blown, arms are raised and bodies move with pure abandonment. But as quickly as we are unified, the track changes and the intensity dies. Arms come back down, and we mingle once again. I make a mental note of the changes in the scene and try to pinpoint the fragmented elements of rave that remain.

As rave was being condemned in the media and coming under increased control by governments, corporations were cashing in wholeheartedly from what they saw as a huge market. Likewise, laws designed to stop raves have assisted in driving it mainstream. Raves were forced into clubs which began to profit from what underground raves had initiated. Raves moved from being illegitimate businesses to booming legal ones that gave everyone a piece of the pie. In Britain legal all-night events began at the superclub Ministry of Sound in 1991. Inspired by the Paradise Garage, Justin Berkman, an English DJ who had lived in New York, opened the Ministry of Sound. In true Paradise Garage spirit he booked Larry Levan to come over and play for its opening. Over the years the club has essentially become a means of selling the Ministry of Sound brand.

Q. Most ridiculous thing you've thrown someone out of a club for doing?

A.
1. Peeing in a garbage can.
2. Including me in "joint rotation."
3. Asking for a bottle opener for beer which had been brought in.
4. Asking if there was "coke in (his) moustache."
5. Snorting coke off of the bar.
6. Having explicit, non-procreative sex on the dance floor.
7. Masturbating on a girl's back.
8. Trying to hide a full beer in a certain exclusively female orifice. And for her boyfriend no less!
9. Relentlessly throwing one hundred dollar bills in the bartenders' faces, screaming, "Why can't I buy the fucking bar?!"
10. For being in the wrong place at the wrong time. Accidents happen.

ILAM NEBRANN, Club/Rave security guard for 6 yrs.

CASHING IN

Compilations, a magazine, clothing and a book are all adorned by Ministry's logo. Pepsi even sponsored a Ministry of Sound tour in 1994.

Initially alcohol was rejected by rave culture. Not only was alcohol accused of bringing out bad vibes but it was rumored to decrease the effects of ecstasy. With a large percentage of alcohol consumers buying water at clubs, alcohol companies tried to get funky and clubby with 1990s versions of the 1980s cooler. Many would advertise their products with rave-style graphics and images of hip club crowds. Coolers such as Vex and GRUV are examples of high alcohol beverages that are aimed at a more dance-oriented crowd. For the all-night crowd, there was Red Bull caffeinated water, Smart Fx and Gurana—drinks that were intended to boost energy and keep you dancing.

Another rapidly growing industry in England, and more recently in North America, is the music and style press. This niche media covers the trends of subcultural sound and fashion and contribute to its construction. *URB* began publishing ten years ago in Los Angeles, *Xlr8r* started as a free 'zine in California, while *DJ* , *Mixer* and *Mixmag* are more recent publications. Some magazines, such as *Wallpaper*, even have their own record compilations. In Canada there are now two magazines that are directly related to raves and clubbing—*Tribe* dates from 1993 and *Klublife* started in May 1997. Free alternative weeklies like *NOW* currently have an underground section that lists upcoming raves, dance nights and parties. Ironically, a few years ago rave promoters were denied any listings in *NOW*'s events calendar because they had no fixed location mentioned. Within the last decade the number of articles concerning drugs in youth-oriented magazines has increased dramatically, no doubt in direct correlation to the growing number of young drug users involved in the club and rave scenes. This phenomenon was evident in magazines designed for young teens as early as October 1992, when the cover of the British magazine *Smash Hits* advertised "8 pages of Rave stuff inside."

A recent HMV ad sums up the ubiquitous presence of rave and how normalized and mainstream illegal pill-popping has become. Their Holiday

Relief Sale advertisement shows an outstretched tongue on which sits a colored pill embossed with the word "sale." Ironically, the image in this advertisement is almost interchangeable with the picture in a front page *Toronto Star* article condemning ecstasy use with the cover for Irvine Welsh's novel *Ecstasy*. The advertising lure of club and ecstasy culture contrasts sharply with the actions and discourse of the governing bodies attempting to control the culture. Most rave flyers are now adorned by a corporate logo, while virtually no club is free of advertising in at least one form. On the back page of Sheryl Garratt's book *Adventures in Wonderland* is an ad for a compilation mixed and compiled by Pete Tong, arguably Britain's most commercial dance/rave DJ, and a staple on BBC radio. This well-placed ad confirms that rave and club culture are so commodified that even a book which analyzes the culture quietly suggests that the reader purchase a commercial compilation.

The Hippie Disco. If rave began in the summer of 1988 as a simulacrum of the 1960s hippie experience, it has surely made the logical progression a decade later to more accurately resemble the last days of disco. As disco gained popularity, the accompanying styles became codified, expensive and gender-based. Any rave clothing store today will suggest a similar relationship to today's scene. What was once a style marked by androgyny and comfort is now a style that is costly and gender-based, with body-hugging women's fashions making a resurgence. Rave culture has undergone the same commodification process that disco experienced. As discos became more popular they also became more segregated, "providing fewer opportunities for those of diverse ethnic backgrounds and sexual orientations to mingle freely."[36] Segregation has also been an inevitable by-product of the growing rave scene, where particular clubs now attract a particular crowd. At one time a rave would attract old, young, gay, straight, as well as a multitude of races. Today there are raves set up specifically by and for the gay community, events that specify a 19-and-over crowd, as well as events that appeal primarily to teenagers.

Mega parties? Thousands and thousands of people gathered together in an overpolished, over-publicized, shiny, clean and SAFE venue with everything in place for people to buy [and] consume. Crowd? Mostly white suburban folks from fairly wealthy families who are looking for cheap thrills, loud music and half-naked people. Men are usually shirtless, body builders or otherwise aware of their overall appearance. Women are dressed to impress, wearing clothes several sizes too small to show their physical attributes. **DJ PSONYK, Montréal, QC, age 30, M, 8 yrs.**

Clubbing and its attendant beliefs has filled a hole in my life that I never knew even existed. **Fluffy, London, England, age 22, F, 2 yrs.**

IN THE 1973 SONG "Midnight Ravers" Bob Marley sang about ravers who were using dance to find hope and meaning in their problem-filled world. His lyrics helped define the nature of rave without any of the limitations of its subcultural definition. Rave started as an alternative, underground, renegade culture, that hid from police and media exposure and rejected the high profile nature of clubs. Having come full circle, rave culture is now a driving force within some factions of club culture and is undoubtedly the impetus behind the increase of all-night clubs.

12

RAVE'S LAST DAZE

Licensing laws and unattainable permits have forced rave-type events into legal club environments, while the ever growing prominence of amphetamine-based drugs such as ecstasy has increased the need for clubs to stay open all night. In England, electronica is the norm in clubland with superclubs such as Ministry of Sound and Cream playing house, techno and its various sub-genres. Other clubs cater exclusively to one particular brand of electronica. This has been paralleled in North America to a lesser extent where rave-type clubs will devote a particular night each week to a particular genre.

Rave culture is no longer a hidden phenomenon; it is what the majority of mainstream youth do for fun on Saturday nights, usually in a legal after-hours club. All that remains of rave's underground nature is illegal drug consumption. The evolution of rave is like the evolution of a town into a city. Like in a small town where you once knew many of the inhabitants, at an old-style rave almost everyone, or at least their faces, was vaguely familiar. Raves have grown to the point where, like in a city, it isn't as easy to find faces you recognize. In a city you have to lock your door at night; at a large rave it is now recommended that you keep an eye on your knapsack.

Subcultures and scenes generally fade after a few years and get reminisced about in books and movies. But as I'm writing this, small and large cities on every continent are preparing for a rave, whether they're still calling them that or not. Whether you think rave is dead is irrelevant. It hasn't died. It lives on in the millions of sub-scenes it gave birth to without planning. Those who have just caught on, who are only now old enough to participate, are undoubtedly having as beautiful an experience as did the initial Shoomers. They weren't willing to let it go in 1988, and these newcomers in 2001 aren't about to let it die either. For some it's just the beginning.

Soon there will be retro-rave parties, where we can get together and listen to those techno classics of the mid- to late '90s. **MAX ,Toronto, ON, age 30, M, 10 yrs.**

Q. What do you feel is the future of your scene?

A. Destruction, change, resurrection. Repeat. **DEVONSHIRE BOY, Toronto, ON, age 37, M, 22 yrs.**

Plur is a bunch of shit! Raving, ravers, raves, whatever, none of that exists no more. Y'all just going through the motions of what you think it's supposed to be. **ANONYMOUS**

Rave is kept alive by the new recruits, new music and new promoters in different cities. Usually, it's the older, seasoned participants that aren't so willing to change with it. Instead they deny that rave exists because it no longer conforms to their definition. It's not that rave no longer exists, it's that rave as they experienced it is gone. Rave is something else now. It's new music, new drugs, new fashions and new faces. Many ravers were only five or six when it all started over 12 years ago. So is this still a rave? What rave is and the emotions one feels are completely dependent on personal interpretation.

Belonging. The last couple of years of my life I've felt disconnected. It's almost like I've moved to a different city. In a figurative sense I have. I had abandoned the community that was my home for six years. Going into some large parties recently I have felt a stranger. I had felt like a stranger at some of my first raves, but that strangeness was constituted by wonder, intrigue, excitement and newness. Now the strangeness is accompanied by judgment, expectation and nostalgic memories of a time long gone.

Unlike other subcultures that have their time in the sun and then quietly dwindle into the archives, rave has already endured countless cycles and resurgences. This has happened not only in Britain, but also in North America. Perhaps it is the lack of overarching ideology and voicelessness of rave that allows it to seep through borders like no other subculture before it. Rave music transcends the limits of words evident in the music of previous cultures, while rave style transcends the parameters dictated by fashion, as each region creates its own style that continuously progresses. Rave events themselves overcome the laws intended to suppress them by finding new locations in fields, cowsheds and even in licensed clubs. This is why rave is limited when it is defined by place. Perhaps it is simply an environment that allows the experience of certain freedoms, and in so doing, the experience of certain emotions. If the environment

Q. What kinds of changes have you noticed in your scene?

A: None, although I'm sure stuff has changed over the years. I think it's more that as you get older you change, and you can deny that and say that the scene is changing, but really I think our interests and outlook change and as a result it seems like the scene has changed. **LAILA, New Jersey, age 18, F, 2 yrs.**

The rave scene has had a considerable effect on my life. Throughout my adventures in the scene, I have played the role of many characters: drug dealer, dancer, promoter, DJ agent, coat check girl, vendor, designer, crew member, "the DJ's girlfriend," financial backer, fashion victim, DJ groupie [and] drug addict . . . just to name a few . . . **SHLOOPY, Toronto, ON, age 28, F, 6 yrs.**

RAVE'S LAST DAZE

allows you to get lost in music, the human connections that surround you, and in dance, then your integral, internal self is found and you are raving.

Rave, much like the Internet, involves more people with each passing year, growing not as a scene but as numerous scenes. As what is considered rave music broadens, it invites a much wider cross section of youth with it. Almost every parent has heard the word rave and most likely hopes their own child is not involved. The probability remains that if the child is not involved yet, he or she soon might be. As rave continues to expand it morphs into a new entity, only slightly similar to its initial form over a decade ago. It is rave's marriage with change that assures its longevity. This cyclical characteristic ensures rave's ceaseless perpetuation and is arguably programmed into its drug of choice: ecstasy. Rave's new recruits experience their own honeymoon periods, but eventually they too will drop out.

The ambiguousness of the definition of rave is evident at the events themselves. Some parties appear spiritual, liberating and even magical; others, however, demonstrate rave's extremist nature where drug use seems excessive and abusive, demeaning its more meaningful attributes. Too often when the drugs wear off, rave's purported ideals diminish, leaving the divisions of race and sex reaffirmed and the barricades of socialized behavior rebuilt. The proof is in the sub-scenes, the war between promoters, the Balearics, the acid Teds and the naming of both.

Syrous Bittersweet. Feb.10, 2001. This marked the first mass event I had attended in well over a year. I wasn't sure if I was hoping to prove my theory of evil-commodifiction-and-commercialization-of-rave or if I was in longful anticipation of the good old days: a rave resurgence of all that was happy and fluffy.

The name of this rave couldn't have been more appropriate. I was bitter that I felt—for the first time—an outsider in a place that had been a home. Was it because I had a camera in one hand and a tape recorder

in the other, ready to judge, assume and depict? An observer instead of a participant?

Tired and jaded I was awkward in this seemingly alien crowd of kids mostly born a decade after me. But the more I searched the more I found sweetness and light. Wrapped in a slightly different package, joy still managed to weave itself into the pulses of sound. There it was in the midst of a breaking circle, holding hands wigged-out in the corner, in a flame held up in homage to the drone of jungle. Joy whispered to me. It was there.

If only ravers could remember the joy they felt when dancing with their eyes closed, not seeing, not judging. Loving, for that instant, themselves, their lives and those around them even if they were strangers, newcomers, or old-timers wearing last year's outfit or dancing last year's dance. They loved them, during that dance, during that song, during that rush, because they assumed those around them were experiencing the same joy they were experiencing. With a simple smile their existence was validated; for at that most vulnerable, intimate and blissful moment, they were acknowledged and allowed to feel more liberated than ever before. If ravers remembered that moment all day every day, perhaps they could live their life not having to go to raves to be a raver.

1 Tomlinson: 197
2 Applegath: 17
3 quoted in Applegath: 3
4 Graham: 66-7
5 Ellis: 479
6 Munday: 46
7 Hill: 42
8 Sanders-Greer: H4
9 Thornton: 56
10 quoted in Collin: 70
11 Gasnier
12 Roberts: 93
13 DeLandri
14 Oh and Atherley: np
15 Kellaway 1989b: 5
16 Cunningham: 31
17 Kellaway 1989b: 5
18 May 1999a
19 Sanders-Greer: H4
20 Findlay: 4
21 Potter: 1
22 May 1999a
23 Garratt: 309
24 DeLandri
25 ibid
26 Sonmor: np
27 Potter: 1
28 Lee-Shanok: np
29 Kingstone: 1
30 Znaimer
31 Roberts: 93
32 Cunningham: 31
33 "The Kick": 10
34 Collin: 297
35 Quoted in Tomlinson: 206
36 Tomlinson: 208

NOTES

Books

Alderson, Evan. "Ballet as Ideology." *Meaning in Motion*. ed. Jane C. Desmond. London: Duke UP, 1997.

Bakalar, James B and Grinspoon, Lester. *Psychedelic Drugs Reconsidered*. New York: Basic Books, 1979.

Barthes, Roland. *Mythologies*. Trans. Annette Lavers. New York: Hill and Wang, 1972.

Bland, Alexander and Percival, John. *Men Dancing*. London: Weidenfeld and Nicolson, 1984.

Broughton, Frank and Brewster, Bill. *Ministry of Sound's The Manual: The Who, The Where, The Why of Clubland*. London: Headline, 1998.

--- *Last Night a DJ Saved My Life: The History of the Disc Jockey*. New York: Grove Press, 2000 (originally published by Headline Book Publishing, 1999).

Cashman, John. *The LSD Story*. Greenwich, CT.: Fawcett, 1966.

Champion, Sarah. "Fear and Loathing in Wisconsin." *The Club Cultures Reader*. ed. Steve Redhead. Oxford: Blackwell Publishers, 1997.

Collin, Matthew and Godfrey, John. *Altered State*. London: Serpent's Tail, 1997.

Cohen, Stanley. *Folk Devils and Moral Panics*. Oxford: Martin Robertson, 1980.

------------------ *The Manufacture of News*. London: Constable, 1973.

"Crackdown on Raves." Letters section. *Time* magazine. April 30, 2001.

Dagan, Esher A. *The Spirit's Dance in Africa*. Westmount, QC: Galerie Amrad African Arts Publications, 1997.

Daly, Anne. "Classical Ballet: A Discourse of Difference." *Meaning in Motion*. ed. Jane C. Desmond. London: Duke UP, 1997.

De Mille, Agnes. *The Book of the Dance*. New York: Golden Press, 1963.

Durant, Alan. "A New Day for Music? Digital Technologies in Contemporary Music Making." *Culture, Technology and Creativity in the Late Twentieth Centruy*. ed. Philip Hayword. London: John Lebbey, 1990.

Eisen, J. ed. *The Age of Rock: Sounds of the American Cultural Revolution, A Reader*. New York: Vintage Books, 1969.

Eisner, Bruce. *Ecstasy: The MDMA Story*. Berkeley: Ronin, 1994.

Ellfeldt, Lois. *Dance from Magic to Art*. Iowa: Wm. C. Brown, 1976.

Ellis, Havelock, "The Art of Dancing." *What is Dance?* eds. Roger Copeland and Marshall Cohen. New York: Oxford UP, 1983.

Erickson, Patricia. "The Selective Control of Drugs." *Social Control in Canada*. eds. B. Schissel. and L. Mahood. Toronto: Oxford UP, 1996.

Ericson, Baranek and Chan. *Visualizing Deviance*. Toronto: University of Toronto Press, 1987.

Foster, Susan Leigh. "Dancing Bodies." *Meaning in Motion*. ed. Jane C. Desmond. London: Duke UP, 1997.

Foucault, Michel. *The Archeology of Knowledge*. Trans. A.M. Sheridan Smith. New York: Pantheon, 1972.

NOTES/WORKS CITED

Garratt, Sheryl. *Adventures in Wonderland: A Decade of Club Culture*. London: Headline, 1998.

Goldberg, Marianne. "Homogenized Ballerinas." *Meaning in Motion*. ed. Jane C. Desmond. London: Duke UP, 1997.

Gottschild, Brenda Dixon. "Some Thoughts on Choreographing History." *Meaning in Motion*. ed. Jane C. Desmond. London: Duke UP, 1997.

Graham, Martha. "I am a Dancer." *The Routledge Dance Studies Reader*. ed. Alexandra Carter. London: Routledge, 1998.

Hanna, Judith Lynne. *To Dance Is Human*. Chicago: University of Chicago Press, 1979.

Hawkins, Erick. *The Body Is a Clear Place and Other Statements on Dance*. New Jersey: Princeton Book Co. Publishers, 1992.

Hebdige, Dick. "Posing . . . Threats, Striking . . . Poses: Youth, Surveillance, and Display." *The Subcultures Reader*. eds. Ken Gelder and Sarah Thornton. London: Routledge, 1997.

----------------- *Subculture: The Meaning of Style*. London: Routledge, 1979.

Henderson, Sheila. *Ecstasy: Case Unsolved*. London: Pandora, 1997.

Kraus, Richard. *History of the Dance*. Englewood Cliffs, NJ: Prentice-Hall, 1969.

Levi-Strauss, Claude. *The Savage Mind*. London: Wiedenfeld and Nicolson, 1962.

Masters, R.E.L. and Houston, Jean. *The Varieties of Psychedelic Experience*. New York: Holt, Rinehart and Winston, 1966.

May, Beverly. *Future Jazz*. Unpublished manuscript. 1999b.

McGrath, John and Scarpitti, Frank. *Youth and Drugs*. Glenview: Scott, Foresman, 1970.

McKay, George. "Evereeebodeee's Freee; Or, Causing a Public New Sense? Rave (Counter) Culture." *Senseless Acts of Beauty*. London: Verso, 1996.

McKenna, Terrence. *Food of the Gods*. New York: Bantam, 1992.

McRobbie, Angela, and Mica, Nava, eds. *Gender and Generation*. London: Macmillan, 1984.

McRobbie, Angela. "Dance and Social Fantasy." *Working Class Youth Culture: Dance, Gender and Culture*. ed. Helen Thomas. London: Macmillan, 1993.

Melechi, Antonio. "The Ecstasy of Disappearance." *Rave Off: Politics and Deviance in Contemporary Youth Culture*. ed. Steve Redhead. Aldershot: Avebury, 1993.

Milestone, Katie. "Love Factory." *The Clubcultures Reader*. ed. Steve Redhead. Aldershot: Avebury, 1997.

Mungham, Geoff. "Youth in Pursuit of Itself." *Working Class Youth Culture*. eds. G. Mungham and G. Pearson. London: Routledge and Kegan Paul, 1976.

Oyortey, Zagba. "Still Dancing Downwards and Talking Back." *Working Class Youth Culture: Dance, Gender and Culture*. ed. Helen Thomas. London: Macmillan, 1993.

Partridge, William L. *The Hippie Ghetto: The Natural History of a Subculture*. New York: Holt, Rinehart and Winston, 1973.

Polhemus, Ted. "Dance, Gender and Culture." *Dance Gender and Culture*. ed Helen Thomas. London: Macmillan, 1993.

Ramsey, Kate. "Vodou, Nationalism, and Performance: The Staging of Folklore in Mid-Twentieth-Century Haiti." *Meaning in Motion*. ed. Jane C. Desmond, London: Duke UP, 1997.

Redhead, Steve. "The Politics of Ecstasy." *Rave Off: Politics and Deviance in Contempo-

rary Youth Culture. ed. Steve Redhead. Aldershot: Avebury,1993a.

------------------- "The End-of-the-Century-Party." *Rave Off: Politics and Deviance in Contemporary Youth Culture*. ed. Steve Redhead. Aldershot: Avebury,1993b.

Reynolds, Simon. *Generation Ecstasy*. London: Little Brown, 1998.

------------------- "Rave Culture: Living Dream or Living Death." *The ClubCultures Reader*. ed. Steve Redhead. Aldershot: Avebury, 1997.

Rietveld, Hillegonda. "Living the Dream." *Rave Off: Politics and Deviance in Contemporary Youth Culture*. ed. Steve Redhead. Aldershot: Avebury, 1993.

Rushkoff, Douglas. *Cyberia: Life in the Trenches of Hyperspace*. New York: Harper Collins, 1994.

Russell, Kristian. "Lysergia Suburbia." *Rave Off: Politics and Deviance in Contemporary Youth Culture*. ed. Steve Redhead. Aldershot: Avebury, 1993.

Sanders, Clinton R. "'A Lot of People Like It': The Relationship Between Deviance and Popular Culture." *Marginal Conventions: Popular Culture, Mass Media, and Social Deviance*. ed. Clinton R. Sanders. Bowling Green, OH: Bowling Green State University Popular Press, 1990.

Saunders, Nicholas. *E Is for Ecstasy*. London: Nicholas Saunders, 1993.

Schultz, Emily and Lavenda, Robert. *Cultural Anthropology: A Perspective on the Human Condition*. 3rd ed. California: Mayfield, 1995.

Shapiro, Harry. *Waiting for the Man: The Story of Drugs and Popular Music*. London: Quartet, 1988.

Starks, Michael. *Cocaine Fiends and Reefer Madness: An Illustrated History of Drugs in the Movies*. New York: Cornwall, 1981.

Stoll, Clifford. *Silicon Snake Oil: Second Thoughts on the Information Highway*. New York: Doubleday, 1995.

Thomas, Helen. *Dance, Modernity and Culture: Explorations in the Sociology of Dance*. London: Routledge, 1995.

Thornton, Sarah. *Club Cultures: Music, Media and Subculture Capital*. Cambridge: Polity Press, 1995.

Tomlinson, Lori. "'This Ain't No Disco' . . . Or Is it? Youth Culture and the Rave Phenomenon." *Youth Culture: Identity in a Postmodern World*. ed. Jonathon Epstein. London: Blackwell, 1998.

Valery, Paul. "Philosophy of the Dance." *What Is Dance*. ed. Roger Copeland and Marshall Cohen. New York: Oxford UP, 1983.

Ward, Andrew H. "Dancing in the Dark: Rationalism and the Neglect of Social Dance." *Working Class Youth Culture: Dance, Gender and Culture*. ed. Helen Thomas. London: Macmillan, 1993.

Walsh, David, "'Saturday Night Fever': An Ethnography of Disco Dancing." *Working Class Youth Culture: Dance, Gender and Culture*. ed. Helen Thomas. London: Macmillan, 1993.

Walton, Paul. "Youth Subcultures, Deviancy and the Media." *Youth Subcultures: Theory, History, and the Australian Experience*. ed. Rob White. Hobart, Tasmania: National Clearing House for Youth Studies, 1993.

Welsh Asante, Kariamu, ed. *African Dance*. New Jersey: Africa World Press, 1996.

Wetzsteon, Ross. "The Whirling Dervishes: An Emptiness Filled with Everything." *What Is*

NOTES/WORKS CITED

Dance? eds. Roger Copeland and Marshall Cohen. New York: Oxford UP, 1983.

Wheless, Joseph. *Is it God's Word?* Kila: Kessinger Publishing, 1997.

Willis, Paul E. *Profane Culture*. London: Routledge and Kegan Paul, 1978.

Wolff, Janet. "Reinstating Corporeality: Feminism and Body Politics." *Meaning in Motion*. ed. Jane C. Desmond. London: Duke UP, 1997.

Yablonsky, Lewis. *The Hippie Trip*. New York: Pegasus, 1968.

Young, Jock. "The Subterranean World of Play." *The Subcultures Reader*. eds. Ken Gelder and Sarah Thornton. London: Routledge, 1997.

-------------- "The Myth of the Drug Taker in the Mass Media." *The Manufacture of News*. ed. Stanley Cohen. London: Constable, 1973.

Periodicals, Internet and Miscellaneous

Applegath, James. "The Divine Creators." *Klublife*. Vol 2, Issue 7. December 1998.

Aslinger, H.F. and Cooper, Ryley. "Marijuana—Assassin of Youth." *The Reader's Digest*. Feb. 1938.

Atkins, Juan. Personal interview. Conducted by Tara McCall, May 2001.

Bains, Camille. "Ecstasy Rules Rave Scene in Vancouver." *Vancouver Sun*. Tuesday, January 2, 2001.

Balon, Emily. "Mayor Mel, Come Rave With Me." *Toronto Star*. Tuesday May 23, 2000.

Banks, Mike. "Techno Rebels: Detroit's Agents of Change." *URB*. Aug./Sept. 1996.

Beck, Clarence V. "Marijuana Menace." *Literary Digest*. January 1, 1938.

Benson, Richard. "Life Over the Rainbow." *The Face*. March, 1996.

Bowling, C.G. "The Trouble with Ecstasy." *Life* magazine. August 1985.

Bragg, Rebecca. "Police say raves can't be stopped." *Toronto Star*. November 2, 1999.

Brown, Ethan. "E-Commerce." *New York* magazine. Monday July 24, 2000.

Brown, Janelle. "Sell a Glowstick, Go to Prison." *Salon.com*. June 20, 2001.

Cichon, Kathy. "The Dark Side of Ecstasy." *Naperville Sun*. Friday October 20, 2000.

Cloud, John. "The Lure of Ecstasy." *Time* magazine. Monday June 5, 2000.

Colorada, Dali. "Feedback." *Fix*. Vol 1, Issue 4 November 1995.

Corwin, Miles. "Psychiatrists Defend New Street Drug for Therapy." *Los Angeles Times*. Monday May 27, 1985.

Crocker, C. "All the Rave." *The Economist*. May 30, 1992.

Cosgrove, Stuart. "Seventh City Techno." *The Face*. May 1988.

Cunningham, Dave. "Celebrating Drug Abuse." *Western Report*. March 16, 1992.

Curtis, Henry Pierson. "Bad Research Clouds State Death Reports." *Orlando Sentinel*. Sunday March 21, 2000.

"The Dangers of LSD." *Time* magazine. April 22,1966.

De Landri (producer). Segment 1. *20/20*. ABC News. January 24, 1997.

"Donna and the Sugar Cube." *Newsweek*. April 18, 1966.

Donut, Tribal. "They Said the Rave Scene Was Dead." *URB*. 6:50 Aug./Sept. 1996.

Edwards, Jeff. "Liquid Cocaine." *Salon.com*. February 2, 2001.

Elliott, Brendan. "Police Thought Drugs Would Be Sold at Rave." *Halifax Daily News*. Friday February 11, 2000.

Evang, Karl. "LSD: New Menace to Youth." *UNESCO Courier*. May, 1968.

Farrel, Barry. "A Remarkable Mind Drug Suddenly Spells Danger—LSD." *Saturday Evening Post*. November 2, 1963.

Feigelson, Naomi. "The Underground Revolution: Hippies, Yippies and Others." New York: Funk and Wagnalls, 1970.

Fields, Gary and Leinwand, Donna. "Drug Dogs Sniff Out Ecstasy at Airports." *USA Today*. April 19, 2000.

Findlay, Alan. "Young Clubbers Ectastic About Rave 'Chemicals.'" *Toronto Sun*. September 25, 1999.

Ford, Jason. Personal interview conducted by Majero Bouman. March, 2001.

Gagliano, Rico. "Ecstasy Without Fear." *LA Weekly*. Friday June 9, 2000.

Gard, Wayne. "Youth Gone Loco." *The Christian Century*. June 29, 1938.

Garcia, Guy. "Tripping the Night Fantastic." *Time* magazine. August 17, 1992.

Gasnier, Louis (producer). *Reefer Madness*. G & H Films. George A. Hirliman (distr.). 1936.

Granatstein, Rob. "Rave Depraved?" *Toronto Sun*. Saturday April 22, 2000.

Guthrie, Ian. "Ian Guthrie Writes . . ." *Transcendance*. Spring 1996.

Heard, Larry. Personal interview. Conducted by Tara McCall. June, 2001.

Hill, Chris. "Destiny." *Lotus*. Issue 11.

"The Hippies are Coming." *Newsweek*. June 12, 1967.

Hissom, Doug. "Taking the E Train." *Shepherd Express*. Thursday December 21, 2000.

Huffstutter, P.J. "We're Not in Woodstock Anymore; Crank Up the Music." *Los Angeles Times*. August 7, 1994.

Ingold, John and Robinson, Marilyn. "Break-ins for Rave Drug Trouble Veterinarians." *Denver Post*. Thursday November 16, 2000.

Jewers, Brent. "Rave Kids Aren't Criminals." *Halifax Daily News*. Saturday February 12, 2000.

Kellaway, Robert and Hughes, Simon. "Spaced Out! 11,000 Youngsters Go Drug Crazy at Britain's Biggest-ever Acid Party." *Sun* (London). June 26, 1989.

Kellaway, R., Hughes, S., Kay, J., Gibbs, W. "Ecstasy Airport: The Sun Cracks Secret Drug Rave-up in Hangar." *Sun* (London). June 26, 1989.

"The Kick." *New Republic*. April 16, 1966.

Kingstone, Jonathan. "Rave Scene Drugs 'Too Easy.'" *Toronto Sun*. September 25,1999.

------------------------ "Chief Raves to PM." *Toronto Sun*. May 5, 2000.

Klam, Matthew. "Experiencing Ecstasy." *New York Times Magazine*. Sunday January 21, 2001.

Kobler, J. "The Dangerous Magic of LSD." *Saturday Evening Post*. November 2, 1963.

Lee-Shanok, Philip. "Chief Blasts Rave Scene." *Toronto Sun*. May 11, 2000.

Leach, H.G. "One More Peril for Youth." *Forum and Century*. January, 1939.

Logan, Bruce. "In NZ We Are Killing Our Kids With Cannabis." *The New Zealand Press*. Monday February 28, 2000.

NOTES/WORKS CITED

Lynch, Lauria. "Officials Cancel Party After Website Bills it as Rave" *Milwaukee Journal Sentinel*. Thursday December 28, 2000.

Mancuso, David. Personal interview. Conducted by Majero Bouman. March, 2001.

Mandel, Bill. "The Yuppie Psychedelic." *San Francisco Chronicle*. June 10, 1984.

"Marihuana [sic] More Dangerous Than Heroin or Cocaine." *Scientific American*. May, 1938.

Marley, Bob. "Midnight Ravers." *Catch a Fire*. Tuff Gong, 1973.

Marshall, Donnie R. Administrator, DEA, U.S. Department of Justice. "Dear Ann Landers." *Arizona Republic*. May 7, 2001.

May, Beverly. Personal interview. Nov. 25, 1999a

--------------"Editor's Commentary." *Transcendance*. Spring 1996.

McCann, Paul. "Boy George: The Queen's Own DJ." *The London Times Magazine*. Saturday June 9, 2001.

McPhee, Mike. "Ecstasy Changes the Fight Against Drugs." *Denver Post*, Monday October 2, 2000.

McKusick, T. "Catch a Rave." *Utne Reader*. Sept./Oct., 1996.

Mead, Rebecca. "Rave On." *New York* magazine. August 20, 1999.

Moore, Suzanne. "Booze—Britain's Real Drug Crisis." *The Independent*. Friday August 7, 1998.

Munday, Matt. "Acid Reign." *WAX*. Vol 1, Issue 7 October, 1996.

Naylor, Tony. "Flashback." *WAX*. Vol 1, Issue 7 October, 1996.

Oh, Susan and Atherley, Ruth. "Rave Fever: Kids Love Those All-night Parties . . ." *Maclean's*. April 24, 2000. Cover story.

"Party Wear or Paraphernalia?" *ABCnews.com*. March 29, 2001.

Potter, Mitch and Powell, Betsy. "Agonizing Over Ecstasy." *Toronto Star*. November 20, 1999.

Raphael, Philip. "Rave Success Spawns Party Fashion Store." *Richmond Review*. Wednesday September 13, 2000.

"Rave Task Force Looks for Way to Tame All-night Parties." Associated Press. April 3, 1997.

Rawnsley, Andrew. "Rawno's Rantings." *XLR8R*. Issue 19 1995.

Ray, Janet. "Trancin' Shoes." *Twin Cities Reader*. April 26, 1995.

Redeker, Bill and The Associated Press. "Feds Crack Down on Raves." *ABCnews.com*. January 13, 2001.

Reynolds, Simon. "British Rave." *ArtForum*. February, 1994.

Roberts, McLean. "My Son Is on LSD." *Ladies Home Journal*. January, 1968.

Romano, Ben, "Ritalin Abuse May Be a Problem." *Oregon Daily Emerald*. April 27, 1998.

Ruryk, Zen. "City Bans Raves." *Toronto Sun*. May 11, 2000.

Rumack, Leah. "They Strangle Raves with a Billion By-laws." *NOW* magazine. November 4, 1999.

Sanders-Greer, Shelly. "Danger Parties." *Toronto Star*. March 22, 1997.

Sanford, David. "LSD Crackdown." *New Republic*. March 16, 1968.

Simpson, Gerald. Personal interview. Conducted by Tara McCall. June 2001.

Sonmor, Jean. "Rave Drugs Are Deadly Serious." *Toronto Sun*. November 13, 1999.

Stallings, Ariel Meadow. "Incense and Glowsticks." *Lotus*. Issue 11.

Tagg, Philip. "From Refrain to Rave: The Decline of Figure and the Rise of Ground." *Popular Music*. 13:2 1994.

Trance, Funk. "Letters to Lotus." *Lotus*. Issue 12.

Turner, Ben. "In Tong We Trust." *Muzik*. October, 1997.

Znaimer, Moses (Producer). *City Pulse News at Six*. March 14, 2000.